AMERICAN NAZI

FROM HATE TO HUMANITY

JEFF SCHOEP

Published by Wilkinson Publishing Pty Ltd
ACN 006 042 173
PO Box 24135, Melbourne, VIC 3001, Australia.
Ph: +61 3 9654 5446
enquiries@wilkinsonpublishing.com.au
www.wilkinsonpublishing.com.au

© Copyright Jeff Schoep 2025

WilkinsonPublishing
wilkinsonpublishinghouse

All rights reserved. No part of this publication may be reproduced, stored in a retrieval system or transmitted in any form by any means without the prior permission of the copyright owner. Enquiries should be made to the publisher.
Every effort has been made to ensure that this book is free from error or omissions. However, the Publisher, the Authors, the Editor or their respective employees or agents, shall not accept responsibility for injury, loss or damage occasioned to any person acting or refraining from action as a result of material in this book whether or not such injury, loss or damage is in any way due to any negligent act or omission, breach of duty or default on the part of the Publisher, the Authors, the Editor, or their respective employees or agents.

A catalogue record of this book is available from the
National Library of Australia.
ISBN: 9781922178985

Cover design: Michael Guillen.

CONTENTS

Preface ... v
Foreword ... vii

1 Flash-Forward: Betrayal ... 1
2 The Early Years ... 12
3 Guns out, but not Outgunned ... 18
4 The Escalation ... 23
5 Battlegrounds ... 32
6 Fear ... 43
7 Entrapment ... 51
8 The End of the Brown House ... 54
9 Arrested ... 59
10 Aryan Nations ... 69
11 Homeless and Hopeless ... 79
12 Bars and Brawls ... 82
13 Wings & Ribs ... 90
14 Taken Hostage ... 96
15 Infiltration ... 103
16 Death By Cop ... 110
17 Surprise! ... 113
18 Assassination Attempt ... 116
19 The System's Court ... 125
20 The Past and Future Collide ... 133
21 The Feds Come Knocking ... 139
22 A Failed Coup ... 142
23 Nazis and Hamas ... 146
24 Valley Forge ... 149

25	Toledo Riot	152
26	Yorktown and Satan	154
27	Deportation: Banned in Canada	159
28	Minnesota Raid	165
29	Adolf Hitler Memorial Museum	170
30	The Road to Detroit	177
31	Counterintelligence Ops	184
32	Betrayals, Raids and Informants	187
33	The Battle of Trenton	195
34	Tragedy Strikes	201
35	Gunned Down in Arizona	206
36	Leith, North Dakota	210
37	Mississippi Burning and The National Conversation on Race	216
38	Losing Family	222
39	Seeds of Change	230
40	Far-Right vs Alt-Right	241
41	Charlottesville	245
42	James	259
43	Court Meddling & Media Circus	263
44	Exiting Extremism	280
45	Formers	284
46	Nazi Hunters	296
47	Justice	307
48	Civilian Life	316
49	Not the End, But a Gateway to the Future	327

| Glossary | 337 |
| Acknowledgments | 341 |

PREFACE

This memoir is a deeply personal account of events that have shaped my journey. In sharing my experiences, I have made every effort to present the truth as accurately as possible. However, to protect the privacy of individuals mentioned in this book, many names and identifying details have been intentionally and thoughtfully changed to ensure anonymity. In certain instances, timelines have been adjusted for clarity and narrative cohesion.

While every effort has been made to preserve the integrity of actual events, this book is not intended as a verbatim historical record, but rather as a reflection of my personal experiences, emotions, and recollections.

Legal Disclaimer

This book is a work of nonfiction. The views and opinions expressed herein are solely those of the author and do not represent those of any organizations, institutions, or individuals, past or present. Any resemblance between characters and real persons, living or deceased, outside of those explicitly identified, is purely coincidental. The author and publisher assume no responsibility for any interpretation of this work beyond its intended purpose.

By reading this book, you acknowledge that the author has exercised discretion in presenting these experiences while maintaining the spirit of the truth.

FOREWORD

A stigma is one of the hardest things from which to separate oneself. It is a negative or set of negative beliefs imposed upon a person or particular group of people by society or by another group of people based upon their perception of those for whom they hold disdain. These stigmas can be deservedly perceived based on behavior such as habitual intoxication or repetitive violence, or criminal activity. Stigmas can also be undeservedly assigned based on skin color, religion, or political party affiliation. The attached stigma reflects a negative connotation impacting those stigmatized long after they have shed their behavior or beliefs which led to them being stigmatized in the first place, deservedly or not.

Take for example a Ku Klux Klan member who decades ago publicly renounced white supremacy and in the ensuing years has worked hard to make amends and reconcile racial and anti-semitic strife. In the media his name always carries the stigmatic prefix "ex-Klansman" John Doe or "former neo-Nazi" John Doe. After redemption, how long must one work and what deeds must one do to shed the stigmatic moniker prefix placed before their name?

For twenty-five years out of his twenty-seven-year membership, the author of this book led a white supremacist group building it into the largest neo-Nazi organization in the United States. His sense of leadership led him to create successful recruitment tactics and maintain full control of his organization with very little attrition. It is rare in the world of white supremacy that a leader has that long a tenure at the top. Most leaders who remain in charge for half that long end up at one of two destinations; prison or death. His toolkit intuition, knowledge, and honed skills kept him from either fate.

Today, he has turned his life completely around and now uses that toolkit to help others from various white supremacist groups to see through the façade of manipulations and falsehoods and also helps others to avoid joining these types of groups. His memoir is a must-read for teenagers and adults alike of every skin color, religion, persuasion, political affiliation, and racial ideology. The similarities between how the author viewed some law enforcement officers and how the law enforcement officers viewed him and his group are mirrored reflections of similarity. Even many commonalities in the experiences of the book's white author and me (a black man) can be found in how we each were treated with hate and violence by those who never took the time to get to know us. I certainly do not advocate for an acceptance of white supremacy or any type of supremacy. Nor do I excuse violence perpetrated upon another human being for their immutable characteristics. However, we both have definitely experienced the negative results of false perceptions cast upon us, giving us each an opportunity and see that as human beings, we have much more in common that we do in contrast.

With this realization now fully absorbed by the author and his half decade of work in the racial reconciliation space, he has written one of the best books on the topic of how one becomes ensnared in a cult and equally important, how one can get out in one piece and rebuild their dignity and integrity. It is not just a wonderful redemptive story, but also a very insightful tool for any- and everyone not involved in destructive ideologies. It teaches how to spot the tell-tale signs of someone getting ready to go down that rabbit hole and it shows us how we can help pull them back out and provide the proper support and perspectives for them to regain their moral footing and humanity. It is the ultimate proof that these ideologies are learned behavior, and what can be learned, can also be unlearned.

It is with great honor and pleasure I was asked and accepted the invitation of the author to write the foreword to his story. If anyone deserves not to have a stigmatizing prefix before his name, I now present my friend, Counter Extremism Specialist Mr. Jeff Schoep.

Daryl Davis
Musician & Race Reconciliator

CHAPTER 1

FLASH-FORWARD: BETRAYAL

The shadowy world of neo-Nazism operates in the margins, hidden from mainstream view. Its influence seeps through the cracks of public consciousness, festering just below the surface, waiting – hoping – for the downfall of American democracy. Occasionally, it erupts into the spotlight through acts of terror – bombings, mass shootings, hate crimes – sudden bursts of violence that shatter lives and leave devastation in their wake.

For me, neo-Nazism wasn't just an ideology – it was my life.

For over two and a half decades, my entire existence was bathed in it. It shaped my thoughts, my choices, my identity. What began as a childhood fascination, reinforced by family ties, dragged me deep into its dark, seedy underworld. I didn't just follow the movement – I led it. I recruited, trained, preached, and prepared for war.

That belief hardened into full-scale conflict with the world itself. Convinced of the righteousness of my cause, I sacrificed my own humanity – while stripping others of theirs in the process.

I became infamous.

For years, I was the face of neo-Nazism in America. A name synonymous with hate. The leader of the National Socialist Movement (NSM) – once the largest Nazi organizations in the

United States.

Breaking free from the cycle of destruction I had built my life around wasn't instant – or easy. It took years. Years of unlearning. Years of reckoning with the damage I had done. Years of clawing my way back to something resembling humanity.

In the end, it wasn't force or punishment that shattered my belief system.

It was the very people I had once vilified who reached out their hands instead of turning their backs. The ones I had dehumanized were the ones who showed me what it truly meant to be human. They didn't just challenge my worldview – they dismantled it, piece by piece, replacing hate with something I never expected to find.

They taught me that race, color, tribe, and ethnicity – things I once saw as insurmountable barriers – were nothing more than illusions. That beneath it all, we are not enemies. We are one human family.

Today, I work alongside the Simon Wiesenthal Center, an international human rights organization, to educate youth across the country about the dangers of extremism – how to recognize it, resist it, and avoid the paths that lead to hate, violence, and division.

I often wonder how different my life might have been if someone had offered me that same guidance when I was young – if someone had shown me another way, before hate took hold, before the damage was done. I can't rewrite the past, but I can help ensure others never follow the same destructive path I once did.

The neo-Nazi movement thrived on paranoia.

It wasn't just an undercurrent – it was the lifeblood.

Every conversation was measured, every action scrutinized. A misplaced word, an intrusive question, even a moment's hesitation could plant the seed of suspicion. Betrayal could come from anywhere. Trust was a rare, fragile commodity – never given freely, only earned over time.

Accusations were constant. Some were baseless, driven by fear, ego, or the desperate need to prove loyalty. Others, disturbingly, turned out to be true. Over the years, we uncovered more informants than I cared to admit. However, the real danger wasn't just infiltration – it was the way paranoia devoured us from within.

I saw men's reputations destroyed, their lives upended over nothing. Innocent people falsely accused, cast out, or worse. Once suspicion took hold, it spread like wildfire – indiscriminate, relentless, impossible to contain.

As the leader of the NSM, I demanded proof before condemning anyone as a rat or an informant. But in a world where survival hinged on loyalty, even a whisper of doubt could be a death sentence, and sometimes, that doubt was justified.

The enemy wasn't always beyond the gates. Sometimes, it was already inside.

One incident stands out.

A recruit named Matt started hanging around. His past was complicated. In high school, he ran with a skinhead crew, but later, he joined a nationally known, predominantly black street gang. Now, years later, he was circling back to the movement. That kind of history didn't just raise eyebrows – it set off alarms.

After an NSM meeting, I pulled him aside. "Matt, if we catch you associating with gang-bangers, we'll put you in the ground. That's not a threat – it's a promise."

I didn't sugarcoat it – his past had people on edge, but I was willing to stake my reputation on giving him a chance.

Matt swore he had cut all ties, and for months, he played the role convincingly. He showed up, put in work, and earned trust. Slowly, the tension around him faded.

Then, one day, he disappeared. No call. No explanation. Just gone.

In a world fueled by paranoia, silence was the loudest warning of all.

Rumors spread like wildfire. Had Matt gone back to his old gang? Had he been a plant from the start? The uncertainty ignited fear. His past, combined with his sudden vanishing act, made him a prime suspect.

I needed to know if Matt was a threat – or if we were chasing shadows. So I set a trap.

Armed with a payphone and a tape recorder, I disguised my voice, mimicking what we considered Ebonics, and posed as an old gang associate. The plan was simple: get Matt talking, gauge his reaction, and uncover the truth.

Would he take the bait?

Or had we been wrong about him all along?

The phone rang.

Matt picked up.

I dropped into character as Tyrone.

"Yo, Matt, what up? This be Tyrone."

A pause. Then, his cautious reply: "I don't think I know you."

"You better know me, muthafucka!" I snapped. "We used to hang at the club."

Another pause. My pulse quickened. Had he figured out the ruse? Then his tone shifted.

"Oh yeah, I remember. What's up, homie?" Feigned familiarity.

Tyrone pressed on. "Word on the street is you've been rollin' with skinheads."

"Nah, not anymore. Screw those guys." His voice wavered, anxiety creeping in.

I pushed harder. "Them skinheads are on our turf and need to be dealt with. If we take out the leader, the rest of them crackers will crumble."

Then came the moment that turned suspicion into rage.

Matt didn't hesitate. Without a second thought, he casually dropped my full name – and didn't stop there. He handed them a strategy. A blueprint.

"Get a white guy to call the NSM hotline, say they want to join. Jeff meets new recruits at a café in St. Paul with his girlfriend and a couple of skins."

Betrayal. Cold. Calculated. Served up without hesitation.

"You're alright, white boy!" Tyrone laughed. "Maybe we'll line it up and do a drive-by."

With recorded evidence of Matt's treachery, there was no room for doubt. No room for mercy. His willingness to expose me, and casually hand over operational details, sealed his fate.

Retribution was inevitable.

Over the next few days, I meticulously crafted a plan. I didn't need an army – just a handful of trusted members. Carol and Maggie were perfect for the task. Matt had always mistaken their friendliness for flirtation, making him an easy mark. I kept the specifics of his betrayal from them, giving them only the role they needed to play: lure Matt from his home and bring him to a nondescript apartment.

The trap was set.

When the girls arrived with Matt, I was waiting behind the door. The second it clicked shut, I slid the deadbolt into place. The sound cut through the air – sharp, deliberate, final.

On cue, the others emerged from the shadows.

I stepped forward, arms crossed, blocking his only exit.

"Hey buddy, where've you been lately?"

My voice was calm, controlled, but carried an unmistakable edge.

Matt's smug grin flickered, barely for a second. Then his eyes darted around the room, searching for an escape that wasn't there. His expression shifted instantly – fear flashing across his face, his body stiffening like a deer caught in headlights. At that moment he certainly knew he'd walked straight into the lion's den. You could see the wheels spinning in his head, scrambling to assess the situation, to calculate his odds.

"Just working," he muttered, voice trembling, betraying the unease he couldn't quite hide.

"Working, huh?" I let the silence linger and the tension coil around him. "Not working with any gang-bangers, hopefully?"

I took a step closer, my eyes locked onto his, pressing the question harder.

"No, of course not," he stammered, shaking his head, trying to maintain his crumbling facade of innocence.

I reached into my flight jacket and slowly pulled out a tape, holding it up for him to see. "You'll want to hear this."

Rich stepped forward, dragging a chair to the center of the room, shoving Matt into it with deliberate force. His hands clamped down on Matt's shoulders, keeping him firmly in place. I moved in slowly, letting the tension simmer as I slid the tape into the stereo. Without breaking eye contact, I let the silence hang a bit longer before cranking the volume and pressing play.

Matt's voice erupted from the speakers, the words he thought would stay buried spilling out for everyone to hear. Each syllable struck like a hammer blow, shattering the thin walls of deception he had built around himself. The room felt smaller, the walls closing in as the gravity of his betrayal sank in.

The girls gasped, hands flying to their mouths in disbelief. Their wide, unblinking stares burned into him.

Matt sat frozen, the color draining from his face, his breath coming in short, shallow bursts. His eyes – wild, darting, desperate – told the whole story.

It was like watching a condemned man forced to witness his own execution in agonizing slow motion. The crushing reality of his betrayal bore down on him like a vise, squeezing out any last flicker of hope he might have clung to.

Rich spat in his face, his voice dripping with venom. "Take off your boots and flight, you rat bastard!"

The command was steeped in tradition.

Being stripped of one's boots and flight jacket wasn't just punishment – it was humiliation. A ritual reserved for enemies and traitors, meant to strip them of their identity and dignity. To lose them was the ultimate disgrace.

Some of our crew wore flight jackets taken from SHARPs or other defeated enemies – trophies of conquest.

Matt knew exactly what this meant.

Without a word, he slumped forward, his hands moving sluggishly as he pulled off his boots and jacket. He handed them over, head bowed, shoulders caving inward like a man already broken. Whatever shred of honor he had left was snuffed out in that moment.

Then, without warning, Rich's fist shot out.

The impact was brutal – bone meeting bone with a sickening crack. Matt's head snapped back, his body whipping sideways as the chair beneath him flipped, sending him crashing to the floor.

What followed was pure chaos – a violent eruption of pent-up rage.

Boots and fists hammered down on Matt as the crew unleashed their fury. He didn't stand a chance. The first blows sent him sprawling, his body curling inward on instinct, but there was no defense against the relentless onslaught. Every hit landed with bone-crushing force, each one fueled by betrayal.

The women recoiled. Carol gasped, hands clamped over her mouth. Maggie turned away, shielding her eyes, unable to stomach the savagery unfolding before them.

Matt had made his choice, and now he was paying for it.

Rich grabbed Matt by the throat, yanking him to his knees. His voice was low, guttural. "This rat bled all over my new flight!" His grip tightened, rage twisting his face.

Matt's rodent instincts kicked in. With a desperate wrench, he broke free, scurrying into the kitchen like a cornered rat. His eyes darted wildly, searching for an escape. Then, in a blur of panic, he grabbed a butcher knife, waving it erratically before bolting through the apartment door.

A thick trail of blood stretched down the hallway, like the path of a gut-shot buck, leading all the way outside.

The commotion stirred the neighbors – doors cracked open, cautious faces peeking out. We hesitated, giving Matt a head start to avoid drawing more attention.

By the time we stepped outside, flashing red and blue lights greeted us. The cops were waiting with guns drawn.

"Get on the ground and put your hands behind your back!" an officer barked, his pistol locked squarely on my chest.

Fueled by bravado and adrenaline, I smirked and lifted my beer. "Yeah, yeah, I'll hit the deck after finishing this."

"Get on the ground now! This is your last warning!" The officer's voice sharpened, the tension crackling like static in the air.

With a slow, deliberate motion, I started to comply – still insolently sipping the beer.

"Drop the can!"

I grinned. "And risk a littering fine? Not a chance."

That was it. A cop stormed forward, ripped the beer from my hand, and tossed it aside before ratcheting the cuffs on extra tight.

I smirked, shaking my head. "Wasting a perfectly good beer? That's alcohol abuse."

A couple of the guys chuckled. The cops weren't amused.

Carol and I were shoved into the back of a squad car together. She was falling apart – tears streamed down her face, hands trembling uncontrollably. She stared blankly ahead, her breathing shallow and uneven, as if trying to process the nightmare she'd just lived through. Guilt hit me like a ton of bricks. This was my fault – she never should've been dragged into this mess.

"Carol, don't worry," I whispered, gently trying to reassure her. "No one's gonna talk to the cops. You'll be home soon."

She nodded weakly, swallowing hard, but her entire body was tense. Then the police radio crackled to life.

"Suspect matching the description – tattoos, white t-shirt, no shoes, covered in blood, wielding a knife – suspected skinhead activity."

Carol tensed beside me, her whole body rigid.

Minutes later, an officer returned and yanked open the squad car door. "Your boy Matt told us he tripped down some stairs. We don't buy it, but with no witnesses willing to talk, it's just another case of skinheads beating the hell out of each other."

They released everyone, except me.

The officer who had drawn his gun on me earlier approached, his gaze steady.

"Do you realize how close you came to being shot tonight?"

I shrugged, bravado still intact. "I didn't do anything that justified lethal force."

He raised an eyebrow, his response calm but firm. "We were responding to reports of a blood-covered suspect running down the street with a knife. If, for even one second, I'd believed my life – or anyone else's – was in danger, I'd have been legally justified in shooting you."

His eyes locked onto mine, unflinching.

"And your attitude while being held at gunpoint? That only made things worse. You escalated the situation. You came off as unstable, which heightened concerns for officer safety."

His words hit harder than expected. The gravity of the situation settled in, gnawing at the edges of my bravado.

Before releasing me, he added, "Next time, give me your word that you'll comply when an officer has a weapon drawn. It might save your life."

I nodded, the seriousness of his warning finally sinking in. "You've got my word."

Matt was branded a traitor, but since he hadn't squealed to the cops, our business with him was over. He wouldn't be hunted down. He was left to his own devices – exiled.

The violence we inflicted wasn't random or impulsive – it was calculated, deliberate. A psychological imprint burned into the minds of anyone who might consider betrayal. To outsiders, it was barbaric, an act of paranoia and an unyielding code. For me, it was routine. Business as usual. Just another day in that world.

Leading an extremist group meant living on borrowed time.

Every day, your life, your freedom, and the lives of those around you hung in the balance. Violence wasn't a last resort – it was the cost of doing business. A dark, ominous shadow that followed you everywhere. Never out of reach.

How did I go from living in that darkness to standing alongside those I once sought to alienate? How did I transform from harboring hatred – rooted in race and religion – to working with human rights organizations, helping others avoid the path I once walked?

This is my story.

CHAPTER 2

THE EARLY YEARS

Born in 1973 in rural Minnesota, my childhood, in many ways, was typical.

My father, an American soldier stationed in Germany, met and married my mother, a German citizen. After moving to the U.S., Mom taught German at the local high school before going to law school while my sister and I were still in elementary school. Dad's career took him from managing a small business to becoming the president of a hunting apparel company.

Our parents worked tirelessly to give us a life filled with opportunities they never had.

Dad's family were farmers – fourteen children under one roof, scraping by, stretching every dollar just to make ends meet.

Mom's upbringing was shaped by an entirely different kind of hardship. She grew up in postwar Germany, where hunger was a constant presence. She once told me about sleeping on a kitchen table because she had no bed, of hiding bits of bread for herself and her brother Harold, never knowing when the next meal might come.

My grandparents, Opa and Omi, immigrated to the United States years after the war, falling in love with a country that offered them a chance to start over.

Omi was from Prussia, a region swallowed by the Soviet Union after World War II. Her family – like millions of other displaced Germans – was expelled from their homeland. Forced into train cars, they were shipped to a refugee camp in Italy before finally returning to Germany with nothing but the clothes on their backs.

During World War II, Opa enlisted in the German army as a teenager, like many young men of his era. By 1945, he was captured by Allied forces and held as a prisoner of war. He wasn't the only member of the family to serve – Omi's brothers, Hardo and Gerhard, also fought in the war.

Uncle Hardo was a decorated officer on the Eastern Front, earning the prestigious Iron Cross and many other medals. He was captured during the brutal battle of Stalingrad – one of the bloodiest conflicts in human history, where 1.2 million lives were lost.

Out of the 91,000 German soldiers taken prisoner, only 5,000 survived the Soviet gulags. Most starved to death. Hardo was one of the last to make it out alive. By the time he was released, he weighed just ninety pounds.

Omi's other brother, Gerhard, fought in the Ardennes offensive. His tank was hit by Allied fire, leaving him with severe burns and permanent disfigurement.

From an early age, I was captivated by Germany's role in World War II. My family's connection to it only deepened that fascination.

It was this interest – this relentless curiosity – that laid the foundation for my later involvement in the neo-Nazi movement. A path I deeply regret.

By the time I reached high school, I was determined to join an active group.

I read every book I could find about Nazism, scouring libraries and bookstores for anything related to the subject. One book about the modern white supremacist movement had an index listing different organizations. That was my gateway. I began writing letters – starting with the Nazi groups.

These days, finding such organizations only takes a few clicks online, but in the early '90s, it required effort. There were no groups listed in Minnesota, but I kept searching. Eventually, I made contact, and the descent began. From a young age, I had been curious about politics.

By 1992, when I became eligible to vote for the first time, I was eager to learn how the U.S. political system worked.

I'd heard that a former Klansman was running for president, and while that piqued my interest, he wasn't on the ballot in Minnesota. Most of the other candidates didn't resonate with me, but Pat Buchanan's populist America First rhetoric struck a chord. He wasn't a white nationalist, but seemed honest, patriotic, and sincere. So, I reached out to his campaign. At 18, I delivered my first public speech at a county Republican convention in St. Cloud, Minnesota.

In the early '90s, these gatherings were filled with men in suits and ties, their speeches polished and rehearsed. Then there was me. Long hair spilling out from beneath a bandanna, stepping up to the podium to advocate for Buchanan. The contrast was impossible to miss.

My speech stirred enough conversation to land in a local news magazine.

Standing before a packed hall was nerve-wracking. I felt the weight of every set of eyes on me, but when I spoke, people listened.

Afterward, attendees shook my hand, telling me my words

had resonated with them. A few even said they were switching their vote from George Bush to Buchanan because of what I had said. It was powerful revelation. For the first time, I understood how words – when spoken with conviction – could shift perspectives, influence decisions, and leave a lasting impact.

PURSUING A DREAM

Though politics intrigued me, music was my true calling. Since childhood, I dreamed of becoming a rock star. My sister, her best friend, and I would pretend we were famous musicians, using Christmas tree lights as stage lighting for our imaginary concerts. By high school, I was fully immersed in music, taking vocal lessons and lettering in choir. Politics was no different than having a side piece – she was there, but my heart belonged to music.

After auditioning for a few bands, I became the lead singer of a rock group that mostly played covers. But the music scene in St. Cloud felt stagnant. My band-mates were content with playing weddings and parties, but for me, music wasn't a hobby – it was my life's ambition.

St. Cloud wasn't the place to chase that dream, so I set my sights elsewhere, and soon heard about a sleaze-metal band in St. Paul looking for a vocalist. I auditioned and made the cut.

The band took me under their wing, helping me refine the raw stage presence I lacked. Before long, we were performing in rock bars and clubs across the Twin Cities. It was electrifying. We had big dreams – Hollywood, the Sunset Strip, playing the legendary Whisky a Go-Go.

To channel that ambition, I wrote the lyrics to an original song: Hollywood Bound.

Music consumed my life, but the interest in neo-Nazism never faded.

One day, a letter arrived from a Christian Identity group. They had a booth at the State Fair. Coincidentally, the fairgrounds were just a short walk from my first apartment in St. Paul. My band-mates didn't share my political views, but we were a tight-knit crew. So, they tagged along.

As we approached the Identity booth, an elderly woman – easily in her eighties – suddenly stood up, her eyes narrowing. She pointed at us, scowling.

"Keep moving and stay away from here – we don't want any trouble!"

For a moment, I was taken aback. Then it hit me. We must have looked like a walking stereotype to them. Dyed hair, black eyeliner, the unfiltered swagger of a rock band straight out of an '80s music video. To the average onlooker, we probably seemed like a pack of reckless outcasts. After all, weren't rock stars supposed to be snorting cocaine off a stripper's backside – not dabbling in politics?

I quickly explained that her assistant, Dale, had invited me. Her scowl faded, replaced by a look of mild confusion. She mentioned that Dale was on break but would be back in about thirty minutes. When we returned, she apologized.

Apparently, a group of Satanists had harassed them earlier in the day. Even with that explanation, she still seemed perplexed by our appearance, struggling to make sense of why we looked the way we did. Dale, sensing the awkwardness, leaned in and gently reminded her, "They're musicians in a rock band – remember?"

After I told Dale that they were the first movement people I'd met in person, he handed me a list of groups operating in Minnesota. I met with all of them. Two stood out: the NSM, then called the National Socialist American Workers Freedom Movement, and the Hammerskins.

Minnesota was home to one of the most infamous skinhead bands in America, aligned with the Hammerskins. Meeting them was eye-opening. They didn't just play music – they used it as a vehicle for National Socialism, turning songs into anthems of ideology. Since we were around the same age, joining them seemed like the obvious path forward.

What ultimately drew me to the NSM wasn't just its ideology – it was its direct connection to Commander George Lincoln Rockwell, the founder of the original American Nazi Party, who was assassinated in 1967.

The group's leader, Cliff, was a Vietnam veteran who had served alongside Rockwell in the ANP. That gave the NSM more than just an ideological foundation – it had history. A living link to the movement's origins. The connection to the past, the feeling of carrying forward a legacy, made the group feel more significant than the others.

Compelled by this connection, I joined almost immediately, and threw myself into the movement. That decision marked the beginning of a 27-year involvement with what would eventually grow into the largest Nazi organization in the United States.

CHAPTER 3

GUNS OUT, BUT NOT OUTGUNNED

In the 1990s, the NSM was based out of Minneapolis, though the city was considered enemy territory. We called it *Red Minneapolis*, emphasizing "red" to underscore its perceived communist leanings. Neo-Nazi activism there was met with fierce resistance, making it a battleground for the movement.

After joining the Party, I was immediately thrust into frontline activism. Cliff, a hardened veteran with a military background, became my mentor. With decades of experience in the movement, he knew how to operate in hostile environments. One of the first lessons he taught me was the One-Man Picket. The concept was simple yet effective – one man, standing alone, could still make an impact. Cliff illustrated this by staging a solo protest in downtown Minneapolis, defiantly wearing a swastika armband and waving a Nazi flag.

One afternoon, Todd – another new recruit – and I accompanied Cliff to a government building downtown. As he pulled the flag from the trunk of his car, he issued a clear directive: "You two stay on the sidewalk, like you're mainstream Jewish media. Film everything." I wasn't convinced and asked, "Why not make it a three-man protest? Wouldn't it be safer if you're attacked?" Cliff didn't flinch. "No. Stay here and keep filming. Even if I'm attacked, don't intervene. This isn't my first rodeo."

Once Cliff was out of earshot, I turned to Todd and muttered, "I don't care what he says – if someone jumps him, we're going in."

Cliff marched back and forth, waving the flag with fervor. Passing motorists reacted as expected – some hurled insults and flashed middle fingers, while others offered thumbs-up or Nazi salutes. It wasn't long before a security guard approached, but Cliff remained unfazed, firmly asserting his legal right to protest. The lesson was clear: even in hostile territory, we couldn't be silenced. A single person, standing alone, could still make an impact.

This tactic became a defining strategy for the NSM over the next 27 years. Whenever a city denied us rally permits, we countered with walking pickets, demonstrating that no matter how unwelcome we were, we wouldn't be deterred.

Another form of activism involved distributing leaflets that included the group's mailing address and phone hotline. Party members were instructed to carry a pamphlet titled *Know Your Rights When Leafleting*, which outlined key legal protections and cited relevant case law. Since run-ins with law enforcement were common while handing out fliers, this document was crucial in preventing unnecessary conflicts with overzealous officers, helping NSM activists avoid arrests and legal trouble.

As the digital era took hold, leafleting became less effective, gradually overshadowed by the internet as the primary tool for spreading propaganda. To remain relevant, the group adapted to the changing landscape. But in those earlier days, the streets were where the movement made its presence known.

THE BROWN HOUSE

In the mid-1990s, I lived at the NSM's South Saint Paul headquarters, known as the *Brown House* – a deliberate nod to the original Nazi base of operations. The house quickly became a flashpoint for violence, especially after our frequent marches through town, Nazi flags held high. Media attention only fueled the confrontations, but the real danger came at night. As soon as the sun went down, the threat of attack was constant, forcing us to maintain strict guard shifts to defend the property.

One night, around 3 a.m., while I was on duty with Tim, something caught my eye. A shadowy figure emerged from the darkness – a black hoodie, face obscured by a bandanna – creeping toward my cherry-red Pontiac Fiero. His arm was raised, weapon in hand, ready to smash the window. Instinct took over. I chambered a round in my AK-47 – chi-chuk! The sharp metallic sound pierced through the silence, stopping him cold. For a split second, he hesitated – then, like a startled alley cat, he spun and bolted, tearing down the street.

Adrenaline surged as I tore after him, my black flight jacket whipping in the wind, steel-capped boots hammering against the pavement. He ducked behind a parked car and suddenly turned, a silver revolver catching the moonlight, its barrel locked onto me. I skidded to a stop, rifle raised in response. The frigid night air burned in my lungs, but my grip remained steady, focus razor-sharp. The world around us faded – just two men in the dead of night, locked in a silent standoff, each waiting for the other to break first.

"Shoot, motherfucker!" I snarled, my voice slicing through

the stillness. "I've got armor-piercing rounds. That car won't save you – so pull the trigger!"

I wasn't bluffing. I'd seen those AK rounds punch through steel like it was paper during target practice at a farm, ripping through both sides of an old truck. At this range, he didn't stand a chance. He crouched behind the car, gripping his pistol, frozen, uncertainty written all over him. Maybe it finally dawned on him that this wasn't a game – that I wasn't just playing at war. His courage crumbled. Without a word, he turned and fled, vanishing into the shadows, leaving me standing alone in the middle of the street, rifle in hand.

As I lowered the weapon, porch lights flickered on in nearby houses. In the distance, the rhythmic pulse of blue flashing lights crept closer. I pulled the magazine, ejected the round from the chamber, and casually stowed the rifle inside the house. Then, I settled into a chair on the porch and waited. As usual, someone in the neighborhood had called the cops.

When the officers pulled up, I recounted the events with the same measured tone I'd use to discuss the weather. They took it in, nodded, and sped off to hunt down the suspect. A short while later, they returned with news – they had found him but were still searching for his pistol. Then came the part that made my blood boil – they had no intention of arresting him.

"You've gotta be kidding," I said, my voice tight with frustration. "The guy tried to wreck my car and then pulled a gun. If you let him walk, he's just gonna come back. Next time he points a gun at me, he won't be leaving in a squad car – he'll be leaving in a body bag."

The officer smirked, shaking his head. "Not a chance. You

scared the crap out of him – literally. He's cuffed down the street, cooling off on the curb."

"How can you be so sure ?" I asked, arms crossed, still unconvinced.

The cop's grin widened, his face turning red as he chuckled. "Because he shit himself."

I narrowed my eyes. "You're serious?"

"Dead serious," the officer said, still grinning. "We don't want him stinking up our cars or the jail. You scared him half to death – trust me, he won't be back."

I exhaled, leaning back against the porch. Maybe they had a point. A man who had just thoroughly humiliated himself would probably think twice before showing his face around here again. In the end, no one ended up in the hospital, jail, or morgue. The only real casualties? The gunman's pants – and whatever was left of his pride and dignity.

CHAPTER 4

THE ESCALATION

Shortly after moving to South Saint Paul, I received an invitation to serve as an alternate delegate at the state Republican convention in Saint Cloud. At 18, before joining the movement, I'd been a delegate there, which was likely why I got the invite. Eager to share the news, I rushed to show the letter to Cliff.

Governor Arne Carlson was scheduled to speak, and Cliff wasted no time in formulating a plan. "We wait for Arne to start his little speech," he said. "Then we put on our armbands and make our presence known."

I hesitated. "Won't we just get thrown out?"

Cliff smirked. "Of course! That's the whole point. Then we take the protest outside and hit them with a walking picket – maximum disruption."

At the convention, a small group of NSM members, dressed in civilian clothes, sat together, ready for the signal. What we didn't anticipate was that the plan would fall apart before the Governor even made it to the stage.

As another speaker announced that Governor Carlson would be stepping up soon, Cliff suddenly shot up from his seat, sending his metal folding chair crashing to the floor with a loud clang that echoed through the auditorium. The room fell into stunned silence as every eye turned toward us.

"Arne Carlson is a traitor to America – and worse, a traitor to the white race!" Cliff's voice boomed, carrying across the hall like a bullhorn. On cue, we rose to our feet and slipped on our swastika armbands.

Security moved in fast, a wave of suits and uniforms closing in to smother the disruption. The tension in the air was thick enough to choke on. As they forced us toward the exits, I felt an odd mix of anxiety and grudging admiration for Cliff's sheer audacity.

Outside, we regrouped with picket signs, hurling our outrage at the Governor, the Republicans, and the establishment. I had expected the stunt to trigger a media firestorm, a major publicity win for the NSM. Instead, the stunt faded into obscurity, barely worth a passing mention in the news.

THE BARBARA CARLSON SHOW

In the early days of my involvement with the NSM, I operated under the pseudonym Jeff Stevens. It provided a layer of anonymity, allowing me to navigate the political landscape without immediate repercussions – and, more importantly, shielded my family from potential backlash. Not long after we disrupted the Republican convention, that protection began to crumble. It was the first crack in what would soon become a shattered life.

Barbara Carlson, ex-wife of the governor and a prominent conservative figure, invited us onto her radio show. We expected a combative environment, but the opportunity to broadcast our message to a wider audience was too tempting to pass up – even if it meant engaging with someone from the very political system we despised.

Cliff and I stepped into the studio, expecting a tense but manageable interview. I slipped into my usual rhythm, spouting the same antisemitic rhetoric I had regurgitated countless times before – ranting about how Jews had been expelled from every nation but America and insisting that history was bound to repeat itself. It was nothing new, just another cycle of hate I had learned to parrot.

Barbara's response was swift and scathing. Her voice dripped with venom as she cut through my facade, stripping away my anonymity in real time. "Your real name is Jeff Schoep," she declared, spelling it out, letter by deliberate letter, for the entire audience to hear.

I froze. *How the hell did she know that?* Worse – she wasn't even close to finished.

With chilling accuracy, she rattled off details that sent an icy jolt through me – where both of my parents worked, and the tiny rural town they lived in. None of it had come from me.

Then, with pure contempt, she drove the dagger in deeper. "How does your mother feel about raising such a hateful son?"

The air in the studio turned suffocating, my pulse hammering as the tension closed in like a noose around my throat. Being exposed was one thing – but dragging my family into this? That was an unforgivable breach. This wasn't just an ambush – it was a deliberate, brutal violation of the one boundary I had always believed was untouchable.

Up until this moment, I had naively believed that family was sacred, even in the dirtiest of political conflicts – a rule honored even by criminal syndicates like the Mafia. My parents had no involvement in my beliefs, yet now they were collateral damage in a war they never signed up for. It was my first brutal lesson in what would later be known as doxxing, long before the term entered public consciousness.

As shock, panic, and regret swallowed me whole, I fought to maintain composure. The false sense of security my alias had provided was gone, leaving my family vulnerable to consequences they had never asked for. In a desperate bid to shield them, I lied – claiming they hated and disowned me, hoping that severing all perceived ties would keep them safe from the inevitable fallout.

The moment those words left my mouth, guilt slammed into me like a freight train. I had been raised on principles – one of which was never to lie. I despised dishonesty, yet here I was, telling the world my parents didn't love me. It felt sickening, like being backed into a corner with no way out. I didn't know what else to say, as terror clawed at my conscience worried that someone might target my family.

It was a sobering realization – extremism doesn't just destroy those who embrace it; its consequences ripple outward, dragging down the innocent along with it. I had prepared for many worst-case scenarios, but never imagined a radio host would publicly dox my family, putting them at risk for choices they had never made.

Barbara wasn't finished. With unsettling enthusiasm, she announced to her audience that after the commercial break, she'd be calling my mother's workplace – demanding to know how she could have raised such a hateful son.

Desperate, I pleaded with her – both on and off the air – not to contact my mother. I warned her of the potential dangers, not just for my mother, but for our entire family. This wasn't about my safety; it was about protecting those I had unintentionally dragged into the crossfire.

The phone lines lit up as the call-screener sorted through a flood of reactions – angry critics, but also, to my surprise, a few voices of support. Even some of her own listeners expressed concern over her decision to target my family. Yet, rather than tempering her resolve, the backlash seemed to stoke Barbara's fury. Her eyes blazed with indignation as she demanded real-time updates from the call-screener between commercial breaks.

It was a surreal moment – watching a radio host face public outrage on her own show.

One caller, a self-identified fan of the show, directly questioned Barbara, asking why she would reveal my family's information on air, warning that unstable individuals could target an innocent family. The atmosphere grew increasingly contentious, as Barbara seemed incapable of handling the mounting criticism and clashed defensively with callers. The interview spiraled out of control and ended abruptly when we stormed out.

At the time, I was barely nineteen, too young to fully grasp the long-term consequences of my actions. It's understandable that Barbara despised my beliefs – any decent person would – but rather than engaging in civil discourse, she went after my loved ones. Those actions severed the last vestiges and connections I had to the mainstream civilian world, and cemented my commitment to the neo-Nazi movement.

After my identity and family were exposed, I believed that any choices I once had in life were now gone. The path ahead no longer seemed optional, but destined. The weight of that realization snuffed out any flicker of hope for change. The isolation was suffocating, leaving no room for reflection or reconsideration.

In today's hyper-polarized world, doxxing has become disturbingly routine, weaponized against individuals with opposing views – often without thought for the long-term consequences. It's essential for society to reflect on the ethics and long-term impact of cancel culture. While accountability is important, creating an environment that fosters the free exchange of ideas is equally vital. By engaging in meaningful conversations and seeking common ground, we can cultivate greater understanding, tolerance, and the potential for positive change.

Music was my passion, my future – the one thing I had always been certain about. Politics had been little more than a background noise in my life, never something I saw as a core part of who I was. After the doxxing, I felt my music career was ripped away, and the path forward was irrevocably altered. It felt like a nuclear bomb had gone off in my teenage mind, reducing every hope and dream I had to nothing but smoldering ruins.

No record label would sign a band whose frontman had ties to Nazism. Worse, staying with the band would inevitably drag them down when my affiliations came to light. It would have been selfish to put their future at risk, especially since they had no involvement in politics. Just as my activism had already stained my parents' reputations, the band would likely be the next to suffer. Everyone connected to me seemed doomed to pay a price – and that was a burden too heavy to bear.

Chasing rock stardom had been one of the greatest thrills

of my life – loud music, beautiful women, wild parties – it felt like we were on the brink of something big. We truly believed a record deal was just around the corner, with our sights set on the Sunset Strip. Now, with my name forever tainted by Nazism, those dreams were dead.

Quitting the band was one of the hardest decisions I ever had to make. It wasn't what I wanted, and I knew my bandmates would see right through me. So, I took a different approach – I shaved my head, hoping it would force them to fire me and spare an agonizing conversation. After all, we had already dropped a talented guitarist simply for not fitting the hairband image.

To my dismay, Dan – the band's founder and lead guitarist – didn't fire me. He shrugged off my shaved head, saying it didn't matter. So much for avoiding the tough conversation. I forced a smile and thanked him for the band's support, telling him only that I needed to focus on politics. I couldn't bring myself to explain the real reason – the truth hurt too much, and I was barely holding it together.

Dan wasn't buying it. He pushed back, insisting there was no reason I couldn't do both – music and politics. He didn't understand why I was willing to throw away something I loved and had poured my heart into. He saw right through me, recognizing that this wasn't what I wanted, and even tossed me a lifeline to stay. Dan was right – I didn't want to quit, but watching my bandmates suffer the way my family had would have been unbearable. Even if I left the movement, I was convinced I'd always be branded by it.

After being doxxed, my life changed forever. When I commit to something, it's all or nothing – no half-measures. So, I let go of every hope, dream, and aspiration I had once held close. Heartbroken, I took all the energy and passion I had once poured into music and redirected it into militantly building the NSM.

JUDGE OR JUDGMENT

While my life was descending further into extremism, my mother was closer than ever to achieving her lifelong dream – becoming a district court judge. She had won her election, had the qualifications, and the support of the voters. However, her appointment still required the Governor's approval.

According to her, the Governor personally called to inform her of his decision. Due to my involvement in neo-Nazism – and her father's past service in the German army during World War II – he believed it would be inappropriate to approve her judgeship.

The rejection devastated her. Years of effort, dedication, and sacrifice were wiped away in an instant. The pain of that moment cut deep, leaving scars that never faded. What made it even more painful was that she had no connection to my extremist beliefs, and had always vehemently opposed them. Yet, she was forced to bear the consequences of my actions.

To this day, I live with the guilt and shame of knowing that my choices robbed her of something she had rightfully earned. My mother's career wasn't derailed because of her own doing, but due to the shadow I had cast over her name.

By the 1990s, the suffering my family endured went far beyond lost opportunities. My sister was interrogated about her connection to a notorious neo-Nazi leader during job background checks, and law enforcement showed up at my father's workplace. These were just glimpses of the larger storm my family had to weather.

For me, every ounce of pressure – whether from authorities or society – only fueled my defiance. The more I was pushed, the harder I pushed back. It became a relentless cycle, reinforcing my resolve and making any chance of turning back feel impossible.

CHAPTER 5

BATTLEGROUNDS

The Brown House and the neighborhood around it felt like a war zone. We were trapped behind enemy lines, constantly on edge. It wasn't normal, but I learned to survive and adapt.

Like a beaten dog returning to its master, I accepted my fate and adjusted accordingly. Resilience takes on different forms – mine was sharpened into survival mode, compacted like a grenade, ready to pop off at any moment.

Then one afternoon, the explosion came.

A violent crash shook the house. My body reacted before my mind could catch up – I sprinted downstairs, heart pounding. The front screen door had been kicked in. Without hesitation. I grabbed the nearest weapon – nunchucks – and charged through the shattered frame, chasing the vandal down the street.

After a block and a half chase, he slipped away. Then came the sirens.

Thinking fast, I ditched the nunchucks under a parked car just before the cops closed in. Someone had called them – said a skinhead was chasing a guy through the neighborhood. I forced my breathing steady, and laid out the facts: our door had been kicked in, I was after the culprit. Hispanic, early twenties, ran that way.

The cops didn't ask many questions. They just sped off.

I stood there for a moment, watching the flashing lights

disappear, the street swallowing the sound of their engines. Then I retrieved the nunchucks and walked home. Back behind enemy lines. Back to a war that never seemed to end.

This was just another link in a chain of rising tensions – a precursor to the storm brewing on the horizon.

Shortly after a TV station aired a segment on neo-Nazis in South Saint Paul, the news spread like wildfire. Then came the tip-off – a credible threat from North Minneapolis, a place so steeped in bloodshed it had earned the nickname Murder-apolis. Street gangs, usually at war with each other, had found common ground in their hatred of us. They weren't just coming; they were coming united.

The Brown House shifted into battle mode. Security tightened. Troops assembled. Conversations were short, clipped, and on edge. There wasn't room for hesitation or doubt. Just the hard, unrelenting instinct to survive.

The police caught wind of the storm brewing and didn't mince words: Do not engage. Their message was clear – there would be zero tolerance for shootouts in the city. Warnings meant nothing. If gang-bangers wanted a war, we were prepared to send them straight to hell the second that first shot rang out.

The Brown House had no shortage of firepower. Rifles lined the walls and pistols were loaded and within reach. Reinforcements rolled in from across the Twin Cities – more bodies, more weapons, more backup.

Yet, beneath the hardened exteriors, something simmered. The slow, gnawing pressure of knowing violence could erupt at any moment. It sat in our stomachs like lead, coiling tighter with every passing hour.

The air was thick with the type of anticipation that precedes an explosion. The kind that makes men reckless. All it would take was one trigger pull and there would be no turning back.

By nightfall, the entire block was in lockdown. Law enforcement from neighboring suburbs had joined the local police, their cruisers forming barricades at every intersection. Flashing lights pulsed against buildings, casting eerie, shifting shadows. Heavily armed officers stood at the ready, scanning the streets with sharp, calculated movements. It felt less like a neighborhood and more like a battlefield – one bracing for an unseen enemy.

The police were on high alert, their message to us crystal clear: Brandish a firearm, and you're going to jail. No negotiations. No second chances.

So we adapted. The assault rifles were stashed just inside the front door, locked and loaded but out of sight. Pistols stayed close – concealed, but within reach.

Tension thickened as the night stretched on. Patrols doubled. Searchlights cut through the darkness, sweeping the treetops like silent sentinels. Somewhere in the distance, a disturbance rippled through the air – subtle but distinct. A sign that maybe law enforcement had intercepted some of the gang members.

Then, an officer broke the stillness. He approached me, his expression unreadable.

"We might have the guy who kicked in your door," he said. "Need you to come take a look."

Stepping past the barricades, I moved through the maze of flashing lights and uniformed figures. The world around me blurred – just motion, noise, and the cold grip of anticipation.

Finally, we stopped at an ambulance. Inside, a black man was strapped to a gurney, wrists cuffed, one eye nearly shut, his face barely recognizable beneath the swelling and blood.

The officer turned to me, "Is this the man who kicked in your door?"

I shook my head. "No, the guy who kicked in our door was Hispanic. This isn't him."

The officer nodded. "Alright, Jeff. Thanks for your honesty."

Curiosity gnawed at me as I glanced at the injured man. "What happened to him?"

Another officer stepped forward. "He's one of the gang members. Tried to fight the police, and... well, it didn't exactly work out for him."

The gang-banger's battered face told the rest of the story.

Had the cops not locked down the neighborhood, the night would have ended much differently – brutally, violently, irreversibly. Their overwhelming presence was the only thing that prevented a massacre. I could feel it in my gut, and shuddered at the thought.

One shot. That's all it would have taken. One panicked squeeze of a trigger, and the entire block would have exploded. Bullets tearing through the night, bodies hitting the pavement, blood pooling in the gutters. The coroner would have had a busy night stacking body bags.

ALTERCATIONS

In the early days, I wore an all-black version of the NSM's brown shirt uniform for official activities but switched to skinhead attire in my personal time. Others, like my roommate Michael, took it further – wearing the full uniform, complete with a swastika armband, while doing everyday things like grocery shopping or running errands.

The NSM's highly visible presence on the streets often led to standoffs, brawls, and sometimes far more violent clashes. Being a walking billboard for neo-Nazism took both a physical and emotional toll, but at the time, it was a price I was willing to pay.

One afternoon, after visiting a girlfriend, I was walking home when I noticed a black man approaching from the opposite direction. His eyes darted nervously. Something about his demeanor felt off – like he was either mentally unstable or under the influence of drugs.

As we were about to cross paths, his hand slid into his coat pocket. I locked onto it, every instinct firing at once. Was it a defensive bluff? A reach for a weapon? My focus narrowed, zeroing in on his hand.

Then – he lunged.

A blade flashed, catching the afternoon light. A cold rush of air grazed my flight jacket as I twisted away. A millisecond slower, and cold steel would have driven deep into my chest – leaving me bleeding out on the pavement.

He didn't say a word. No threat. No warning. Just silent, calculated violence.

After his first strike missed, he became frenzied – slashing wildly, each swing more erratic than the last. I backpedaled, barely staying ahead of the blade as it cut through the air, inching closer with every desperate lunge.

My mind raced. Should I break his wrist to disarm him? The

risk was high – one miscalculation, and he could sever an artery. The chaotic pursuit stretched down half a block, an agonizing eternity compressed into seconds, until the sharp glare of a squad car's lights flickered across the pavement. For once, I was relieved to see the police.

The officer confiscated the knife, but to my shock, let him go without charges. I was furious. A cop had witnessed a man trying to stab me – multiple times – and still, he walked free.

I turned to the officer, voice tight with disbelief. "What would happen if the roles were reversed? If I was the one trying to stab a black man on a public sidewalk?"

He didn't answer. So I pressed further.

"It would be national news. I'd be in a courtroom by morning, facing a decade in prison with hate-crime enhancements tacked on."

The man who had just tried to stab me in broad daylight, right in front of them, walked away. His knife was gone, but that didn't matter? He could get another. Next time, maybe he'd grab a gun. Why not? There were no consequences.

Incidents like that only reinforced my beliefs, deepening my commitment to neo-Nazism. A core tenet of the movement was that white people were treated unfairly – discriminated against – while minorities were handed special rights, affirmative action, and privileges that poor and working-class whites weren't eligible for.

When you're already entrenched in that mindset, and something like this happens – a minority tries to stab you in front of a cop and walks away without consequence – it doesn't just confirm your beliefs. It cements them.

Back then, I truly believed that's how the system worked.

I knew plenty of men who had gone to prison for hate-crimes, some serving exceptionally long sentences for what were, in comparison, minor offenses – vandalism, graffiti, a bar fight that got out of hand. Meanwhile, our enemies could attack us – attempt to kill us – and walk free. The double standard seemed glaring and unjust.

I'm not seeking sympathy, nor am I excusing the hateful ideology I was caught up in back then. But I ask you to pause and consider this: If a complete stranger tried to stab you in broad daylight, unprovoked – if the police watched it happen and still let your attacker walk free – how would you feel?

In that moment, I felt like the entire world was against me. That the system wasn't just broken – it was corrupt, rotten to the core.

Cliff had always advised us to avoid weapons and follow the law, but after the stabbing attempt, those rules seemed untenable. Our street-level forces adapted. Improvised weapons became the norm. One guy fashioned a vicious whip out of a bicycle chain. Another filled a metal bar with a lead-like substance – I confiscated that one because it could kill someone.

Carrying anything was high risk, as cops frequently stopped and searched us whenever they spotted us on the streets. After what happened, the bigger risk was not being armed.

Not long after the first stabbing attempt, it happened again – this time in the middle of a packed crowd at the Mall of America. There were six of us, decked out in skinhead gear – boots, braces, flight jackets – roaming the mall. When an interracial couple came into view, the floodgates of racial slurs opened. I didn't participate in the name-calling, but didn't stop it either. Looking back, I often wonder – was that really the kind of person I was back then? The sad truth is, yes.

It happened in a split second. The black man in the couple pulled a knife and came straight at me. Unlike the last attacker, this guy knew what he was doing. His movements were sharper, more controlled. My instincts fired – I saw it coming – but his speed caught me off guard. The blade sliced the air, barely missing me.

Then, just as fast as it started, it was over. The couple fled, disappearing into the crowd.

A bystander had seen everything and tipped off mall security, who arrived shortly after. The witness confirmed the attack, the details lining up exactly as it happened. Then one of the security guards scoffed.

"When you wear racist attire, you should expect stuff like this to happen."

Those words hit like a gut punch. That response further cemented my belief that any crime against us would be justified or swept under the rug by the system. While our rhetoric, behavior, and beliefs were repulsive and despicable, it still does not grant anyone the right to stab, maim, or kill over offensive words. It sets a dangerous precedent when name-calling is considered sufficient provocation for violence.

Weeks later, Michael and I were walking near the Brown House. As usual, he was in uniform. Up ahead, I spotted two men stepping off a basketball court – followed by a small crowd.

"Check it out," I motioned. "Two big Jews are headed our way."

Michael squinted in disbelief. "Jews don't get that big. You're wrong, Jeff."

In neo-Nazi circles, there's a stereotype that Jews are weak, small in stature, and inept at fighting. Encountering large Jewish men who towered over us shattered that stereotype. Whether they were actually Jewish or not remains unknown, but I assumed they were.

As they closed the distance, their body language was unmistakable – aggressive, ready to strike. One of them pointed at Michael's uniform.

"What the hell are you doing wearing a swastika?"

I shot back. "What are you Jews doing in our neighborhood?"

The explosion was instant. One of the men threw a devastating right hook. It connected with Michael's jaw, snapping his head sideways and sending him crumpling to the pavement. His legs buckled, body folding like a house of cards.

Now, it was two against one, and the crowd from the basketball court was closing in fast. With the odds stacked against us, it was time to level the playing field.

My hand shot into my pocket, fingers closing around the canister. Time seemed to slip into slow motion as I yanked it free, aimed, and squeezed the trigger.

A thick stream of burning yellow mist erupted, cutting through the fight like a miniature fire hose. It hit everything – the two men, the crowd, anyone caught in the line of fire.

Screams tore through the air. The group staggered, shielding their faces, stumbling back. Within seconds, they were retreating – blinded, coughing, disoriented, breaking apart like a panicked herd.

Michael groaned, stumbling to his feet, shaking off the hit.

"Whoa," he exhaled, dazed. "I never saw that coming! He sucker-punched me! Did you get hit?"

Still gripping the canister, I smirked. "Nope. Saw it coming, took a step back, and used this."

Michael cracked a grin, rolling his jaw to make sure it wasn't broken. "Yes! Victory by pepper spray!"

Then came the sirens. Police arrived fast – faster than I expected, and with them came a wave of anxiety. It didn't matter that we had acted in self-defense. Who were the cops going to believe? The Nazis or the crowd gasping for air, eyes red, soaked in pepper-spray?

The angry mob surged toward the officers, shouting for our arrest. In the middle of the chaos, one man stood out – red-faced, shrieking at the top of his lungs. "The Nazis maced me!"

The shrillness of his voice made me wince. A grown man, shrieking like a toddler afraid of the dark. At first, I thought he was a woman – his pitch was that high – but there were no women in the crowd. The absurdity of it all hit me, and for a fleeting moment, I felt secondhand embarrassment for him.

An officer moved through the mass of complaints, taking statements.

Michael and I, used to clashes like this, stayed still, silent – calm. The crowd, on the other hand, was a mess of flailing arms and wheezing outrage. Then, a voice broke through the noise.

"Officer, I saw the whole thing," a shopkeeper declared, stepping forward. "I can tell you exactly what happened."

The officer instructed us to stay put. We watched anxiously as the shopkeeper pointed toward the basketball courts, then at us, then at the crowd. For a moment, our fate seemed to hang in the balance.

"You two are very lucky," the officer said when he returned. "That witness backed up your story – otherwise, you could've been charged."

It was a pattern that had become all too familiar – once again, we had been just a breath away from imprisonment.

CHAPTER 6

FEAR

I've always had a strange relationship with fear. While guilty of instilling it in others, I rarely felt it myself – or at least, I never let it show. Guns, knives, threats – it didn't matter. I remained composed, unnervingly so. To say I was fearless would be inaccurate. Everyone has a breaking point, and one night, someone found mine.

It started with flashing lights appearing in my rear-view mirror. I pulled over, rolled down the window, and waited. The officer approached, but instead of the usual routine – license, registration – he just said, "Step out of the vehicle and get in the squad car."

Something felt off. When I reached for the back door, it didn't budge.

"No, up front," he said.

There was no standard protocol – just silence. He hadn't asked for ID, proof of insurance, nothing.

"Do you need to see my driver's license, sir?" I asked, trying to gauge his intent.

He turned and glared. "Schoep, I know exactly who you are."

The unease in my gut turned to a knot. "May I ask why you pulled me over?"

His jaw clenched. "I just want to talk," His voice was edged with barely controlled rage.

He was older, gray creeping into his hair, temper simmering

just beneath the surface. "What do you think your grandfather would say about this Nazi shit you're into?"

The question landed like a slap. I snapped back. "What would you know about my grandfather?"

"I know he fought for the Germans during the war," he sneered, tone dripping with condescension.

"Yeah, well, my family is none of your business."

I rarely discussed my family background, even within the Movement. I worried that German World War II veterans living in the U.S. could be accused of war crimes or mis-labeled as camp guards. The thought of my grandparents being deported or wrongfully accused because of my activism was unbearable. I'd already seen how my choices impacted my mother's career. What if my grandparents were next?

The cop leaned in, his voice ice-cold. "We know everything about you."

A chill shot down my spine. He pressed harder, relentlessly circling back to my grandfather, demanding to know what he would think of my views. I held my ground, evaded his questions, but his persistence was rattling.

His knuckles whitened as he gripped the steering wheel. "I bet your grandfather's ashamed of you. Even though he fought for the Nazis, I'm sure he regrets it now – just like he regrets having you as a grandson."

My usual cockiness evaporated. He was getting under my skin. No matter how vigilant I was about protecting my family, incidents like this kept happening. It took every ounce of restraint to keep from lashing out.

Sensing he had me on edge, the officer doubled down. He

kept trying to shame me, throwing out remarks about how embarrassed my grandparents must be. Each comment more invasive and inappropriate than the last. I was consumed with fear for my grandparents, worried they'd be targeted next.

By dragging my family into his twisted game, he gained the upper hand. My composure was slipping, and he knew it. He toyed with my emotions, smirking, chuckling under his breath, watching me squirm in the passenger seat.

After tolerating more than enough verbal abuse, it was time to go on the offensive. Civility and respect didn't resonate with this guy, so I flipped the script.

"I know exactly what this little talk is about – you're Jewish!" I shot back, patience gone.

"I'm German!" he snapped, temper flaring.

"Nice try, Jew-boy," I taunted, as the conversation devolved into childish bickering.

Fed up with the back-and-forth, I demanded, "Either charge me or let me go."

He flashed a smug grin. "Alright, skinhead, you can go," but the door stayed locked.

A slow, deliberate motion – he reached over and switched off the dispatch radio. The car plunged into a suffocating silence. I went for the door handle. His glare stopped me cold.

"I won't stop, do you hear me? He hissed through clenched teeth. "Not until you're rotting in a cell for the rest of your life, you Nazi bastard. If I could, I'd make sure you disappeared forever."

Those venomous words hung in the air.

I'd stared down threats before, but this was different. This wasn't a street fight or a rival crew looking to settle a score. This was a cop – someone who could act above the law with impunity and bury me.

I swallowed my pride and kept my mouth shut. At barely 20 years old, hearing a police officer say he wouldn't stop until I was locked up – or worse – was the most terrifying moment of my life.

Then – click. The lock disengaged. "You're free to go – for now."

I stepped out, body moving on autopilot, mind racing. The night air felt heavier. Streetlights cast jagged shadows. Every instinct screamed that this wasn't over.

As I walked away, I could feel his eyes drilling into my back, his words replaying in my head. *Not until you're rotting in a cell... If I could, I'd make sure you disappeared forever.*

This wasn't an enemy I could fight in the usual way. This wasn't a battle with fists, knives, guns, or even strategy. This was someone with the law on his side – someone who could erase me from the streets and chalk it up as just another skinhead getting what he deserved.

By the time I got home, my pulse was still hammering in my ears. I picked up the phone and called Cliff.

He didn't hesitate. "File a police report. Get it on record."

I scoffed. "Skinheads don't file police reports."

"That's exactly what he's counting on," Cliff shot back. "Think strategically. If he follows through on his threats and there's no record, who do you think the system – its courts – will believe?"

I hated that he was right. Ignoring it seemed easier, but doing nothing meant giving that cop free rein to follow through. Filing a report went against everything I stood for, but this wasn't about pride. This was about survival.

The incident shattered any illusions I had about being invincible. Part of me wanted to move away, but running from problems reeked of cowardice.

I thought about history – my ancestors fighting on the Russian front, facing the communist hordes with little more than sheer will. I remembered Opa's stories of yanking boots and gloves off dead Soviet soldiers just to survive the brutal cold. My situation wasn't even close to that level of hardship. If they could endure, so could I. Time to stand my ground.

The next day, I walked into the police station and approached the bulletproof glass. I gave the dispatcher the officer's name and a brief explanation of what had happened.

She nodded. "Wait here. Someone will be with you shortly."

A few moments later, the door to the dispatch area swung open.

To my dismay, the very same officer who had threatened me stepped into the room.

"Schoep!" he bellowed, voice dripping with disdain. "Are you here to file a complaint against me?"

A chills ran down my spine, anxiety levels spiked. I felt sick. How the hell was this possible? The irony was almost too much to bear – he was the one assigned to take my complaint.

I struggled to stay composed. "Yes, I'm filing a report over the threats you made."

He shoved the complaint form through the window slot, hard. "Go ahead, file it!" His tone oozed hostility.

As I stared at the paper every muscle in my body screamed to think carefully. Filing this report wasn't just paperwork – it was a declaration of war.

I met his gaze. "Actually... I think I'll just head home."

A slow smirk crept across his face. He was enjoying this. "Fine. Suit yourself."

Then, as if to drive the point home, he stepped out from behind the bulletproof glass and casually strolled toward the only exit.

"I'll even hold the door for you, skinhead," he sneered. "Have a nice day. Stay safe out there."

I moved toward the door – then hesitated.

"I'll just wait for you to go first," I said, voice steady, "since you seem to be heading that way."

His tone shifted instantly, growing darker, more threatening. "I'm holding the door for you. Get the fuck out now!"

A surge of fear shot through my veins. I stepped toward the exit, every muscle coiled, every instinct urging caution.

Then – bam!

He slammed his shoulder into me, sending me staggering backward. I barely caught my balance, eyes locking onto his hand as it wrapped around the grip of his service revolver. Time slowed to a sickening crawl.

"How dare you attack me!" he roared, voice thunderous in the small room. "Are you assaulting a police officer, you Nazi piece of shit? I'll blow your head off right here, right now!"

Terror gripped me, cold and absolute. I threw my hands up, praying with every fiber of my being that he wouldn't pull the trigger.

"Are you seeing this?" I called out, voice tight with panic. "This is why I came to file the complaint!"

The female officer behind the bulletproof glass didn't speak or react. She just stood there, frozen in place, eyes wide with disbelief.

"If you assault me again, Nazi," he spat, "I'll shoot you. That's a promise."

Petrified but refusing to yield to intimidation, I held my ground. "I'm not walking past you for anything. I'll stand here all day if I have to."

His fingers twitched against the grip of his gun. His other hand gestured impatiently. "Come on. Just walk through the door, and go."

The standoff stretched, seconds dragging like hours. Then – suddenly – he scoffed, muttered something under his breath, and stormed off. I didn't move, not right away. I needed to be sure.

Then, heart hammering, I stepped outside, every nerve on high alert. The walk home felt endless, my head on a swivel, glancing over my shoulder every few steps. All trust in law enforcement utterly decimated.

Even now, this memory is as sharp as a blade, lodged deep in my mind.

The most disturbing part wasn't just the threats. It was his unhinged behavior – inside a police station – with a witness standing mere feet away. If this could happen there, in a place meant to uphold the law – what hope was there for justice?

Of all the battles, the close calls, the moments where death felt just a breath away – this incident holds a prominent place in my relationship with fear. I was more afraid in that police station than at any other moment in my life.

Instead of breaking my spirit or making me question beliefs, every lash of the proverbial whip only strengthened my resolve. The psychological toll was immense, but I refused to be intimidated or driven off the battlefield. I'd rather face prison or death than be bullied, shamed, or coerced into submission.

CHAPTER 7

ENTRAPMENT

Before the internet became widespread, the NSM's primary contact point was a phone hotline. No caller ID. No way to verify who was on the other end. A vulnerability that, on more than one occasion, was exploited. One such call nearly altered my life forever.

The caller, who I'll refer to as Gordon, claimed to have military surplus gear he wanted to donate. At twenty years old, I was naive, impressionable – and enticed by the thought of free military equipment. The offer felt like a rare opportunity.

A flicker of caution reminded me: Survival depends on not jumping blindly into anything – even offers from supposed allies. I told Gordon that while we appreciated his support, such donations had to be cleared through our chain of command. It was beyond my authority.

We arranged to meet at a local café, bringing a small security detail along. Cliff usually took the lead in vetting new recruits, but this time, he was unusually quiet. His eyes locked onto Gordon, unreadable, watching. Something felt off.

Curiosity gnawed at me, so I asked Gordon how he'd acquired the gear.

"Logistics," he said casually, stirring his coffee. "I work on base. This stuff gets written off all the time."

Then, as if reciting a shopping list, he started naming off items. Rifles. Explosives. A charged silence settled over the table.

The hum of conversations around us faded into background noise. Cliff remained motionless, but when he finally spoke, his voice was cold, sharp, deliberate.

"We have no interest in what you're offering. Do not contact us ever again."

Each word landed with precision. Gordon's brow furrowed. His confidence wavered.

"What do you mean, don't contact you?" His voice held a tinge of desperation, bravado cracking. "How about Jeff – he seemed interested."

Cliff leaned forward. "Listen," he said, his tone lethal. "I know exactly what you are. You are not to contact anyone from the NSM ever again."

The mask slipped. Gordon's frustration flared. "Not sure what the issue is. Don't you guys realize how many people would line up for free gear like this?"

Cliff's stare hardened.

"Sir," he said coolly, "put your wallet on the table. Now."

The words stunned me. I'd never seen Cliff act like this before.

Gordon stiffened, insulted. His body tensed like he was ready to walk out. Just as he reached for his wallet to pay, Cliff's hand shot out – gripping his wrist.

In that instant, everything changed. Gordon's posture stiffened, his expression hardened. The sympathetic stranger vanished – replaced by something cold and methodical. Authority.

A tense pause stretched between them. Then, reluctantly, Gordon flashed his wallet just long enough for Cliff to see it.

No words were spoken. He shoved it back into his pocket and stormed off.

I exhaled, only now realizing how tight my chest had become.

"What the hell just happened?" I asked, still trying to process the scene.

Cliff leaned back, arms crossed, a smug satisfaction flickering in his eyes.

"You didn't get caught in a sting operation and end up in prison," he said.

He uncrossed his arms, his expression dead serious.

"That man was an undercover agent."

The truth hit hard. Like a warning shot, reverberating deep in my gut. That moment crystallized the dangerous tightrope I was walking. A single misstep could cost me everything. It was a lesson in the necessity of staying within the confines of legality.

Not long after, we heard about a skinhead crew from the West Coast who hadn't been so fortunate. They'd fallen into a similar trap, with devastating consequences. Allegedly, they were planning domestic terrorist acts – derailing trains, attacking infrastructure. Their leader was sentenced to eight years, despite his insistence that he'd been coerced and entrapped.

Being part of the NSM meant living in constant conflict with the US government. The offer of free military gear was just one attempt at entrapment – many more would follow in the years ahead. Each one a direct threat – to my life, liberty, and freedom.

CHAPTER 8

THE END OF
THE BROWN HOUSE

The writing was on the wall – our time at the Brown House was drawing to a close. One by one, roommates moved out, until only Michael and I remained. Our meager blue-collar jobs couldn't sustain the rent, let alone the gas, water, and electric bill. The last few months were a slow descent – ice-cold showers, darkened rooms, and peanut butter sandwiches for breakfast, lunch, and dinner.

We weren't completely alone. We had one other roommate: Stuka, a Rottweiler I'd rescued from a shelter. Michael had resented that from the start. Having a dog when we couldn't even afford to feed ourselves seemed like madness to him.

One afternoon, his voice erupted from the kitchen, raw with anger.

"Just look at what your animal did!"

I rushed in. The scene told the story before he did. A shredded bread bag, crumbs scattered across the linoleum, muddy paw prints tracking the crime scene. Then Stuka trotted in – completely unbothered – nose to the floor, sniffing for leftovers. Like it was just another day.

"We don't have the money to feed that thing – we can't even feed ourselves!" Michael's voice trembled with restrained fury. Then Stuka nudged his boot, still hunting for crumbs. That was the last straw. Michael reached into his jacket, unholstered his Magnum .44 – a weapon that looked eerily like Clint Eastwood's in Dirty Harry – and aimed it directly at Stuka's head.

"If this dog eats another scrap of my food, I'll blow its brains out."

My emotions flipped from mild sympathy to blazing rage. "Don't you dare point that gun at my dog."

Michael held his ground, hand steady on the gun. I took a slow breath, my voice dangerously calm. "If you pull that trigger – you'll be next."

His expression shifted from fury to disgust, but I didn't blink. "Put the gun away, Michael, or you'll be dead before you hit the ground."

For a moment, neither of us moved. Then – color drained from his face. His fingers trembled against the cold steel of the gun. Finally, he lowered it.

"We're supposed to be brothers," he muttered, voice thick with bitterness. "And you'd murder me over a damn dog?"

I didn't answer. He shoved the .44 back into his holster, grabbed his keys, and stormed out. The next day, Cliff called.

"Did you threaten Michael's life?"

I didn't hesitate. "It wasn't a threat – it was a promise."

If Michael had pulled that trigger, there would've been consequences.

Cliff exhaled, his tone measured. "You need to control your anger, Jeff. Michael never actually threatened you. You should apologize."

Apologizing felt like a lie, so I couldn't do it.

Though Michael and I eventually salvaged our friendship,

the Brown House was finished. Soon, I was on the verge of homelessness. Thankfully, Cliff's family took me in, providing a stable place to reset.

At the time, I was working downtown, about ten miles from Cliff's house. That morning, I climbed into the Fiero, cranked up the stereo, and merged into the rush-hour chaos. Something felt off. I tapped the brakes – no response. Pressing harder, I felt nothing beneath my foot. A sickening realization hit. The brakes were completely gone.

The traffic thickened, a semi-truck loomed ahead, blocking the lane. Swerving hard, I narrowly missed one car, then another, as horns blared and tires screeched. I was hurtling down the road in a fiberglass deathtrap, weaving through rush-hour traffic with no way to stop.

Then I spotted it – a gas station just before the freeway entrance. It was my only chance.

Slamming the gearshift, I downshifted hard. The engine roared in protest, but the speed dropped just enough to give me a shot at making the turn. I yanked the wheel and veered toward the gas station exit. The Fiero bounced violently, suspension groaning under the strain. The gas pumps rushed toward me – too close – way too close.

I forced the wheel toward a concrete parking block – aiming to kill the momentum. At the last second, I cut the ignition, yanked the keys, and braced. With a sickening jolt, the car lurched to a stop. Heart hammering, I exhaled, knuckles white on the wheel. Then, stepping out, I crouched beside the car and looked underneath. Just as I suspected – the brake lines had been slashed.

I had no money for repairs until payday, but the gas station owner was kind enough to let me leave the car there for a few days. That night, back at Cliff's house, he wasted no time letting me have it.

"What's it gonna take, Jeff?" His arms were crossed, expression sharp with frustration. "When are you going to start taking security seriously?"

I bristled, defensive. "No one ever had their brakes cut at the Brown House."

Cliff scoffed. "Yeah? And we had round-the-clock guards at the Brown House. We don't have that luxury here. While you're off dreaming about beer and women, anything could be happening in that parking lot."

He leaned forward, voice cold. "My car's been sabotaged twice since we moved here. Both times, I caught it before getting in," he continued. "There's no room for mistakes, Jeff. Mistakes cost lives." Those words landed heavier than I expected.

His tone dropped, stare sharpening. "Maybe you haven't noticed, but every time we leave the house, I inspect the car." He let that sink in before delivering the final blow.

"Think about it. What if you'd crashed into kids walking to school this morning? Could you live with that on your conscience?"

I smirked, trying to lighten the moment. "Got it. Inspect the car for sabotage before getting in, or risk becoming Minnesota's most hated, child-murdering freak."

Cliff's expression didn't change. His voice softened, but the weight behind it remained. "I don't think a guy who came that close to dying today should be making jokes so soon after. This isn't a game, Jeff. I couldn't bear it if something happened to you under my watch. Just do better, okay?"

It wasn't the last time my car was vandalized, but from that day forward, I never let my guard down again. Nearly every aspect of my life became rooted in conflict and security precautions.

Paranoia is a constant companion in extremist movements, but real-world consequences were always lurking just beneath the surface. Imagine checking your car for sabotage every single time you leave home. Civilians don't worry about that – but for a prominent figure in an extremist group, it becomes second nature.

At the time, I downplayed Cliff's warnings about mistakes costing lives. But in hindsight, those lessons saved me more times than I care to remember – especially as the targeted attacks escalated.

CHAPTER 9

ARRESTED

One afternoon, a group of us headed to the mall, pockets stuffed with stickers and mini-leaflets for distribution.

In the food court, I spotted a young white guy dressed in what we derisively called a 'whigger' look – sideways baseball cap, oversized sagging pants, embracing hip-hop culture. As warped as our beliefs were, his appearance immediately set us off.

I confronted him with a flyer titled Act Your Color, featuring a cartoon mocking white youth mimicking hip-hop culture. "You look like a damn clown dressed like that. Read this," I sneered, shoving the flyer at him. He kept his head down, avoiding eye contact, and quietly took the flyer before shuffling off – likely to tattle.

Mall security soon approached, informing us that leafleting wasn't allowed and ordering us to leave. Refusing to comply, I replied, "Hell no, we did nothing wrong and aren't leaving."

They explained that the swastika armband one of our guys was wearing had upset customers. I scoffed, "If someone's that damn sensitive, tell them not to look at it!"

Just then, a woman in a short skirt strutted by, so I paused to make a point. "Check this out – mall rent-a-cops are hassling us, and that's upsetting. Watching that smoking hot girl walk by? Not upsetting at all. Maybe I'll go get her number. See? It's all about perspective."

Tensions flared further when they asked us to turn our flight jackets inside out so the patches wouldn't offend anyone. I pushed back, "Are you saying if someone's clothes are offensive, they're banned from the mall? What if someone walked in draped in an Israeli flag, wearing a gold Star of David necklace? Would you ask them to leave?"

The guard looked confused. "Of course not; that isn't offensive."

"Wrong!" I snapped. "It offends us! We're customers too, and Jewish symbolism offends us, but we're not demanding anyone leave."

Mall security had had enough. One of the guards exhaled sharply, clearly out of patience.

"Take off the armband. Stop handing out materials. You can stay."

We weighed our options. They couldn't force us out, and agreeing to their terms felt like a minor victory. We took the deal.

About thirty minutes later, we noticed two men shadowing us, trailing from store to store. One of them wore a prominent gold Star of David necklace. It didn't feel like a coincidence. Not after our argument with mall security. To test if we were actually being followed, we ducked into a women's boutique. Sure enough, they followed us inside.

I put my arm around Kari and whispered, "What do you think the odds are of two Jews stalking us after what I said to mall security?"

She giggled. "Probably about six million to one."

They hadn't spoken, hadn't confronted us, but their presence was grating on my nerves. It felt like a silent challenge, one I wasn't willing to ignore.

Hoping to drive them off, I loudly told a highly offensive anti-Semitic joke, making sure they heard every word. It seemingly worked. They left.

I smirked. "See? Tell a joke they won't like, and just like that – problem solved."

But I spoke too soon. As we neared the mall exit, we were met with an unwelcome sight – a sizable contingent of police officers, backed by mall security. We were completely encircled. Stares came from every direction. Before I could process what was happening, my arms were yanked behind my back and cold steel snapped around my wrists.

Dragged into a holding area inside the mall, I was shoved into a chair as a police investigator loomed over me, arms crossed. His expression was hard, tone accusing.

"Our witnesses informed us that you said you were planning a second Holocaust, starting with them. Is that correct?"

I shook my head, stunned. "Absolutely not. I told a joke. Either they misheard, or they're deliberately lying."

After the interrogation, we were released with a warning – a court date would be coming in the mail. The charges were unclear, and I couldn't wrap my head around how telling an anti-Semitic joke was considered a crime. The only explanation I was given was that it fell under a new law: ethnic intimidation.

For weeks, I called the courthouse, checking for updates. Every time, the answer was the same – my name wasn't on the docket. With no official notice arriving in the mail, I assumed the case had been dropped as frivolous. It seemed like a dead issue. However, fate had a different plan.

One evening, the police arrived at Cliff's place and hauled me off to jail. Later, I was told that the court notices were supposedly sent to an outdated address and never forwarded. The irony was hard to miss – they sent the notices to the wrong place but knew exactly where to come for the arrest.

The Bloomington Police took me to jail, and after a few hours in a cell, I was transferred to downtown Minneapolis. For a twenty-year-old white kid from rural Minnesota, being sent to the infamous Minneapolis jail was a nightmare scenario. The transfer happened in the dead of night, and upon arrival, I politely asked for contact lens solution. The guards shrugged it off, saying the day shift would handle it in the morning. Agitated, I protested with an obnoxious level of insolence.

"This is jail," a guard replied flatly. "It's not meant to be accommodating. Deal with it."

"Fine, I'll kick the cell door all night until contact solution is provided."

"Waking up the entire cell-block probably isn't the brightest idea," he warned.

WHAM! I kicked the cell door, then again, and again. The entire cell block erupted with shouts and threats as I pounded on the door like a petulant child, kicking until I wore myself out.

"Cut the noise! Shut the hell up! Go to sleep! We'll kick your head in tomorrow!"

The next morning, contact solution was finally provided. As my contacts soaked, an inmate covered in jailhouse ink – whom I'll call Tattoo – approached. "Hey, new guy, it's time for breakfast."

I shook my head. "I'm good."

He raised a brow. "Seriously? Lunch is a long way off. You should eat."

Figuring he knew better, I went. It was my first time being locked up, and Tattoo started filling me in on jail life. He explained that most guys in the pod were chill and didn't pose a threat – except for one, Tito.

I glanced at him. "What's his deal?"

Tattoo lowered his voice. "He's the only black guy in this pod, just caught his second murder charge. He's got nothing to lose, likes to throw his weight around, and has a wicked temper."

Another inmate smirked, "Yeah, I bet Tito's been itching to meet you after last night, since you kept us all up banging on the door."

Before I could respond, a tray slammed down across from me. I looked up. A black man, muscles tense, eyes locked on me. "Who the hell was making all that noise last night?" Then – casually – another inmate pointed his spoon at me.

Tito's glare was intense. "What the hell's wrong with you? Withdrawals or something?"

I explained the contact lens issue, and he seemed to relax slightly. "Man, that's messed up. The guards always do shit like that."

Then, without missing a beat, he pointed at my tray. "Give me your egg!" His words hung in the air as silence descended upon the entire table. Although I was young and unfamiliar with jail, it would be a cold day in hell before I let someone disrespect or take advantage of me. Expecting a fight to pop off, I went all in.

"No, you cannot have my egg," I said firmly. "But I'll trade you for it."

I picked up a banana and held it out. "You give me your egg for this."

Tito stood up, jaw clenched, fists tightening, eyes locked on the fruit in my hand. Around the table, guys gripped their trays, ready to bolt at the first sign of trouble.

Then, Tito reached for the banana, slid his tray toward me, and grinned.

"I think my cholesterol's a little high these days anyway." He laughed, shaking his head. "I like this new guy!"

Tension drained from the table as conversations picked back up, but Tito kept studying me.

"You look familiar." I shrugged. "Don't think we rolled in the same circles."

"Nah, not that." He squinted, eyes scanning my face. "I remember faces. I've seen you on TV."

A jolt shot through me. Before being doxxed by Barbara Carlson, I had appeared on The Montel Williams Show under a fake name. My long hair was tucked under a black hat, sunglasses shielding my identity.

Ironically, that appearance had also marked my first interaction with what many would call a black supremacist group – the Black Hebrew Israelites. Their rhetoric mirrored much of the white supremacist Christian Identity ideology – only in reverse.

I'd also been featured on the news. If that's what Tito was remembering, things could get dicey fast. At the breakfast table, my mind drifted back to that day on Montel Williams.

"For sure, I've seen you on a talk show!" Tito squinted, trying to place me. "The Arsenio Hall show, right?"

"No," I said, shaking my head, bracing for all hell to break loose. "It was Montel Williams. I was on with some Black Hebrews."

Tito's expression shifted as the memory clicked.

"Oh yeah, that's right! It was Montel." He nodded, thoughtful but still guarded. "So, what's it all about? Y'all trying to put chains back on all the Black people?"

He didn't sound hostile – more curious – but the rest of the table seemed to be holding their breath.

I shrugged. "The system wants to put chains on all of us," I said, gesturing around the jail.

As the conversation continued, I steered it toward NSM policies – racial preservation, a drug-free lifestyle. To my surprise, Tito didn't immediately dismiss it. Instead, we found unexpected common ground discussing the destructive effects of drugs on our communities and the importance of preserving cultural identity. Despite our vastly different backgrounds, we shared stories of struggle and discovered unexpected commonalities.

Not long after, a guard pulled me aside and warned, "You better stop spreading that Nazi bullshit in our jail." I smirked, promising to keep preaching until they released me.

"Alright, inmate," the guard replied coldly, "if you don't stop, we'll throw you into solitary confinement." Normally, I'd fire back with sarcasm or defiance, but this time, held my tongue.

Tito smirked as he walked up. "Bet I know what that scolding was about."

"Yeah, it seems freedom of speech is dead in here," I replied, feigning indifference.

In a somber tone Tito said, "Jeff, if you're looking for any sort of freedom, you'll never find it here."

After a couple of nights behind bars, my family posted bail. As I changed out of jail clothes, I couldn't resist taunting the guards on the way out. "Hey, I've got some NSM cards in my pockets. You guys want any?"

No response. Just cold, disapproving stares.

Despite despising my political views and poor choices that landed me in jail, my family's love never wavered. They were determined to intervene. A few miles down the road, Dad broke the uncomfortable silence.

"Jeff, we really want you to leave the movement," he said firmly. "We've arranged for you to stay with your uncle for a while." After a pause, his voice softened, "Your mother has been worried sick about you being in jail."

He tried everything to get through to me, but I felt like a source of shame, being shuffled between relatives like a recovering addict. Reluctantly, I went to stay with my uncle in the far-flung suburbs. The plan was clear: after a short stay, I'd be sent to an aunt's farm in rural Iowa. It felt like exile. Hundreds of miles from the NSM. Hundreds of miles from my girlfriend. The thought was unbearable.

So, one afternoon, I walked to a payphone, called a friend, and waited beneath a highway overpass for extraction.

RISING TO THE TOP

It was around 1994, and I had no idea how drastically my life was about to change.

Out of the blue, I was appointed Commander – the National

Leader of the NSM.

Cliff was stepping away to focus on his family, retiring from active duty, though he would remain Chairman Emeritus. Overnight, the weight of day-to-day operations fell on my shoulders. Leading the Party had never been my ambition. It never even crossed my mind. Yet, with reluctance, I accepted the role – becoming the youngest national leader in the neo-Nazi movement.

Skepticism followed. Veterans of the party questioned whether someone so young was qualified to lead. Earning trust and establishing credibility wasn't something that happened overnight – it was an uphill battle that took years.

Within the ranks, disloyalty and disruptive behavior were not tolerated. Those who challenged leadership faced swift demotions or outright purges. The movement had no patience for weak links. Those who joined expecting a fast-track to power were quickly outmaneuvered, unable to command respect or cooperation from their peers.

Time and again, it was the reluctant leaders – those who never sought power, but had it thrust upon them – who proved to be the most effective.

Leadership within the NSM meant juggling multiple roles: authority figure, mediator, teacher, enforcer, coach, and confidant. It was all-consuming. From preparing troops for conflict to steering clear of criminal influences, leading effectively required a delicate balance – firm but fair, with a steel resolve and, at times, an iron fist.

Over time, I implemented a military-like structure, establishing a clear chain of command. I introduced handbooks and protocols, ensuring the organization operated like a well-oiled machine.

After Cliff's departure, I relocated to Saint Paul, where the bulk of the NSM forces were based. Soon, I'd lay the groundwork for nationwide expansion.

CHAPTER 10

ARYAN NATIONS

In the mid-1990s, I was invited to speak at the Aryan Nations World Congress near Hayden, Idaho. White Nationalist groups from around the globe flocked to the annual event. Being invited as a speaker was considered a great honor, so I made the trip with my girlfriend, Shannon.

When we arrived at Aryan Nations, the first thing that caught my attention was the guards at the gate, all dressed in blue uniforms. Unable to resist, I joked, "You guys look like cops! We almost turned around, thinking the event had been raided."

They didn't laugh.

We parked and took in the surroundings – a church with stained glass windows, towering flagpoles, an imposing guard tower, and several buildings scattered across the compound. It was a strange mix of religion, paramilitary aesthetics, and ideological zealotry, all concentrated in one place.

Inside the church office, we approached Pastor Butler, the leader of Aryan Nations. As we got closer, a low growl rumbled from beneath his desk. Hans, one of his German Shepherds, didn't take kindly to anyone getting too close to the Pastor.

That year's speakers included some of the biggest names in the movement. Louis Beam, who introduced the concept of Leaderless Resistance, was there. So was Pastor Neuman

Britton, along with JB Stoner, whose history traced back to the founding of the National States' Rights Party in 1958. Stoner had once served as an attorney for James Earl Ray, the man who assassinated Dr. Martin Luther King Jr.

The featured speaker from Canada was John Ross Taylor, a relic from another era. In the 1930s, he had been involved with the Canadian Union of Fascists, and during World War II – like many of his American Nazi counterparts – he was imprisoned in an internment camp. It was a reminder that history had a long, tangled way of repeating itself. After all, Japanese-Americans had also been interned during the war – one of America's darker chapters.

Among the speakers at the Congress, I felt like a kid surrounded by elders – men who had spent their entire lives devoted to white nationalism. These weren't guys who had joined some Aryan gang to survive prison or hobbyists going through a phase. They were the architects of the movement. Anxiety crept in. How could I possibly add anything of value, sharing the stage with men who had been shaping this ideology since before I was born?

Pastor Butler delivered a fiery sermon, and Louis Beam spoke of his experience being tried for sedition by the U.S. government in 1987. For me, Pastor Neuman Britton stood apart. His delivery was mesmerizing – a hellfire-and-brimstone sermon that shook the audience to its core. He didn't just speak. He commanded. After the speeches, I sought him out.

"Incredible speech, Pastor. One day, I hope to learn to speak as powerfully as you."

He placed a hand on my shoulder, his gaze steady.

"Son, you'll far surpass me in time. I sensed it the moment I heard you speak today."

His words hit like a surge of electricity – a defining moment.

It was time to sharpen my skillset and grow into the role of a political leader.

KICKED IN

Alcohol was forbidden on Aryan Nations grounds. Anyone caught drinking risked expulsion. Still, some managed to skirt the rules. One night, a group of us headed to a fishing dock near the church. With no moonlight to cut through the darkness, the lake stretched out like a vast, endless void, its surface barely visible in the night. The air was cool, the water eerily still – and the beer and vodka were flowing freely.

Shannon, irritated with my drinking, insisted on leaving. Others were heading back to the compound, so she caught a ride with them.

I had other priorities that night – specifically, Cassie, a petite blonde who had been batting her eyes and flirting with me since we first met. I had every intention of seeing what kind of trouble we could get into together.

Earlier that day, I had caught my share of judgmental stares and whispers warning me to steer clear of her. Sure, I already had a beautiful girlfriend – but always preferred having two, and in the Christian Identity faith, multiple wives were permitted.

Bird, a kickboxer from the West Coast, had his eye on Cassie, too. Even in the darkness, I could feel his jealousy simmering as she giggled at my jokes. But she wasn't his, so what he thought wasn't my problem.

I couldn't resist poking at him.

"You're not going to get drunk and start crying over there, are you, Bird?" I smirked.

The group erupted with laughter, picturing a tough fighter like Bird shedding tears after a few beers. Teasing was normal. It was part of the camaraderie.

Then – suddenly – the pitch-black night erupted with a flash of white lightning.

I blinked – stumbled – BOOM. Face-first, I hit the dock.

Distant shouts echoed around me, muffled like background noise, barely registering as the metallic taste of blood flooded my mouth. Disoriented, I tried to process what had happened. Bird had blindsided me – with a brutal kick to the face.

I had never experienced such a sudden, violent outburst from a so-called movement brother. Kicking someone in the face over a harmless joke was unthinkable. The brotherhood that had once defined Aryan Nations felt like it was corroding, rusting away like cheap iron.

Furious, I forced myself up, wiping the blood from my face.

"Where the hell is Bird?" I shouted. "I want to face that coward right NOW!"

Jamie, one of the guys from the Church, pressed a cold beer can against my nose. "Lean back – it'll slow the swelling."

I shoved it away.

"If Bird wants a fight, he should face me like a man instead of taking a cheap shot and running like a little bitch. Where is he?"

"He took off," Jamie said.

He hesitated before adding, "Jeff, you're very lucky. If you'd lost consciousness or fallen just a couple feet in any other direction, you could've drowned. It's so dark out here – if you ended up in those deep waters, you'd be gone."

Violence had always been a part of my world, but until that night, I had never experienced this level of savagery – not among brothers. It wasn't the physical pain that stung the most – it was the betrayal.

Back at the compound, Jamie brought me to the infirmary, where an old Klansman tended to the injury. The pain was excruciating as he reset the broken bone; I clenched my jaw, bracing against each jolt.

Suddenly, the door flung open. Tim, the Aryan Nations chief of staff, stormed in. "What the hell's going on here? Jeff, what happened to your face?"

The old-timer spoke up, "Some of the youngsters were horsing around. That kick-boxer fella kicked Jeff in the face and broke his nose."

Tim's mouth dropped, as he pressed Jamie, "Did this happen on church grounds?"

"No, sir, at the docks."

Tim scowled. "I'm well aware of what you kids do at the docks. Where is Bird now?"

"He took off after kicking Jeff," Jamie replied. "Probably at the men's bunkhouse."

Tim looked down at my blood-soaked shirt, his expression hardening. He turned and stormed off. Minutes later, I was summoned to the bunkhouse, where the commotion had woken everyone. Tim – face red with fury – had dragged Bird out of his bunk and forced him onto his knees in the middle of the floor.

"Tell him!" Tim growled, nudging Bird with his boot.

With a blank, emotionless stare, Bird muttered, "Sorry. What I did was dishonorable." He hesitated, then added, "You can kick me in the face if you want... since that's what I did to you."

The room fell deathly silent, like time had slowed. I glanced at Tim, unsure how to respond. I'd been fixated on revenge, but this moment required something else – accountability and a measured response.

Bird represented a dangerous level of unpredictability, one that put the unity and stability of our cause at risk. He displayed a pathetic sense of entitlement, expecting others to tolerate his shortcomings. His lack of self-control rendered him a loose cannon – a liability to us all.

This felt like a defining moment for leadership – one that could shape my reputation and set an example for others. True strength wasn't found in aggression – it was in the ability to rise above base impulses, to demonstrate restraint.

There was no honor in kicking a man while he was on his knees – even if he deserved it.

I met Bird's vacant stare and spoke with deliberate calm.

"Bird, I'm nothing like you. What you did was pure cowardice, and I refuse to stoop to your level. A fair fight would've been better, but this ends now – for the sake of the cause."

As Tim and I left the bunkhouse, he patted me on the shoulder. "Good man. I figured you'd do the right thing."

"But was it really the right decision?" I asked, feeling uncertain.

Tim paused, then said, "There's no easy answer. Both choices had merit, but you put the well-being of the cause above personal revenge. That was impressive – and it showed true leadership."

CROSSING PATHS WITH MURDER

After the Congress, Shannon and I decided to stay at the compound, leaving behind our modest possessions and skipping out on our rent back in Minnesota. Finding work in northern Idaho proved almost impossible – especially with Aryan Nations as our mailing address. About a month later, with no job prospects, we knew it was time to return to Minnesota.

Even after leaving, I kept in touch with Pastor Butler, Tim, and others for years. But one name – one face – faded from memory entirely. Until it resurfaced on the news.

THE MONSTER WE OVERLOOKED

During our time at Aryan Nations, we met an unassuming security guard named Buford. I never gave him a second thought, not until 1999.

That year, Buford walked into a Jewish community center with an Uzi sub-machine gun and opened fire. He shot three children, a counselor, and an office worker. Then, after fleeing, he murdered a postal worker – someone who had simply been in the wrong place at the wrong time.

It's hard to reconcile having crossed paths with someone who later committed such atrocities. So, why didn't that make me walk away?

For many involved in extremism, a deep psychological disconnect develops. I, like so many others, had convinced myself that acts of terrorism and murder were carried out by the mentally unstable – never recognizing how the ideology itself fueled such actions.

Mental health issues can amplify the potential for violence, but when combined with extremist beliefs, they create a volatile mix. When isolation, fear, and desperation build, it can spiral into deep-seated, irrational hatred. Extremist ideologies – rooted in an 'us versus them' mentality – create an environment where those already struggling with mental health issues are far more likely to cross the line into violence, justifying it as self-defense or a duty to their race.

This justification of violence isn't exclusive to white supremacy. Extremism – whether ideological, religious, or political – operates on the same rationalizations.

For instance, rioters incensed by perceived injustice might burn down neighborhoods, directing their rage toward unrelated people or businesses. Just like white supremacists, they frame their violence as justified retaliation, as self-defense – normalizing it, making it seem reasonable. At its core, extremism operates on the same principle, no matter the belief system.

After decades immersed in that world, I understand how it warps the mind – and I see it seeping into society today. It's a pervasive problem, stretching far beyond any single ideology.

THE SURVIVOR

Fast-forward to 2021 – I had the chance to meet Josh, a survivor of Buford's hate-fueled mass shooting. The meeting – graciously arranged by Rabbi Abraham Cooper and Rick Eaton, Director of Research at The Simon Wiesenthal Center in Los Angeles – was filmed by an NBC TV crew.

Meeting Josh was deeply emotional. It brought me face-to-face with the consequences of violence unleashed by someone I had once crossed paths with at Aryan Nations.

I had no idea how Josh would feel about meeting someone with my past – and I was keenly aware of the possibility of causing him further pain.

My only hope was that our meeting, in some small way, might contribute to his healing.

Josh's courage was evident from the start.

As a child, he had survived a near-fatal attack by a white supremacist – yet here he was, willing to meet a former neo-Nazi leader who had only turned away from that world two years earlier.

In Josh, I found something unexpected, a kindred spirit – a man committed to Tikkun Olam, the Jewish principle of repairing the world. Meeting him was an honor, and today, we stand together as allies in the work of peace-building.

Coming to terms with the fact that the ideology I once embraced was responsible for such horrific acts has left a deep scar on my conscience. Through self-reflection, I've learned the importance of taking responsibility for past actions and striving to make amends. Acknowledging the harm done is a crucial step toward healing – both for myself and for others – and may help prevent more people from falling into similar destructive patterns.

We must work toward a society that rejects extremism, fosters inclusivity, and encourages civil discourse. Only then can we prevent future tragedies and create a world that values peace.

CHAPTER 11

HOMELESS AND HOPELESS

As Idaho faded in the rear-view mirror, Shannon and I grew anxious about what awaited us in Minnesota. Could we negotiate more time to pay the rent? Would our jobs still be there?

Our return was a rude awakening. We arrived around 2 a.m., only to find an eviction notice tacked to the door, and the locks changed. Catching up on rent was no longer an option – but what about our belongings?

There was only one way in. A bathroom window that didn't lock, overlooking the roof. I climbed through, barely avoiding a head-first dive into the toilet. Unsure if this was even legal, we grabbed what we could – two garbage bags' worth of essentials – and stepped into the cold reality of homelessness.

Shannon's eyes filled with tears. Everything we owned was gone, except for two trash bags stuffed into the tiny trunk of the Fiero.

"Please try to cheer up," I said, trying to sound hopeful. "We'll have paychecks and another apartment soon."

The next morning, we found a payphone and made the dreaded call to our employer. The news hit like a gut punch – our jobs had been filled. It felt like we were drowning, gasping for air with no hope in sight.

With nowhere else to go, we set up camp in the woods at

a park near St. Paul. Shannon was resilient, sticking with me through hell, but I worried this might be her breaking point.

That night, I pushed a can of chili toward the campfire, hoping to ease into a conversation. Shannon sat staring into the flames, silent.

Then, her voice shook. "Jeff, I have to tell you something."

She hesitated, her breath unsteady. Then, finally – "I'm pregnant."

We were still kids ourselves. What should have been a joyful moment felt overwhelming in the face of our circumstances. Now more than ever, we needed to escape homelessness and build a stable life – for the sake of our unborn child.

Our search for work dragged on, but most employers wouldn't hire anyone without a phone number, complicating job-seeking opportunities in an era prior to affordable cellphones. Meanwhile, the daily ritual of breaking camp had grown exhausting.

One morning, I suggested, "Let's leave the tent up today so we have more time to job hunt. No one's going to find it out here, and who'd mess with a tent and some blankets anyway?"

After another fruitless day of searching, we returned to a ravaged landscape. Our tent was gone, its ties left dangling mockingly from tree branches. Our pillows and blankets had been shredded, trampled, and smeared with mud. We stood there, surveying the wreckage in stunned silence. It felt like the final nail had just been hammered into our coffins.

That night, we scraped together a meager meal of cold canned vegetables, then tried to sleep upright in my cramped two-seater car. Sleep never came.

I stared into the darkness, my mind cycling through the same question – what's next? I didn't even want to know the answer to that question.

A week later, desperate for some semblance of normalcy, we went to a party with people from the Movement. It was a break from the suffocating confinement of the car – at least for one night.

While refilling my cup at the keg, Paul, a skinhead from another crew, approached.

"Jeff, I heard a rumor that you and your pregnant girlfriend are living in a tent?"

I stiffened. "Who told you that?"

Paul didn't blink. "Don't worry about who told me – just tell me if it's true."

I hesitated. "Maybe, but we're figuring it out."

"Bro, you need to learn to reach out when you're struggling. You can't expect people to just find out and come to your aid."

I bristled. "Paul, I don't expect anyone to help me with anything."

His demeanor softened. "Jeff, everyone knows you're the last person who'd take advantage of anyone. Enjoy the party, but when it's over, you and Shannon are staying at my place – and I won't take no for an answer."

Despite my unwillingness to ask for help, Paul and his family showed us kindness and compassion when we needed it most. Their generosity gave us a chance to regroup – a rare moment of stability that helped us begin to get back on our feet.

CHAPTER 12

BARS AND BRAWLS

In my early twenties, the nightlife in Saint Paul was a whirlwind of excitement, women, and the occasional barroom brawl. We'd start the night with a semblance of decorum, but as the drinks flowed, inhibitions dropped fast, and things often descended into hooliganism. A seductive glance from a beautiful woman or a provocation from a wannabe tough guy was usually all it took to set things off. I was always primed for whatever would light that fuse.

One night, on the way to a bar, I picked up Justin, a skinhead who was new in town. He mentioned he usually avoided bars because trouble seemed to follow him wherever he went.

I scoffed, "So, you're always the target in a bar fight?"

"Every time," Justin sighed. "If there's a punch thrown, it's like it's got my name on it."

I laughed. "Well, maybe it's because you're a skinhead. That can rub some folks the wrong way, you know?"

Justin shook his head. "Even as a kid, way before I was a skin, if a rock got thrown on the playground, it was aimed at me."

"So, are you saying you'd rather not go out?" I asked.

He shrugged. "I like going out. Just don't blame me if something kicks off."

When we arrived at the bar, our crew – including a massive guy I'll call Ox, standing 6'6" and tipping the scale at over 300 pounds – saluted us as we walked in.

"Hey, bro, I'm gonna grab a CD from my truck to show you," he said as we settled in.

Then, a black man tapped me on the shoulder. "Mind if I pull up a chair? I need to tell you something."

"Are you sure you want to sit with us?" I asked. There was no mistaking who we were – we were practically billboards for neo-Nazism. Still, I was curious, and offered him the seat next to me. In a hushed tone, he said, "The bar owner's talking about picking a fight with you guys. He's kinda crazy, and once he's had a few drinks, he gets really stupid."

"Who's the owner?" I asked.

"Hang on," he whispered, scanning the bar, then subtly pointed out the owner.

The bar owner looked furious, but hardly like a real threat. He looked like a tubby, middle-aged alcoholic – better suited for backyard grilling than picking fights with skinheads.

"Yeah, the owner starts fights in here all the time," the man continued.

I laughed. "Seriously? There are ten of us. Even our smallest guy could wipe the floor with him."

"Yeah, but he's got a few screws loose. Just remember, I gave you a heads-up, alright?"

I lifted my mug in acknowledgment. "Thanks, man. Much appreciated."

"You sure you don't wanna leave, avoid the trouble?"

I chuckled. "Nah, we're not going anywhere."

The words had barely left my mouth when the bar owner lunged at Justin. Grabbing him from behind, he flipped him backward off his bar stool. Justin's beer bottle shattered as his head hit the concrete floor with a sickening thud.

"Nazis! Get the fuck outta my bar!" the owner bellowed.

The place exploded into chaos. A cook burst from the kitchen, swinging a baton, as punches flew, chairs flipped, and glass shattered around us. Some guy started hurling billiard balls like a baseball pitcher – one whizzed past my head as I charged into the fray. Narrowly avoiding a skull-cracking hit, I set my sights on the guy throwing them.

Before I could reach him, a huge, burly man grabbed me like I weighed nothing and slammed me into the wall. The air rushed from my lungs as he yanked my shirt over my head – like a hockey fight – and started raining down punches. Blow after blow landed. I was stunned – but still in the fight, and responded by unleashing a barrage of quick strikes to his face.

His grip loosened, I had him. Then – WHAM! Another guy jumped in, and together they slammed me back against the wall. One of them pinned his forearm against my throat, choking me, while the other buried a fist in my gut, knocking the wind out of me. This fight was going downhill fast.

I struggled to break free from the choke-hold while absorbing punches. Across the bar, Charlie dropped the guy throwing billiard balls. Then – BOOM. The crowd split like the Red Sea as Ox stormed in from his truck. Plowing through bodies like a raging bull tearing through a wheat field, he snatched the burly man off me and flung him across the bar like a discarded ragdoll. Breaking free, I drove a fierce uppercut into the other guy's jaw. He stumbled backward but was still standing. I wound up for the knockout punch, then a massive hand clamped onto my shoulder and dragged me toward the exit.

"Let's go!" Ox thundered.

Inside, the bar owner and his staff were barricading the door while some of our crew tried kicking it down, desperate to get back in and restart the brawl. Through the window, I caught a glimpse of the man who had warned us, shaking his head in disappointment – one of the few who had stayed out of the chaos.

"Ox, why'd you break up the fight? I had it under control."

Ox scowled. "Oh really? You call getting pummeled into a wall by two guys 'under control'? Your shirt is barely hanging on by threads. Yeah, sure, Jeff – totally under control."

I sighed. "Yeah, I suppose you're right. Thanks for stepping in."

With sirens closing in, we scattered to evade the cops. Some of us weren't so lucky; those who got caught faced legal consequences, despite the bar owner's unprovoked attack on Justin. Predictably, no one from the bar – including the owner who'd started the fight – was held accountable. The newer members struggled to wrap their heads around how we could be charged while the other side walked away without consequence.

By then, I was numb to what we bitterly called the "INjustice system." But for those who were caught, it hit hard – they grew twice as angry and even more defiant. Facing charges for a fight they hadn't started, while the bar owner who'd triggered everything got to play the victim, only reinforced our belief that the system was out to crush us.

It didn't matter whether we were the aggressors or the victims – we were always the ones paying the price. That was our reality, as we saw it.

DETOXED

Another weekend rolled around, and our bar-hopping antics continued. This time, a small group of us walked from my apartment to a bar. The night started off chill, but as the drinks flowed, our behavior grew more confrontational, obnoxious, and laced with hate.

Then, an interracial couple walked in. Our table erupted with hate-filled slurs directed at them. They ignored us, refusing to engage, and quickly left the bar.

The atmosphere was tense, ready to ignite. Then, a Hispanic man approached our table chastising us for the racist comments. He was right; our remarks were vile and wrong. That being said, confronting a group of drunken skinheads was a recipe for disaster.

I stood up, locking eyes with him. "Mind your own business."

His buddies stood up – so did our crew. The air thickened with tension – it was about to pop off. Then, the barmaid rushed in, stepping between us.

"Sit down. All of you. Now."

Her tone left no room for argument. After a few tense seconds, we backed off, finished our drinks, and stumbled outside.

As soon as we hit the sidewalk, I saw them – a lineup of cop cars waiting for us. Shit, I straightened up, trying to play it cool. "Is there a problem, officer?"

The cop smacked his nightstick into his palm, eyes locked on me.

"You know damn well there is." His voice was flat, dangerous.

"Get in the squad car, or I'll throw you in headfirst."

He wasn't bluffing. He ratcheted the handcuffs so tight they cut off circulation. Then – BAM! He slammed my head against the roof of the car before shoving me into the back seat.

Brad was livid, spitting a string of profanities as they cuffed him and slammed him face-first onto the hood of another cop car. The rest of us were cuffed without much incident and carted off to the drunk-tank.

At detox, they ran breathalyzer tests. When it was my turn, the worker tested me twice.

His brows furrowed. "This thing's gotta be broken."

He reset the machine and tested me again, same result. He gave me a long, hard look.

"I don't get it. At this level, most people would be unconscious. Hell, some would be in critical condition."

I shrugged. "Guess I've built a tolerance."

His expression didn't change. "You should see a doctor when you get out."

The conditions in the holding cells were appalling. A drain hole in the floor – meant for urine and vomit – reeked of overuse. The walls were grimy, the air stale with sweat, piss, and regret. The only way to cope was to detach – to shut down basic hygiene and dignity.

When we were finally moved into the detox common area,

I did a headcount. Everyone was accounted for – except Brad. I asked the guard, who barely looked up.

"He's still in holding. Refused to comply with staff orders to leave."

I chuckled. "So, he's just... sitting in there?"

The guard smirked. "Still deciding what to do with him."

Amusing as it was that Brad chose to marinate in a piss-soaked cell, I was more concerned that his defiance would land him in jail.

"Show me where Brad is, and I'll bring him out."

The guard shook his head. "Only employees are allowed back there."

I sighed. "Fine, then tell him the NSM Commander ordered him out – and it's not a suggestion."

A few minutes later, Brad strolled out, sporting a mischievous grin.

"So, you had to pull rank and ruin all my fun? Were you guys scared without me?" he teased.

I shook my head. "No, we just needed you out here for entertainment since you're such a ray of sunshine. Seriously though – why the hell did you stay in that nasty cell?"

Brad smirked. "Maybe I enjoy the lovely aroma of rancid piss and squalor?"

Within 48 hours, we were released into the custody of our furious wives and girlfriends.

After a string of incidents like these, the mounting consequences forced us to shift course. Bar-hopping took a backseat – not because we'd grown up, but because it became a liability. Instead, we started hosting our own parties, where we could control the environment and avoid run-ins with the cops.

Even though we cut back on bars, the real problem never went away. Alcohol abuse ran rampant in the ranks. The bar brawls may have decreased, but other alcohol-related issues and poor decisions still plagued us.

CHAPTER 13

WINGS & RIBS

After another night of heavy drinking, Trevor and I found ourselves in an unfamiliar, predominantly black neighborhood, looking for a late-night meal. We stumbled upon a dingy sub shop, parked the Fiero, and went inside. The place was rundown, with grime caked onto nearly every surface and reeking of neglect. Behind the counter, a teenage boy and a heavy-set woman worked the late shift, looking like they wanted to be anywhere else.

Trying to sober up, I ordered a meatball marinara – the messiest thing on the menu. One bite, and it was a disaster. Sauce dripped down my hands, chunks of meatball tumbled onto the table. I went up to the counter.

"Can I get some napkins, please?"

The teen fumbled around, unsure where to look, until the woman shoved him aside. With a look of rude indifference, she slid a single brown napkin across the counter. One. I stared at it. It wasn't much, but given how often we were refused service elsewhere, I let it slide.

The sandwich kept falling apart, and that flimsy napkin was as useful as an umbrella in a hurricane. Desperate to clean up, I asked, "Can I use your restroom?"

She barely looked at me. "We don't have one. Try next door –

the Wing and Ribs place."

The teenager glanced nervously at my t-shirt. His voice shaky, he muttered, "It's probably not a good idea to go there... that's a black establishment."

I had nearly forgotten what I was wearing – a t-shirt with a large KKK Knight-rider emblazoned on both sides, framed by the words: Invisible Empire Ku Klux Klan.

I never cared much for the KKK, but reveled in the shock value of the shirt.

"What the hell are they gonna do?" I snapped.

We walked over to the rib joint, where every seat was filled. The restroom line was long, and we were the only white faces in the place. The man in front of me nodded a quick hello, but when his eyes landed on my shirt, he recoiled, "Whoa, I'm staying outta this."

Then, a huge man emerged from the restroom, spotted my shirt, and froze, blocking the doorway.

His voice boomed, loud enough to cut through the restaurant's hum. "What the fuck!" He snapped, "KKK! What are you crackers doing in here?"

"Just here to wash my hands," I replied, trying to sound nonchalant.

"Oh, HELL nah." His voice rose – heads turned. Conversations died. The entire place seemed to shift in an instant.

"Racist motherfucker! HEY, Y'ALL – THE KKK'S UP IN HERE!"

His arms shot out, waving for attention. A ripple effect swept across the restaurant. Gasps. Chairs scraping back. Glares turning deadly. The energy snapped tight – a loaded spring ready to explode.

I clenched my fists, and said. "I suggest you step aside."

He crossed his arms. "I ain't moving. Get the fuck outta here, honky."

Tension skyrocketed as about a dozen angry men surrounded us. The moment he yelled KKK, the place became a tinderbox, ready to ignite. We turned and walked out under a hail of profanity, somehow managing to avoid an all-out fight.

Foolishly, I went back to the sub shop to ask if I could use the sink behind their counter. The workers looked stunned that we'd actually gone next door and, without a word, let me wash up.

Trevor looked dismal as he glanced outside. "There's a mob forming around your car. Why the hell didn't we just leave? What's gonna happen when we step outside?"

It looked like the entire rib joint had emptied into the street, with everyone waiting for us. We silently pushed through the enraged crowd, who hurled expletives about the KKK as we finally reached the car. The moment we got inside, the passenger window shattered, spraying shards of glass all over Trevor. A barrage of kicks and punches followed as they tried to rip the door off.

I reached down, grabbed my knife, flicked the blade open. Trevor's hand shot out, gripping my wrist. "What the hell are you doing?! GO!"

I slammed the Fiero into gear – and floored it. Tires screeched. The mob scattered.

A few blocks away, I pulled into a gas station, to assess the damage.

Trevor was still breathing hard, his hands shaking. Glass was everywhere.

"Why are you stopping?" Trevor hollered.

"Because we have to call the cops."

His eyes snapped to me. "Are you out of your damn mind?"

"Listen," I said, forcing my voice to stay calm. "There were civilians around. Someone definitely called this in – and they probably got my plate. If we don't report it first, they'll twist the story. I can already hear it – 'The KKK tried lynching us.'"

I gestured to the wrecked Fiero. "If we don't get ahead of this, we're looking at hate-crime charges."

The gas station was in a high-crime area, bulletproof glass shielded the cashier. I burst through the door, adrenaline surging. "Sir, we need to use the store phone to call the police!" I thrust my hand beneath the transfer box. "We were attacked by a bunch of n*ggers down the street!"

Even back then, it wasn't a slur I typically used. But that night, my inhibitions were gone, and hateful words poured from my mouth more than anytime ever before – or since. The bitterness came from the fact that I'd worked since I was twelve, saving every cent to buy that car, and now it was trashed – door ruined, window shattered.

The attendant barely blinked. "Our phone isn't for customers. You'll need to find a payphone."

I slammed my fist on the counter. "I'm not searching for shit!" I snapped. "If you don't hand me that phone, a full-on race war might start – right here!" Fear flickered in his eyes as he slowly handed over the phone. I called the cops, and we waited outside.

As my rage spiraled, a low-rider packed with gang members

in matching colors rolled into the station. They overheard my ranting and rolled down the window.

"What the fuck did you say, white boy?" one of them snapped.

I fired back, spewing racial epithets, too angry to care. They exchanged glances.

One of them shook his head. "White boy's gotta be crazy. Probably strapped."

Without another word – they drove off. Didn't even get gas. Two skinheads spitting racist slurs in the heart of the ghetto? Either we were insane – or armed to the teeth. They didn't stick around to find out.

When the patrol car finally rolled up, the cops stepped out and asked if we could identify who attacked us. Trevor, still seething responded with racial slurs, and I suggested they check the rib place.

The cop glanced at his partner, then chuckled. "No way. You guys came here from South Saint Paul, wearing that crap, looking for trouble – and got more than you bargained for. Now you want us to start a riot over it? We know what happens when they come to your turf. You guys tool them up. Well, tonight you got a taste of your own medicine."

I knew exactly what he was referring to. A recent news story had reported a black man was dragged from his car and beaten in broad daylight in our neighborhood by skinheads. The NSM wasn't involved, but everyone assumed we were.

The cop shook his head. "You're damn lucky you didn't get shot tonight. Stay in your own neighborhood, and don't let us catch you around here again."

Blinded by youthful invincibility, we hadn't realized just how dangerous the situation really was. "Lucky" was how the cops described us, but driving home with a wrecked car door and a shattered window sure as hell didn't feel lucky.

CHAPTER 14

TAKEN HOSTAGE

Around the same time, Joe – a friend from the NSM – helped me land a job on the siding crew where he worked. With both of us earning steady paychecks, we moved into a large apartment in a newly built complex, which doubled as our residence and a local meeting place.

One morning, when Joe was running late for work, a couple of members stopped by with whiskey, eager to hang out. He told them they could stay, as long as they locked up when they left.

That evening, when we returned home from work, the apartment was in ruins. Entire walls had been torn down, exposing electrical wires and framing. The damage looked as if it had been wrought by a railroad hammer – the only tool in our apartment capable of such destruction. It was clear who was responsible, yet we couldn't fathom why so-called brothers would trash our home.

I called the property manager, who explained that, given the extent of the damage, the police needed to be involved. The very thought of cops showing up filled me with dread – especially since we were already teetering on the brink of eviction for loud parties and the armed skinheads that roamed the halls.

With the lease under my name, I faced two options: rat

out the culprits or deal with the legal fallout myself. The men responsible were being purged from the NSM, but turning them over to the police wasn't even on the table. To an outsider, it might seem irrational – why not report the guys who destroyed the apartment? The answer was simple: I wasn't a snitch. We operated on the principle that problems were dealt with internally. Justice was our responsibility – not something to be outsourced to the system or its lackeys.

After multiple failed attempts to confront those responsible, I called an emergency meeting. I had refused to snitch – and now, I was paying the price. With a court date looming, I fully expected the guilty parties to step up and take responsibility.

During our internal investigation, one of our men finally reached the culprits by phone.

He didn't sugarcoat it: "The Commander caught charges for what you guys did. He's got a court date coming. Do the right thing."

Unfortunately, they didn't possess a shred of honor or dignity, and I ended up taking the fall for their actions.

Our investigation confirmed their guilt, and they were expelled in absentia. We made it clear – if our paths crossed again, justice would be served.

As fate would have it – that day arrived sooner than expected.

THREE ROCKS

Mounds Park was one of our usual hangouts in St. Paul,

especially a secluded spot we called Three Rocks. That night, Mike, a new recruit, and I lit a bonfire, cracked open a twelve-pack, and settled in – talking about the movement and women.

Suddenly – a searing pain shot through my spine. I lurched forward, spun around and saw two of the exiled members. One clutching a hunting knife, the steel glinting in the firelight.

They hadn't come down the trail – they'd flanked us, sneaking through the woods. Unarmed and caught off guard, Mike and I were at a serious disadvantage.

"You know what we're here for, asshole," snarled the one holding the oversized knife.

"To settle your debt for trashing my apartment?" I shot back, scanning the area for anything I could use as a weapon.

The traitor didn't appreciate my response. The blade pressed harder against my throat, his grip unsteady, dangerous. His glazed eyes, dilated pupils – he was wired, mental state as flimsy as a house of cards.

"Hand over the NSM mailing list," he snarled, "or you're both dead men. Understood?"

That list wasn't just names on paper – it was our lifeline. It contained – contacts, organizers, business owners, even active military personnel who'd kept their affiliations hidden.

In the wrong hands, it could destroy careers, families – lives. No way in hell was I giving it up. Our lives hung in the balance, but the consequences of relinquishing that list seemed far greater.

"It's not here," I said flatly.

"You better tell us where the fuck it is!" he growled, his voice shaking like a junkie in withdrawal.

"Jamie has it. After traitors trashed my apartment, I stopped keeping it around."

"Then tell us where Jamie lives," he demanded, blade digging in. "Then we'll be done with you both."

"I don't know the address, only how to drive there." I replied, stalling for time to form a plan. The truth was, Jamie didn't have it. The list was hidden, and I wasn't surrendering it.

The traitor smirked. "Alright, then. We're all going to Jamie's. No tricks. You go in alone, get the list, and come back alone. Otherwise..."

He flicked the blade toward Mike.

"Your buddy gets filled with holes." He grinned, mocking. "Nothing personal, bro."

With the knife pressing into my spine, we were forced down the dark trail – each step an invitation to death.

Meanwhile, the other traitor bragged to Mike about their delusional plan. They wanted to start their own skinhead crew and thought stealing NSM's mailing list would give them an edge. They were high on something, which made them twice as volatile and unpredictable.

Mike took the wheel as we crammed into his car. In the backseat, I was held at knifepoint. The defector in the front turned around, his tone almost casual, "We've been around enough to know you're not the right man to lead the movement. You're a good guy, Jeff, but act like the white man's Martin Luther King."

Then his voice hardened. "If we're going to win, it'll take blood flowing in the streets."

Beside me, the knife-wielding lunatic let out a sinister laugh, "Blood, huh? Let's start with his!" He jabbed the knife toward my chest, again and again, just a breath away from sinking cold-steel into my ribs.

"You call us traitors, Schoep, but you're the real traitor. You've got a nice car, a pretty girlfriend – you've gone soft. You're not hardcore enough to lead. I should pluck out one of your eyes to teach you a lesson."

The defector in the front seat snapped. "Bro, stop swinging that knife around. We could hit a bump and accidentally kill him. We don't need to go that far with white brothers. Once he hands over the list, he can go back to playing movement, and we'll be set."

The knife-wielding traitor had that vacant, glassy-eyed stare – the type you see in serial killers and psychopaths. His partner had a plan, and killing us wasn't part of it. The entire situation was as unstable as the guy gripping that knife.

They didn't seem suspicious that Jamie's place was so far away, but eventually, they'd realize it was a stalling tactic. Then what?

Suddenly, the knife-wielding traitor blurted out, "Dammit, I gotta piss."

Mike pulled into a gas station. The lunatic tucked the knife under his shirt before heading to the restroom. The second he was out of sight, I lunged over the seat and slammed my fist into the defector's jaw. Mike ripped open the door, and together, we dragged him outside. We put the boots to him – pent-up fury unloading in seconds – until he curled up in the fetal position, bleeding on the pavement. Then we dove back into the car and sped off before his knife-wielding buddy returned.

"Hold on, Mike!" I snapped. "Do you have any weapons in the trunk? We left the main scumbag untouched. We need to go back and take care of business."

Mike shook his head. "The cops are probably already looking for us after we left the other guy bleeding back there. Besides, once word spreads about what those traitors did tonight, they'll be hunted like vermin."

He was right – going back would've gotten us arrested. So, we called it a night and spread the word among the troops.

THE HUNT BEGINS

After the incident, our crew was determined to track down the traitors. We roamed their neighborhoods, searching for them, but something was off. Locals – people who had never given us trouble before – were hostile.

One afternoon, a man stepped off his porch, cursing about skinheads being degenerate junkies who steal from children. I was appalled – we'd been called many things, but that was a first. I needed to know why he felt that way.

After talking to him, it turned out he was after the same men we were. He explained that skinheads had stolen his kids' bikes from their backyard and even named one of the culprits, who lived nearby. I explained why we were looking for them, and he confirmed our suspicions – they were likely on drugs. He mentioned a string of thefts in the area and was convinced they were responsible, having caught them stealing from his yard.

It gnawed at me – the same traitors who trashed my apartment and held us hostage were now stealing from working-class families. This wasn't just personal anymore.

I had already taken the fall for them, keeping my mouth shut instead of snitching, even after they wrecked my home.

Now, they were preying on the very people we claimed to fight for – families just trying to get by. It was infuriating. I didn't know what bothered me more – the betrayal, the lack of honor, or the fact that I ever trusted them at all.

After the hostage incident, they vanished. No one saw them again. Maybe they skipped town. Maybe they ended up in a ditch somewhere. Either way, they were gone – and nobody missed them.

CHAPTER 15

INFILTRATION

In the 1990s, most of our local crew was based in Saint Paul's working-class neighborhoods. Minneapolis was considered enemy territory, and the NSM members operating there were behind enemy lines.

One of our biggest street-level adversaries was the ARA (Anti-Racist Action) – a militant far-left group that served as a precursor to Antifa in the U.S. The ARA originated in Minneapolis in the late 1980s, but Antifa's roots went even deeper, tracing back to 1930s Germany, where it was created and funded by the Soviet Communist Party.

The hatred between Nazis and Communists had never truly died.

One afternoon, Joe told me about a skinhead girl from Minneapolis – his latest love interest and, apparently, a prospective recruit. Her name was Aubrey. She had a Chelsea cut – a signature skinhead girl hairstyle – and, according to Joe, she was the one, it was love at first sight.

The details immediately raised alarms. Joe claimed he'd met her in a neighborhood known for far-left socialist activity, a place we typically avoided unless we were looking for a fight. He said he'd gone there to buy boots, spotted a lone skinhead girl outside a store, and struck up a conversation. It didn't add up.

A skinhead girl – unaffiliated – just hanging out in Marxist territory? Too convenient. Some of us suspected she might be a SHARP (Skinheads Against Racial Prejudice), one of the enemy. Joe dismissed our concerns, convinced she was the girl of his dreams.

I suggested he bring her around so we could vet her properly. At a pool hall meet-up, Joe walked in with Aubrey and saluted. She flinched – just a little – but I caught it.

Still, lacking any proof she was a plant, we welcomed her like anyone else.

Days later, at an NSM meeting, I kept operational details minimal since she was present. Afterward, while we were socializing, several members mentioned that Aubrey had been asking intrusive questions about where they lived and worked. Such probing questions are always suspect in movement circles, whether innocent or nefarious. I promised to address the issue with Joe privately once no new recruits were around.

The next morning, I confronted him. "Why the hell is Aubrey asking our people where they live and work?"

Joe exhaled sharply. "Commander, please relax. She's moving to Saint Paul and needs help finding work. I appreciate you looking out for me, but she's just learning our rules and protocols."

This wasn't about looking out for Joe – it was about safeguarding the NSM.

Weeks later, Aubrey was still showing up at meetings, lingering in the background like a nervous shadow. Something about her presence unsettled me. After one session, I pulled her aside, my voice firm but steady. "Are you planning to enlist, Aubrey?"

She shifted uncomfortably, avoiding eye contact. "I just want to meet more members first."

I sighed, feeling irritation simmer beneath my skin. "You've already met around thirty locals. Meeting more won't make a difference."

She hesitated, then said quietly, "I'd still like to keep coming."

My patience wore thin. "You've reached the limit on meetings for prospective recruits. Rules are rules."

Before she could respond, Joe stepped forward, his voice edged with defiance. "That's not fair, Commander. NSM policy says members can bring a guest."

A ripple of anger surged through my veins. Joe was technically correct, but I didn't appreciate his insubordination or tone. My jaw tightened, eyes blazing with authority. "Policy or not, my decision stands. Aubrey isn't welcome until further notice."

Joe's face flushed deep red, anger clashing with humiliation. Without another word, he grabbed Aubrey's arm and led her out, their departure abrupt and tense.

Moments later, Brad rushed over, panic etched across his face. "Commander, did you move the clipboard from the literature table?"

My stomach twisted into knots. "No, I didn't. Why?" That clipboard wasn't just paperwork – it was a local roll-call list tracking who showed up for meetings, a dangerous list if it fell into the wrong hands.

"It's gone," Brad gasped, his eyes wide with dread. "I've looked everywhere. It's just... gone."

My pulse quickened. Suspicion locked into place, zeroing

in on the only people unaccounted for – Joe and Aubrey. The room seemed to close in, the stakes mounting with each passing second. I snatched the phone, fingers slightly trembling as I paged Joe. Minutes crawled until he finally called back from a payphone, his voice unsettlingly calm, oblivious to the storm raging.

"I'm just taking Aubrey home," he said casually, unaware of the disaster unfolding.

I cut him off. "The clipboard's missing. It vanished right after you and Aubrey left."

A heavy silence hung on the line before he responded, suddenly uneasy. "I – I don't know anything about it."

"Joe," I said, my voice shaking with accusation, "your girlfriend took it."

"No way," he protested immediately, his voice trembling. "She'd never..."

"Damnit, wake up!" I exploded. "You've known her a month! Search her backpack – I guarantee it's there. We've torn this place apart, shaken down everyone here; it has to be her!"

Joe hesitated, his voice uncertain. "I – I can't just go through her things. I trust her. She trusts me."

His naivete was a blade twisting in my gut. Furious, betrayed, I slammed the phone down so hard it echoed through the apartment. Joe had been played by a pretty face, too blinded by infatuation to see the truth. Aubrey didn't care about him – she was using him, preying on his vulnerability to gather Intel on the NSM. Now we were compromised, trust shattered.

We expected Joe to do the right thing – check Aubrey's backpack, realize she was an infiltrator, and drag her and the clipboard back for questioning. As the night wore on, frustration mounted. Every hour that passed without Joe's return only amped up the tension, pushing the group to the edge.

The phone finally rang, breaking the crushing silence. It wasn't Joe; it was Cindy, my girlfriend – a stunning exotic dancer with the magnetic allure of a Hollywood starlet. Her gentle voice cut through the fog of anger, offering me an escape.

"Come over," she whispered softly, sensing the strain in my voice. "Just for a little while. You need to clear your head."

Desperation won out. I slipped away to Cindy's place, losing myself in the warmth of her embrace, desperate to push aside the chaos unraveling back at the apartment. That peace was fleeting. Soon, my mind was flooded with dark thoughts – Joe's betrayal, Aubrey's deception, the impending fallout. Anxiety clawed at me, unrelenting.

"Sorry, Princess, but I have to leave,"

She looked up, eyes soft, filled with concern. "Can't it wait until tomorrow, please?"

"I wish it could," I sighed, heart aching. "If I don't go back now, things might spiral out of control."

She squeezed my hand gently, understanding mixed with worry. "Just promise me you'll stay safe," she whispered. "Don't let anger take over."

Her words echoed painfully as I drove back, bracing myself for whatever awaited. Yet nothing could have prepared me for the nightmare lurking behind that apartment door.

The moment I stepped inside, dread gripped me in a suffocating vise. Robert sat in the dark, eyes blazing with icy fury. His hands trembled, knuckles white as he clutched a large knife

– its blade gleaming ominously, reflecting his deadly intent. The air felt thick, charged with menace. My stomach churned. This was far worse than I'd anticipated.

"What the hell are you doing, sitting in the dark with a knife?" I demanded.

A slow, sinister smirk crept across Robert's face as he raised the knife, letting its cruel edge catch the dim light. "Oh, this?" he sneered, voice dripping with malice. "This is to gut Joe like a pig when he shows up."

A surge of conflicting emotions hit me – relief that Joe was still alive, but a fierce need to defuse this madness before blood was spilled.

"So, you're planning to stab Joe right here in the apartment?" I asked, disbelief lacing every word.

"Yes, sir," Robert replied, his tone cold, disturbingly detached. "He compromised the group over some bitch."

Taking a steady breath, I extended my hand, infusing my voice with authority. "Hand over the knife."

Robert hesitated, eyes flashing with inner turmoil before he finally, reluctantly, surrendered the weapon. Turning to the others, I made one thing painfully clear: Joe's reckless actions had endangered us all, but murder was never an option. Appropriate consequences would be delivered – cold, calculated, and controlled.

Shortly afterward, Joe endured a brutal, merciless beating – nose shattered, eyes swollen black, ribs cracked. The violence was savage, almost ritualistic, a grim demonstration of discipline. While undeniably excessive, this punishment was seen as a necessary response to a devastating breach of trust. Its cruelty meant to deliver a message: putting the group at risk wouldn't be tolerated.

When Joe confronted Aubrey about the missing clipboard, she coldly abandoned him, leaving him utterly devastated. His gamble had proven costly, and while his physical injuries were severe, they paled in comparison to the torment of his broken heart.

Reflecting on this incident still churns my stomach with regret and shame. Joe had been a loyal friend – first manipulated and preyed upon, then brutally beaten by those he had called brothers. Seeing him drag himself to work in such a battered state tore at my conscience, leaving me drowning in guilt. I adored Joe's family; the thought of facing his mother after what we had done was unbearable. How would she react, seeing her son like this? Would Joe shield them from the horrifying truth?

It's hard to fathom now, how a young man nearly lost his life over something as trivial as a few sheets of paper. In the relentless pursuit of loyalty and strength within the NSM, I had severed all ties to empathy and compassion, sacrificing my humanity along the way.

The scars left on my conscience are permanent reminders of the darkness I embraced – and the price paid in blood and broken trust.

CHAPTER 16

DEATH BY COP

One tragic night near Saint Paul, Adam, a member of the NSM, was fatally shot by police while in the passenger seat of a stolen truck following a high-speed chase. According to reports, after the chase ended, officers approached the vehicle with guns drawn. Adam allegedly made a sudden movement, which police interpreted as reaching for a weapon, prompting an officer to shoot him point-blank in the head.

Later, it was confirmed that Adam was unarmed, and the officer involved was cleared of misconduct. In the ultra-paranoid echo chamber we lived in, we believed the government was using any excuse to execute our members. The driver survived, but our friend was gunned down like a rabid dog. There was no public outcry, no outrage – just silence. Adam's death was reduced to a footnote on the evening news.

In the wake of Adam's death, I delivered a furious tirade at a meeting, convinced that a grave injustice had been committed. I declared that the system had initiated an act of war upon us and told members it was time to choose: walk away or prepare for the battles ahead. I expected some might leave, but no one did.

Today, my perspective has evolved. I now see the essential role law enforcement plays and the complexities of their responsibilities. It's unfair to paint all officers with the same brush. They are fundamental to the fabric of civil society.

Without them, nations would plunge into chaos, becoming breeding grounds for anarchy, violence, and crime. Extremists on the fringes often wait for such breakdowns, eager to impose their radical ideologies in place of order.

When immersed in extremist ideology, nuance disappears, and independent thought is overshadowed by group-think. Radicalized individuals rarely realize how they've voluntarily surrendered their autonomy. The tribalistic, cult-like worldview feels deceptively secure and comforting – something I, along with many others, embraced without even noticing.

Adam's death epitomizes the confirmation bias embedded in extremist thinking. We assumed, without question, that the government was targeting us – a belief fueled by our paranoid and narrow perspective. This all-consuming mindset is mentally crippling, deeply isolating, and fosters a dark, hopeless view of the world.

Rather than investigating the circumstances surrounding Adam's death, we saw it as a targeted assassination of a party member. To an outsider, this might seem irrational, but the human psyche is complex, and trauma plays a powerful role in shaping one's perspective. My own experiences with law enforcement – including an incident where an officer threatened me – only amplified my biases, further obscuring my judgment. While these experiences don't justify radicalization, they show how personal trauma can make someone more vulnerable to extremist ideologies.

This pattern often appears in individuals affected by trauma. For example, a woman who has survived sexual assault may develop a pervasive distrust of men, her emotional scars shaping her worldview.

Another parallel can be seen in police shootings. Imagine officers shoot a black man who was resisting arrest and reaching for a weapon. Even if video footage shows him struggling with police, public outrage may still erupt, driven by historical patterns of injustice. For many, these past tragedies reinforce a belief that police systematically target black individuals – a form of confirmation bias rooted in real trauma.

These examples reveal how trauma, whether individual or collective, can distort perceptions, fueling reactions that may seem extreme or irrational to outsiders. Unaddressed trauma can alter how we interpret events, creating a cycle of mistrust and conflict.

CHAPTER 17

SURPRISE!

One morning, as I prepared for work, I discovered all four tires on my Fiero had been slashed – a disheartening act of vandalism. My heart sank as I stood there, helplessly staring at the limp rubber and deflated dreams. Living paycheck to paycheck, this was more than just an inconvenience; it was a devastating blow, forcing me into an impossible choice: replace the tires or pay rent. The suffocating dread triggered painful flashbacks of homelessness – a fate I desperately feared revisiting.

Thankfully, a friend loaned me a spare car to get to work, a glimmer of hope in the darkness. Determined to save enough for new tires, I took on a side hustle shoveling snow after work, cutting back on groceries and scraping every penny. Exhaustion weighed on me, but the promise of restoring my car kept me going.

Then, one evening, that fragile hope shattered. I returned home, the Fiero was gone.

Property management had it towed, citing a rule about leaving non-running vehicles parked for over a month. I explained that the car worked fine until the tires were slashed – likely due to their lack of security. Instead of understanding, their response was a condescending remark about my chances of affording a "more secure" place to live. Fury surged through me, and I slammed the phone down, insulted, only realizing after that I'd never even asked where my car had been taken.

Weeks of infuriating silence followed. When management finally disclosed a towing company's name, hope sparked – but was quickly extinguished. The company had no record of my car. Desperation deepened with each subsequent call to other companies; no one knew anything. The Fiero had vanished.

Since childhood, I'd dreamed of owning a sports car. At twelve, I began mowing lawns; by thirteen, I was working farm jobs and part-time at my dad's company. While my peers splurged on the latest trends, I saved every dime toward that car. Designer clothes or brand-name shoes were never in my wardrobe, but none of that mattered – what mattered was turning my dream into reality.

The loss of my Fiero was more than losing a vehicle; it felt like all those years of hard work and sacrifice had amounted to nothing. Months passed, and even if I somehow located it, the impound fees would be impossible to pay. Eventually, I came to terms with the Fiero being gone forever, but the bitterness lingered.

That winter, my temporary car got stuck in a snowstorm on the way home from work. I tracked down a payphone and called for a tow. During the drive home, the driver remarked that my compact car was no match for the snow. I shared that my previous car, the Fiero, had been even worse in winter – and how it disappeared after its tires were slashed.

The driver's curiosity piqued, and he asked for a description: damaged passenger door, custom racing stripes, and, of course, the slashed tires. Suddenly, he exclaimed, "Hang on – I think we have your car. It's been in the lot for months, and nobody remembered how it got there."

My heart leapt, but as we discussed impound and towing fees, my excitement quickly faded. The staggering costs were impossible; with just $80 to my name, it felt hopeless. The driver saw my disappointment and, after a quiet pause, confided that he'd faced tough times too. He promised to talk to his boss about lowering the fees, then cautioned gently, "No promises."

Two days later, the driver called back. His voice had a triumphant edge: "Jeff, the boss turned down your offer, so I reminded him of a huge favor he owed me from way back. I cashed it in to get your car out."

Emotionally overwhelmed, I barely managed to thank him. When he arrived with the flatbed, I watched in awe as the Fiero rolled onto the pavement – tires and all, fully intact.

He grinned, noticing my astonishment. "I remembered your story. I didn't want it getting towed again for flat tires, so I found some spares in the lot and put them on. Haven't told the boss yet, but I'll tow after-hours to cover the cost."

I handed him the $80, insisting on repaying him somehow, but he waved it off with a smile. "It was fate our paths crossed," he said simply.

Standing there, overcome with emotion, I struggled to find words. This stranger's kindness felt like a lifeline – a powerful reminder that even in the darkest times, human generosity can break through, shining brightly and unexpectedly. It's a memory I'll carry with me forever, proof that hope could still be found, even amid despair.

CHAPTER 18

ASSASSINATION ATTEMPT

One evening, a news report caught my attention: Somali immigrants had started moving into Rochester, Minnesota, igniting racial tensions. At the heart of this conflict was a local crew called the All-American Boys (AAB), aggressively resisting the newcomers. My mind immediately saw opportunity – this was exactly the chaos the NSM thrived on. Sensing a chance to assert influence, I pitched an idea at our next meeting: we'd travel to Rochester, lend support to the AAB, and lay the groundwork for a new NSM chapter. With such short notice, only three of us could make the journey: my roommate Charlie, a new recruit named Slick, and myself, eager to capitalize on the unrest.

On the day of departure, something felt off. Slick arrived with an unfamiliar face – a guy named Nate. Instantly alarmed, I pulled Slick aside, reprimanding him for bringing an outsider without approval. He apologized nervously, stammering excuses about not knowing NSM's strict rules against outsiders. It was a rookie mistake born of ignorance, but left a bitter taste in my mouth. Against my better judgment, I let it slide, but an uneasy feeling lingered. In our world, trust was a currency we couldn't afford to waste, and Slick had already spent more than he had earned.

Days earlier, Slick had raised suspicions during a hike in the woods. He seemed unusually on edge, repeatedly asking if we were planning to jump him. His paranoia was hard to miss, so I confronted him, demanding to know why he had such ridiculous fears. He stammered through his response, unable to provide a logical explanation. His behavior irritated me, but I chalked it up to cowardice. Most of our crew came from tough, working-class neighborhoods, while Slick was from a distant suburb – a background we considered privileged. Suburban recruits often lacked the street-level grit of our inner-city guys, so I dismissed his anxiety as the product of a sheltered life.

Slick's friend Nate, however, was much different. Disheveled, shifty, he carried an unsettling, creepy energy – like the type you'd expect from a child predator. There was a dark, ominous aura surrounding him that I couldn't quite place. Nate seemed detached, self-absorbed, and unreadable, as if he was mentally checked out or on something. From the moment we met, I felt uneasy, but didn't dwell on it. After all, he was just another body to help pass out literature, and Slick vouched for him.

After arriving in Rochester, we linked up with the AAB guys in a mall parking lot and spent the evening distributing hundreds of NSM fliers. Once we finished, the four of us from the Twin Cities swung by a local bar to hand out the last few leaflets. As we were leaving, two out-of-shape, middle-aged men waddled out of the bar, confronting us about being Nazis. A heated exchange erupted between Charlie, myself, and the two men, but eventually, they backed down and retreated inside.

On the drive back to St. Paul, Slick asked, "Do you think those guys were actually going to fight us?"

Charlie chuckled. "Please, they were so out of shape they could've had heart attacks just getting off their bar stools."

I laughed, sharing a funny story about a drunk who tried

to pick a fight with me in a bar, but ended up pissing himself before anything popped off.

Nate, who had been silent most of the trip, suddenly spoke up, his voice cold and smug. "Those two guys would've done just fine. They had something you guys didn't know about."

Curious, Charlie and I pressed him for more details, but he evaded our questions, refusing to elaborate.

Slick, sensing the tension, quickly changed the subject. "There weren't many skinheads in Rochester, definitely not like Saint Paul. Were there many where you're from, Nate?"

"Yeah, a bunch of assholes. They beat me up for no reason," Nate replied bitterly, voice tight with resentment.

I interrupted, puzzled. "Hold up – why would skinheads beat you up? Were you part of some sort of commie group or something?"

He flatly denied any far-left affiliations, but his response did little to ease my suspicion.

Nate hardly spoke the entire night, and when he did, his comments were either cryptic, nonsensical, or riddled with contradictions. After his bizarre remark about the guys at the bar having something we didn't know about, the car fell into an uneasy silence. No one uttered a word for miles, until we stopped for gas.

I pulled Slick aside by the restroom. "Hey, your friend is really weird."

Slick shrugged defensively. "I swear, he's a solid dude. He'll join NSM."

I shot him a hard look. "We'll reject his application. Something's off about him. Don't ever bring him around us again, got it?"

Photograph of Jeff as a baby.

Elementary Years.

Jeff fishing as a child.

Photograph from Middle School years.

High School photograph.

Jeff's Great Uncle Hardo, World War II.

Above and below: Jeff circa 1990s.

Jeff circa 1990s.

Minnesota, 2000s.

National Socialist Movement Rally in Yorktown, Virginia, 2005.

Above: Kentucky, 2012.

Right: Jeff speaking to news reporters at NSM Rally. Georgia, 2013.

Below: Jeff speaking Chattanooga, Tenessee, 2014.

NSM Rally in Toledo, Ohio, 2015.

Above and below: NSM Rally, Pennsylvania, 2016.

Above: Pikeville, Kentucky, 2017. Below: Georgia, 2016.

Speaking before NSM Rally in Pikeville, Kentucky, 2017.

NSM Rally - Shelbyville, Tenessee, 2017.

Above: Jeff speaking at NSM Rally in Rome, Georgia, 2018.
Below: Swastika and rune lighting. Georgia, 2018.

Pikeville, Kentucky, 2017.

Little Rock, Arkansas, 2018.

Above: Daryl Davis and Jeff. Screenshot from the film "Accidental Courtesy: Daryl Davis, Race & America", 2016.

Right: Screenshot from the film "White Meeting the Enemy", 2017.

Below: Jeff and Deeyah Khan.

Jeff, Daryl Davis and Scott Shepherd at the Florida Holocaust Memorial Resource and Education Center, 2022.

The Simon Wiesenthal Center's Associate Dean & Director, Global Social Action, Rabbi Abraham Cooper and Jeff. Chicago, 2020.

The Jewish News article, 2020.

Assembly Select Committee on the State of Hate, California, 2019.

Jeff speaking at the International Symposium on Radicalization and Extremism. Ankara, Turkey, 2019.

Jeff speaking at the California Assembly Select Committee on the State of Hate in California, with The Simon Wiesenthal Center.

Professor Ding-Jo Currie and Jeff at California State University Fullerton.

Jeff with "Free Hugs Ken" Nwadike Jr and Santiago Canyon College faculty.

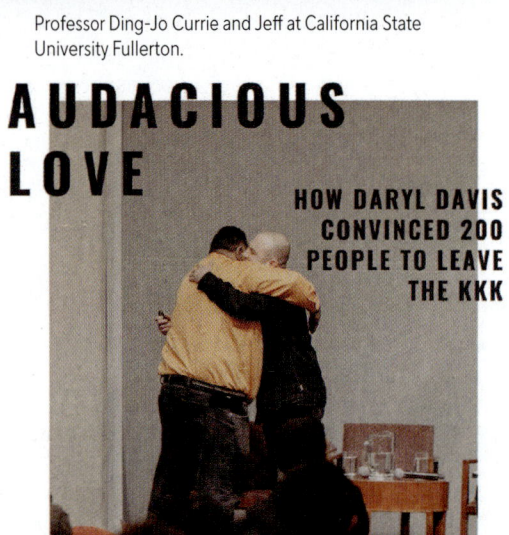

Jeff speaks with Deeyah Khan at the Nobel Peace Center, Oslo, Norway, 2022.

Jeff and Daryl Davis. Detroit, 2020.

Jeff speaks at the New America Foundation in Washington DC "Combating Violent Extremism & Terrorism", 2020.

Despite my growing reservations about Nate, I kept things cordial. When Charlie and I were dropped off at our apartment, we shook hands with Slick and Nate, thanking them for helping pass out the fliers.

Then, as I leaned into the trunk to grab the box of merchandise we'd brought along when, suddenly, everything went white – like I'd been struck by lightning. A searing pain exploded through my skull, blurring my vision, my legs nearly giving out beneath me.

"Anti-Nazi league, motherfucker! We're here to kill you!" Nate's voice roared from behind me, dripping with murderous rage.

In that vulnerable moment, with my back turned, Nate had swung a tire iron with brutal force, smashing it into the back of my skull. Pain exploded like a bomb, fire searing through every nerve in my body. Time slowed to a surreal crawl as the box slipped from my arms, falling back into the trunk with a hollow thud. Staggering backward, somehow still upright, I instinctively reached up to my head. The sensation was horrifying – soft, pulpy, like pressing into a wet sponge. My scalp had been torn loose, dangling grotesquely, raw bone exposed beneath.

Blood surged from my wound, hot and thick, blinding me as dizziness overwhelmed my senses. Staying conscious felt like an impossible task. Through my blurred vision, I saw Charlie rush forward, blocking two more vicious blows from Nate's tire iron. Charlie's quick reflexes were all that kept me from a fatal strike. Then Nate's fury turned to Charlie, leaving me with a grim choice: succumb to this savage assault or take a desperate gamble by hurling myself into the traffic roaring past us.

I chose survival.

Summoning every ounce of strength, I threw myself blindly into the street, stumbling into a chaos of blinding headlights, roaring engines, and screeching tires. Vehicles whipped by at fifty miles an hour, horns blared in panic, and brakes shrieked in desperate attempts to avoid hitting me. Disoriented by the deafening noise, blood loss, and the searing pain radiating from my skull, I staggered aimlessly forward, vision clouding further with each faltering step.

Suddenly, a firm grip seized my arm – Charlie. He'd sprinted recklessly into traffic, grabbed hold of me, and hauled me to safety on the opposite sidewalk. Behind us, Slick and Nate screeched away in their car, tires spinning furiously as they vanished into the night, leaving nothing but echoes of their escape.

Back at the apartment, the adrenaline drained away, replaced by overwhelming, relentless agony. My hands trembled violently as I tried to manage the wound, blood soaking my jacket completely. Struggling to focus on a plan of action, I tossed the jacket into the laundry, but my thoughts unraveled. A crushing wave of fatigue hit, knocking me back onto the couch as darkness threatened to swallow me whole.

"I need to rest... my head's too foggy to figure out what to do next. I just need to sleep," I muttered weakly, barely able to keep my eyes open as exhaustion dragged me under.

Charlie gripped my shoulders urgently. "You've lost a lot of blood and have a concussion! If you fall asleep, you could die! You need to get to a hospital – now!"

What followed was a back-and-forth argument, my stubborn refusal clashing with Charlie's persistence. Eventually,

I reluctantly agreed to go, but when Charlie's car wouldn't start, my resistance flared up again. I didn't want to get blood all over the Fiero. Frustrated, Charlie threatened to force me into the car himself, but I wasn't having it.

"Alright, fine, we'll go, but you're not driving my car," I said firmly.

Charlie was stunned, but before he could protest, I slid into the driver's seat, started the engine, and drove hunched forward, desperate to keep blood off the upholstery. Throughout the drive, Charlie hovered anxiously, one hand nervously near the wheel, annoyingly prepared to take over if I showed any sign of blacking out.

At the emergency room, pain barely registered anymore; my mind was fixated on a single burning thought: revenge. When medical staff asked about my injuries, I didn't hesitate – I lied, claiming it was an accident. Hospitals report violent crimes, and I couldn't risk triggering law enforcement involvement. If Nate and Slick ended up on missing persons posters, I needed to ensure nothing traced back to us.

Waiting impatiently for stitches, I paced through a pool of my own blood that had spread across the white linoleum floor. The scene was like something straight out of a horror film – but this wasn't a movie. It was real, and the blood was mine. The pain was intense, but the burning desire for vengeance kept me sharp, focused.

The wound was severe, split down to the bone, requiring two layers of stitches – dissolvable ones deep inside, and Frankenstein-style metal staples on the outside to hold the scalp together. At first, I stubbornly resisted the tetanus shot, but

Charlie wouldn't stop snickering, teasing me about being afraid of needles. With a cute nurse nearby, I had no choice but to save face and take the damn shot.

The doctor stitching me up was breathtakingly beautiful, possessing an elegance impossible to ignore. Despite my head split open and blood staining everything around me, I couldn't help but flirt, telling her she looked far too young to be a doctor. Her eyes sparkled as she smiled softly, almost bashfully, admitting she'd just finished med school. Amid the surreal chaos and agony, her presence felt otherworldly – like a Valkyrie who'd descended not to carry me off to Valhalla, but to gently piece me back together.

Just as we turned to leave, Charlie couldn't resist tattling to the doctor that I'd driven us there. She crossed her arms, giving me a look both stern and tender. "You're not driving home after suffering head trauma," she ordered gently but firmly.

Reluctantly, I handed Charlie the keys, but my eyes followed her as she walked away, drawn to her like a magnetic force. Something primal stirred inside me – like a lion stalking its prey, or the Big Bad Wolf fixated on Little Red Riding Hood, captivated by innocence and the thrill of pursuit.

Charlie rolled his eyes in disbelief. "Seriously, Jeff? You were inches from death, and now you're hitting on the doctor like she's some stripper swinging on a pole?"

I sighed. "My only regret is not asking for her number." he next morning, I woke up in a pool of dried blood that had seeped from the stitches onto my pillow. The pain was excruciating, the crippling migraines making it impossible to think, let alone work. Desperate for answers, I returned to the hospital for more advanced testing. They ran an MRI and a brain activity scan. Thankfully, no visible brain damage was detected, but the neurologist found troubling irregularities in my brainwave patterns – abnormal spikes similar to those seen in epileptic seizures. The doctors were baffled, attributing these anomalies to severe trauma. Those debilitating migraines would plague me for years – a lasting consequence of the attack.

A week into healing, it was time to deal with the infiltrators. Several members of our inner circle immediately volunteered for retaliation. Every fiber of my being screamed for personal vengeance, yet the severity of my injuries kept me sidelined, powerless and seething with frustration. The stakes were dangerously high – rumors swirled that Nate and Slick might have ties to a government agency. This chilling possibility forced a painful dilemma: risk one of our own getting arrested, or entrust the legal system to deliver justice.

After agonizing consideration, I reluctantly chose to trust the courts. Surely, Nate would face charges for attempted murder, and Slick, as his accomplice, would at least be charged with aiding and abetting. My faith in the system was thin at best, but this was different – it was attempted murder, plain and undeniable. With a witness, permanent scars, and hospital records as proof, even the most corrupt legal system in a third-world banana republic would be forced to deliver justice.

At the police station, Charlie and I reported the crime. The officer asked bluntly why we hadn't come in sooner. I responded coldly, explaining that we had originally planned to handle it ourselves. His jaw dropped as he paused mid-report, then he reassured us that coming in was the right choice, reminding us that vigilante justice wasn't the answer. He noted that it appeared to be a clear-cut case of attempted murder, but the decision was in the hands of the prosecutors.

Walking out of the police station, I firmly believed that choosing the legal system over violence was a defining moment. It symbolized a shift from the impulsive, alcohol-fueled vengeance of a street gang to the calculated, disciplined approach of a legitimate political organization. I hoped it would set a powerful precedent for others in our movement, proving that trusting the system was a better alternative than descending into cycles of endless violence.

Yet, as I reflected on involving the police, doubt crept in. Had I made the right choice? Would my decision be seen as a sign of weakness by our men, or would it demonstrate that I valued their well-being, refusing to risk their freedom for the sake of vengeance?

CHAPTER 19

THE SYSTEM'S COURT

A trial date was set, and Charlie and I were summoned as witnesses. Moments before it began, I met briefly with the prosecutors, only to be blindsided by the single charge Nate faced: assault with a deadly weapon – nothing more.

"Why isn't he being charged with attempted murder? What about the theft of merchandise? And his accomplice – the getaway driver? Why isn't he facing charges?" I pressed, seeking some semblance of justice.

The prosecutors explained that attempted murder would be difficult to prove, the stolen merchandise wasn't worth pursuing, and they'd decided not to charge Slick at all.

"Nate explicitly stated they were there to kill me, acted on that intent, and it's backed by a witness," I argued, but my words were brushed aside with cold, bureaucratic indifference.

Taking the witness stand, a wave of revulsion hit me. The courtroom's back rows were filled with ARA/Antifa activists there to support Nate, openly smirking and mocking the proceedings. Some flipped me off, others laughed, and one kept making throat-slitting gestures, pointing directly at me as I testified. The judge appeared oblivious – or perhaps deliberately indifferent – to the open intimidation.

As I recounted the attack and mentioned the stolen

merchandise, an Antifa supporter jeered and pointed to what he was wearing – my hoodie, taken from the stolen box. From the stand, I called out the Marxist wearing it, but my words fell on deaf ears.

It felt painfully clear that Antifa already understood what was obvious to me now: this trial would never be impartial. Equal protection under the law wasn't extended to me as it was to them. That message was being driven home like a bullet – cold, ruthless, and undeniable – from the start.

Then, the defense wielded the stolen items like weapons, twisting them into tools to assassinate my character. They paraded the Neo-Nazi paraphernalia as a smokescreen to portray me as irredeemable, shifting focus away from the crime itself. In that courtroom, it felt like my life meant absolutely nothing. Why had I been so naive to believe that justice would be served? The taunting from Antifa – shielded by the system that was failing me – was a bitter, humiliating pill to swallow.

When the defense asked me to read song lyrics, I objected, arguing that music was irrelevant to the case. The judge swiftly reprimanded me, asserting that he alone determined relevance. Frustration boiled over, and I sarcastically asked if the court had a favorite album they'd like me to read from. Nate's attorney smugly handed me the most visibly offensive CD from the stolen box – its cover depicting a pig in a yarmulke on a blood-splattered Israeli flag. The band promoted Christian Identity, like Aryan Nations, so I selected a song laden with Biblical references, quoted Scripture, then insolently asked if the court wanted to hear any other Bible verses.

"Where are you going with this line of questioning?" the

judge finally demanded of the defense.

The defense quickly pivoted, playing a recording from the NSM hotline, then asked if it was my voice. "Yes, Sir," I answered sharply, "but that's irrelevant unless my political beliefs are on trial."

The judge's gavel slammed down hard. "Mr. Schoep, must I remind you again, this is my courtroom! I'll decide what's relevant." It wasn't the first time he'd warned me, and it wouldn't be the last.

Agitated and fed up with the defense's irrelevant side-stepping, I finally lost composure. "You know what?" I snapped. "The only thing missing from this courtroom is a juggling bear on a unicycle. With the ARA clowns in the back, it's just short of a full-blown circus!"

The judge's gavel slammed down again, the sound ricocheting off the courtroom walls like a thunderclap. His eyes narrowed in sharp disapproval. The attorneys mirrored his glare, their cold, contemptuous stares locked onto me. The room fell eerily still, every breath held captive beneath the suffocating, oppressive tension. In the back, the ARA supporters leaned forward, grinning with predatory delight, like sharks circling at the scent of fresh blood.

The atmosphere crackled, electric – a live wire ready to snap. I'd struck a nerve, but a quiet dread whispered, this was only the beginning.

The defense's next tactic was infuriating. They spun an implausible fairy-tale, casting Nate as the innocent victim and me as the violent aggressor. As if that wasn't absurd enough, they dramatically produced a knife as evidence, claiming I'd attacked

Nate with it. I demanded they check the knife for fingerprints, but my request fell on deaf ears. The accusation was not just ridiculous – it was insulting, a slap in the face.

The attorney shamelessly demonstrated his client's supposed self-defense technique, flailing his arms in childish windmill motions – like a toddler caught in a tantrum. He insisted this awkward flailing allowed Nate to dodge being stabbed while simultaneously landing a precise blow to the back of my skull.

I countered, pointing out that his story defied both physics and common sense. Facing an attacker head-on, injuries would naturally be to the torso, arms, or face – not the back of the head. Unless Nate had octopus-like limbs or moved like a cartoon ninja, their scenario was physically impossible – a laughable, desperate fiction.

How could his client avoid getting "clipped" by a non-existent knife while flailing like a windmill? Even a harmless 90-year-old grandma would have landed a hit, but somehow, I didn't?

The more I exposed these absurd inconsistencies, the harder he clung to his fantasy. The glaring fact that I had no weapon at all was conveniently ignored.

The closing arguments remain burned into my memory as vividly as if they happened yesterday. Nate's attorney brazenly proclaimed that his client should be celebrated as a hero for standing up to me and the hatred I represented. When the judge announced a not-guilty verdict for Nate, the Antifa activists in the courtroom erupted in cheers and mocking laughter. It felt like being victimized all over again – this time with the court system itself joining the mockery.

Within the NSM, the prevailing sentiment was that Antifa could commit crimes and acts of violence without consequences, especially when their targets were marginalized, working-class individuals from the far-right. What transpired in that courtroom only cemented my belief that the legal system wasn't just turning a blind eye – it was actively complicit in shielding their crimes.

Initially, I'd believed that reporting the attempted murder would set a precedent – that we could trust the legal process over resorting to violence. That belief disintegrated into a Kafkaesque nightmare; the entire ordeal felt more like a twisted charade than a pursuit of justice.

The trial left me emotionally shattered, reinforcing every radical and prejudiced view I'd ever held. Any last glimmer of hope for meaningful change or escaping the extremist path was extinguished. Experiencing such a blatant miscarriage of justice – where my would-be murderer was hailed as a hero – inflicted psychological wounds that shaped my life for years to come.

The thirst for revenge was all-consuming; I felt an intense urge to grab a rifle and go to war. But, by reporting the attack to law enforcement, I'd forfeited any chance for payback. Any retaliation post-verdict would only land me in prison. The ordeal taught me a brutal lesson about the futility of relying on the legal system. I swore never again to bow to its courts or endure such humiliation.

Denied even the possibility of justice, my resolve hardened, and focus shifted to battling the system that had shielded my attacker. I vowed to devote every ounce of energy to tearing down the corrupt establishment that had failed me and countless others. The injustice I endured in that courtroom was, without question, the single most radicalizing moment of my entire life.

FORCED RETREAT

Shortly after the sham trial, my life fell apart. Chronic migraines from my head injury cost me my job, and without income, eviction loomed. Once again, the threat of homelessness hovered, like a dark ominous cloud on the horizon. My notoriety as a Neo-Nazi leader only compounded the nightmare – background checks were a hurdle I couldn't overcome. The walls were closing in fast.

With dwindling options – either face the streets in a debilitated state or swallow my pride and seek help – I reluctantly reached out to my father. Asking for help felt like the ultimate defeat, a crushing blow to my battered ego. Instead of lectures or judgment, I was met with empathy, understanding, and an outstretched hand. He offered me a place to stay and a job – generosity I felt deeply unworthy of, given the pain and chaos I'd brought into our family's life. Living under their roof, I followed their rules, distancing myself from the movement.

One evening, after a minor disagreement with Dad at work, I vented my frustrations to my mom. She shut me down abruptly, her words sharp and bitter, revealing that my father was the sole reason I was even allowed back home – apparently against her wishes. Her firm, icy tone shocked me, exposing the deep strain my return had caused their lives.

Quietly, without fanfare, Dad had gone to bat for me, holding back the storm despite fierce resistance. The realization cut deep, leaving me humbled, burdened by guilt, yet profoundly grateful. After Mom's reprimand, I took time to reflect. Knowing she hadn't wanted me back hurt deeply, but it magnified my gratitude and respect for my father. In the weakened state I'd been in after the attempt on my life, I might not have survived another stint on the streets if he hadn't taken that stand.

Once I regained the ability to work full-time, I moved into my own apartment. Transitioning from years of intense, street-level conflict to the quiet stillness of rural Minnesota felt unsettling, even surreal. It was like trading a life of purpose, adrenaline, and constant battle for one dominated by endless prairies, crushing boredom, and suffocating mediocrity.

Craving excitement, I took a job as a bouncer at a strip club – a blend of duty and pleasure. It offered a sense of purpose: protecting beautiful women while injecting a much-needed thrill into an otherwise mundane existence.

After surviving the assassination attempt and relocating, my dating life was in shambles until Jennifer – a nineteen-year-old dancer with long, cascading black hair – entered my world. She brought a peace I hadn't felt in years, offering a rare glimpse into a life that didn't revolve around conflict and chaos. With her, I saw that life could be something else, something calmer. Still haunted by what I saw as a gross miscarriage of justice, I felt compelled to return to the movement rather than retreat. Leaving felt like surrendering to Antifa and their powerful allies within the system – a notion that reeked of cowardice. How many others would be crushed if no one stood up? Despite glimpses of a better life, I felt drawn back into the fray.

The court ruling felt like a declaration of war – a sobering reminder that our lives were expendable and that equal protection under the law was nothing more than a cruel illusion. The verdict sent a chilling message to our adversaries: they had carte blanche to attack – even kill us – with the system's tacit approval.

Witnessing the blatant manipulation of the legal system by powerful interests didn't break me; it ignited an unquenchable fire deep within. My resolve to fight back grew fiercely, fueling a relentless determination to elevate the NSM from mere street-level activism to a legitimate, formidable political force. I swore I'd transform the group into a powerhouse, a hundred times stronger than it had ever been at its peak – and that's exactly what I did.

CHAPTER 20

THE PAST AND FUTURE COLLIDE

When I took the reins of the NSM, Cliff emphasized the importance of finding Allen Vincent – the former youth leader from George Lincoln Rockwell's original American Nazi Party. Allen's story was detailed in the 1975 film *California Reich*, but he'd vanished from the scene in the 1980s. His return could lend historical gravitas to the NSM, merging the legacy of the old guard with the vigor of the new generation. My mission was clear: bridge the past and present to elevate the organization to unprecedented heights.

Out of the blue, a letter arrived from Allen, detailing his past involvement in the movement and his reasons for stepping away – primarily a lack of leadership and momentum. Yet, after reading NSM newsletters passed on by a friend and seeing the surge in activism, his passion was reignited, and he wanted to join forces. It seemed as though fate was aligning.

Driving a Volkswagen van reminiscent of Rockwell's infamous Hate-Bus, Allen arrived in Minnesota from California just in time for the NSM national meeting in Saint Paul. The timing felt almost destined, reinforcing the NSM's claim as the rightful successor to the original American Nazi Party. This alignment sparked a surge in membership and momentum, propelling the group forward with renewed intensity.

Around this time, we enlisted a professional graphic designer named Merlin, who transformed the NSM newsletter from basic photocopy into a polished, professionally designed magazine. Though it rivaled mainstream publications in quality, it was filled with racial animus, Nazi propaganda, and dehumanizing rhetoric. In the late 1990s, the publication displayed disturbing images of lynchings, bombings, and implied threats. We leveraged the magazine as a platform to herald Allen's comeback, prominently featuring him on at least one cover.

Past skepticism about my youthful leadership quickly faded as the NSM solidified its position as a dominant force: Appointing Allen as my Chief Advisor drew more remnants of Rockwell's old-guard back into the fold. What had been a small, fragmented organization with scattered chapters was now poised for nationwide expansion.

To hold our national meeting discreetly, we booked a hall under the name Norwegian Social Movement, preserving the NSM initials under a less contentious guise. The plan unraveled when the reservation was abruptly canceled due to "misrepresentation." Undeterred, we pivoted, announcing a press conference in downtown Saint Paul instead, advising out-of-state members to stay home.

As we scrambled to adapt, unknown to us, Anti-Racist Action had already caught wind of our intentions and was mobilizing. The stage was set for another confrontation, and this time, we had no idea what was coming.

BRAWL IN SAINT PAUL

As we mobilized downtown, Cliff, who'd traveled from out of state to join us, mentioned having a bad premonition about the day. I brushed off his concerns, confident we could handle whatever came our way. When I asked if he wanted to sit this one out, he chuckled, "Miss out on all the excitement? Not a chance."

Backing down from the press conference over threats wasn't an option. For us, danger was par for the course. The NSM's street-level activism and direct confrontations set it apart from other white nationalist groups in the 1990s, most of whom avoided such risks. We wanted front-line soldiers, not armchair intellectuals or tough talkers. In our eyes, those unwilling to take to the streets were cowards – part of the problem, not the solution. Meanwhile, far-left shock troops dominated the streets, unchallenged, but we stood ready and willing to confront them head-on when few others dared.

On our way to the press conference, ARA activists ambushed us, hurling rocks, spitting, and attempting to block our path. Despite their aggression, we adhered to strict self-defense protocols, knowing that striking first would result in legal trouble. The double standard was maddening – our opponents incited violence and wielded weapons without consequence, while we were held to a different standard, always one step away from serious legal repercussions.

Tensions exploded into a full-scale brawl at the downtown press conference, where Antifa unleashed a disturbing new tactic: using their women as human shields. They shoved women to the front as barriers, allowing men behind to punch and retreat rapidly, forcing us into reluctant restraint to avoid harming the women. In contrast, our women were shielded by men on both sides. Amid the chaos, Cliff was blindsided – an attacker lunged from behind a woman screaming inches from his face, landing a brutal punch to his jaw.

In the heat of the street battle, Antifa seized one of our flags. Enraged, I charged through their ranks, snatched a banner emblazoned with the communist hammer and sickle, and slammed it into the ground, grinding it beneath my boot. One of their men charged at me, desperate to reclaim it. In self-defense, I drove my fist into his face. He shrieked like a toddler and scrambled back, retreating behind their women, abandoning the banner in the dirt.

Outnumbered and hemmed in, it was time to withdraw. Suddenly, one of our men collapsed, struck in the head by a chunk of concrete hurled by Antifa. He hit the ground hard, blood gushing from his skull as he vomited violently. Cliff rushed to his side, shouldering him up and guiding him through the chaotic streets as the scene descended further into madness.

As we tried to leave, the Marxist mob was unrelenting, fighting us every step of the way for blocks. By the time we reached our vehicles, violence had reached a fever pitch. They pounded on our cars with clubs, flagpoles, and hurled rocks. A large chunk of concrete smashed through the side window of the car I was in, spraying shards of glass all over the young woman beside me. Another vehicle had nearly every window bashed out as they tried to leave. Surrounded, Antifa did everything possible to prevent us from leaving – a tactic I'd witness countless times in the years ahead.

This clash exposed Antifa's habitual disregard for human life, as they wielded weapons and wreaked havoc in downtown Saint Paul with impunity, even as cameras rolled. Predictably, none of the far-left militants faced charges for their violent assaults or destruction of property. Emboldened by a legal system that continually turned a blind eye, they didn't even bother using Black Bloc tactics to hide their identities. Why mask up when the courts consistently let your comrades walk free – even after attempted murder?

Several skinheads who arrived late to the press conference, unaware of the earlier ambush, were attacked by ARA, igniting another scuffle. According to news reports, a far-left activist lost his front teeth in the fight. The next day, I learned that Antifa had forcibly seized a photographer's camera lens, throwing it down a storm drain – a calculated effort to erase visual evidence of their violent rampage. Despite their attempts at suppression, fragments still surfaced in the media.

After leaving the scene in our battered vehicles, we regrouped at a diner. Cliff, usually talkative and upbeat, sat silently, his meal untouched. Concerned, I asked if he was alright. Wincing, he spoke through clenched teeth, finally admitting his jaw was either broken or dislocated from the earlier sucker-punch. Despite the severe pain, he'd put off going to the hospital to stay with us.

"I'll head there afterward," he assured, flashing a strained grin before reminding me that his bad premonition had been right all along.

In time, we discovered that the mole who had tipped off the ARA about our press conference was based in Chicago. This incident exposed critical vulnerabilities in our intelligence network – but it also offered a valuable lesson. Determined to prevent future breaches, I bolstered our counter-intelligence operations, embedding our own informants within enemy camps.

The realization that Antifa would brazenly attack us with improvised weapons in broad daylight – even in front of the media – was a major wake-up call. Previously, our protests had led to minor skirmishes, but this was different. It was the first time we'd encountered such a calculated, coordinated assault. Their tactics went beyond physical violence, extending to systematically destroying our vehicles as we tried to leave. As demonstrations grew increasingly hostile, protecting vehicles became a necessity. To counter these rising threats, we began using shields to fend off projectiles and adjusted tactics, to meet the escalating aggression head-on.

CHAPTER 21

THE FEDS COME KNOCKING

As a neo-Nazi leader, I was no stranger to being under surveillance by law enforcement. Unannounced knocks on the door weren't uncommon – each time unsettling, each one leaving me wary about when they might show up next.

During one such visit, agents questioned me about an associate allegedly making threats against the U.S. government. They produced a photo of me standing beside the man, who was holding an assault rifle.

"Do you know this individual?" one asked, voice measured. "Do you know where he might be now?"

I studied the photo, then looked back at them, unfazed. "Well, the picture suggests I know him," I replied dryly. "Beyond that, I have nothing to say."

Another knock came just as I was preparing lunch for my kids. This time, the agents were investigating the theft of ammonium nitrate and believed I knew something.

Confused, I asked what ammonium nitrate was. They explained it was a fertilizer sometimes misused in explosives, referencing the Oklahoma City bombing.

Typically, I wouldn't have let them in without a warrant, but the accusation of harboring bomb-making materials struck a nerve, and curiosity got the best of me. I offered them a seat at the kitchen table and pressed for the basis of their claim.

They finally admitted a prisoner had implicated me but refused to elaborate. Typically, I brushed off these visits, but this felt different – there was an urgency in their tone, an unspoken tension that made my skin crawl. My distrust of the feds ran deep, and paranoia began to creep in. Was someone trying to frame me, or was the government orchestrating a setup?

"You're questioning me based on a prisoner's word but won't reveal who's behind the accusation?" I pressed, trying to get a sense of their motive.

"Their identity must remain confidential to ensure their safety," the agent responded.

"If they're in your custody, how does disclosing their name pose a risk?" I challenged.

The agent's tone sharpened. "Mr. Schoep, we're well aware of your connections behind bars. We won't endanger the witness."

I forced a smile as my youngest daughter wandered into the kitchen, oblivious to the tension. She reached up for a hug, and as I lifted her into my arms, I turned back to the agents. "Just to be clear, I'm not involved in any criminal activity, especially anything related to explosives."

The female agent persisted, her eyes narrowing. "Why wouldn't you be?"

I glanced down at my daughter, her innocent face nestled against my shoulder. "Because I don't want to go to prison – and more importantly, because of this little girl right here."

"So you're saying if there weren't consequences, you'd be involved with explosives?" she shot back sharply.

"No, ma'am," I responded firmly. "Consequences or not, I'm

not involved in anything illegal."

She locked eyes with me, her gaze cold. Then, shifting her focus to my daughter, she remarked quietly, "She sure is a beautiful little girl. It would be a shame if something were to happen to her because of what you're involved in."

A chill shot through me, and the conversation was over. I immediately demanded they leave my home. Maybe her comment was just a careless observation, but it felt like a veiled threat. As a father, my first duty was to protect my family, and whether intentional or not, her words felt like a warning. Far from intimidating me, it deepened my distrust and resentment toward the authorities.

After the legal system had already marginalized me following the attempt on my life, the possibility of entrapment or being framed by law enforcement felt disturbingly real – just another consequence of the life I'd chosen.

CHAPTER 22

A FAILED COUP

Three new recruits – whom I'll call Lurch, McLain, and Lacy – had recently moved to Minnesota from out of state, eager to immerse themselves in the day-to-day operations of the NSM. Before long, they became fixtures in our household, so familiar that my children even began calling McLain 'Uncle.'

Both Lurch and McLain soon began pushing aggressively to be named second-in-command, or Deputy Commander. That title carried a dark history – it was tainted by the assassination of Commander Rockwell, murdered by his own deputy. We'd decommissioned the title for precisely this reason, eventually replacing it with 'Chief of Staff.' Despite their persistent lobbying, I had no intention of elevating either of them. They'd shown a spark of dedication, but hadn't put in the years or proven the loyalty needed to earn such a role.

Their fixation on the title soon became unsettling. While long-standing members rarely spoke of succession, Lurch and McLain obsessed over it, constantly speculating about the future of the NSM "if something happened" to me. Gradually, they began neglecting their responsibilities, increasingly offloading their tasks onto Lacy.

Then, one day, Lacy pulled me aside, visibly shaken. Her voice trembled as she revealed something chilling: she'd overheard Lurch and McLain plotting to seize control of the

NSM. Their obsession with the Deputy Commander title wasn't merely ambition – it was part of a calculated scheme to stage a coup. She recounted, eyes wide with fear, how they'd coldly discussed removing me by any means necessary, even murder.

At first, I wondered if Lacy might have misinterpreted their intentions or exaggerated, due to tension with her boyfriend, Lurch. As she described overhearing their whispers while she pretended to sleep, the terrifying reality of her words sank in. They'd deliberately excluded her from their plans, but her quiet observations had exposed a meticulously plotted betrayal.

Lacy's courage in coming forward, even at the cost of her relationship, had revealed their sinister intent – and likely saved my life.

Challenges to leadership are inevitable, but I hadn't anticipated such insidious betrayal from within our ranks. Discovering that they'd infiltrated my inner circle under false pretenses – gaining access to my family – cut deeply. The idea that I'd allowed these snakes so close filled me with rage and regret.

After warning the crew, I asked Lacy to secure a recording to provide undeniable proof. She delivered, capturing a damning conversation that erased any doubt. Simultaneously, troubling messages trickled in from out-of-state members, who shared screenshots of private exchanges from McLain hinting at a "leadership shakeup" and my imminent ouster. The accumulated evidence confirmed their treachery beyond question.

Furious that these cockroaches had infiltrated my home and gotten near my children, I couldn't confront them myself; my anger ran too deep. Losing control wasn't an option.

Instead, I entrusted a reliable NSM contingent to handle the situation. With the proof in hand, they made sure Lacy was safely out of harm's way before storming the apartment to confront the traitors.

The account relayed to me was as follows: When confronted with the incriminating recording, McLain panicked, lunging desperately to grab it, only to be slammed to the ground. Chaos erupted as one of our men stood over him, pressing a pistol firmly against his forehead.

Just then, Lurch burst through the door, demanding answers. He froze instantly, his eyes widening in shock at the scene before him. Mark stepped forward, voice deadly calm.

"Take another step, and your boyfriend here gets a new mouth," he warned. "For the record, neither of you will ever be anything in the NSM – not Commander, not Deputy, not even water boy. Your new orders are simple: leave Minnesota while you still can."

The crew began tossing Lurch and McLain's belongings out the front door, scattering them across the sidewalk. Lurch stood there speechless. He hadn't heard the incriminating tape but knew the jig was up.

Mark suddenly halted one of the crew. "Hold on, that looks like Lacy's stuff – put it back."

In that moment, it all clicked for Lurch. His face twisted with rage, fists clenched. "I can't believe this is all because of that stupid bitch, Lacy!" he bellowed.

Mark moved in close, eyes burning with fury. "This has nothing to do with her," he growled. "If you want someone to blame, take a long look in the mirror. The traitor staring back at you is the problem. Lacy's safe, and she's not coming with you. Don't even think about contacting her again."

Before leaving, Mark paused at the door, turning back with a cold glare. "My brother here was itching to kneecap a couple of traitors today," he said evenly, "but the Commander said to send you packing without bloodshed – if possible. Consider yourselves lucky. The way we usually deal with rats is far less forgiving."

CHAPTER 23

NAZIS AND HAMAS

The movement had a constant turnover rate, like a revolving door – people came and went, though some stuck around. Mike was one of the few I trusted around family. I still remember our first meeting at a café. I'd asked the waitress to leave the bacon off my salad, and suddenly Mike blurted out in front of everyone, "What's wrong with bacon? Are you Jewish or something?"

The table fell silent, tension in the air. Still, Mike pressed on, waiting for an answer. His bluntness could've easily sparked conflict, but I saw something different in him – boldness. Though unfiltered, his approach had a raw honesty that reminded me of my Omi's straightforwardness, where truth mattered more than sparing feelings. That quality laid the foundation for a lifelong friendship.

There are countless stories I could share about Mike, but this one could have altered our lives forever. It began with a member we knew as Pat, who mentioned an encounter at a convenience store while wearing an NSM t-shirt. The Middle-Eastern clerk there had expressed support for the group. Pat handed him a business card and jotted down his number. While it may seem unusual, support for the NSM from people of color wasn't unheard of. Historical figures such as Jerusalem's Grand Mufti Hajj Amin al-Husayni who allied with Hitler, and the Waffen SS

Muslim Handschar Division, demonstrates that Middle-Eastern ties to Nazism had precedents.

Curious, Mike and I agreed to meet the clerk for coffee at a local mall. We wore NSM insignia to make ourselves easily identifiable. The moment we shook hands, alarm bells went off – his grip was limp and clammy, like holding a dead fish. He radiated nervous energy, sweating profusely, eyes darting around constantly. His jitteriness was so severe, he appeared almost paranoid schizophrenic. While we were always alert to our surroundings, his anxiety was next-level.

The clerk wasted no time bringing up Hamas, a group that the State Department would later classify as a terrorist organization. Although we shared opposition to what we viewed as Zionist control, our methods were worlds apart. Hamas used violence, while the NSM focused on legal and political channels.

As we talked, the clerk suddenly mentioned needing safe-houses for their supporters within the U.S. Noticing his frequent, anxious glances toward the mall's upper level – where onlookers seemed to be observing us – Mike asked, "Why do you keep looking up? Got friends posted up there?"

Clearly, we were under surveillance, and my stress levels surged. Convinced this was yet another law enforcement sting, I kept my composure, firmly making it clear we didn't engage in illegal activities. Undeterred, the clerk persisted, suggesting Hamas had significant financial resources and could fund NSM's activities.

"It was nice meeting you," I said sharply, rising to leave.

The clerk, sounding desperate, urged, "We'll make it worth your while."

Mike cut him off. "Go ask your own supporters. Apparently, you didn't hear us – we're not interested!"

As we left the mall, we were certain the clerk had been part of an entrapment operation targeting the NSM. It never occurred to us that Pat, who'd introduced us to this man, could be involved. Pat had always adhered to NSM guidelines, avoided drama, and never raised any suspicion within the group.

In time, Pat moved to Arizona, joining NSM's border operations. There, he allegedly convinced someone to build explosives – a decision that resulted in that individual's imprisonment. During the trial, a shocking truth emerged: Pat was a long-term undercover informant who'd previously infiltrated a 1% motorcycle club. Unlike many informants, who typically keep some distance, Pat fully immersed himself, even bringing his girlfriend and her family around us. His deception ran deep.

Many informants would try to incite illegal activities and withdraw if unsuccessful, but Pat was different. He was patient, calculated, never pushing openly for criminal acts until the Arizona incident. This approach allowed him to stay hidden for years.

Once we realized Pat had been a mole, the incident with the supposed Hamas supporter suddenly made sense. After the setup in Minnesota failed, the strategy was repurposed in Arizona, where someone took the bait.

Pat wasn't the first informant we'd encountered, nor would he be the last. Each time we thought we'd figured out their tactics, their handlers adapted, changing their approach. As we sharpened detection skills, the informants grew subtler, more sophisticated, and harder to spot.

CHAPTER 24

VALLEY FORGE

Mainstream media coverage was central in amplifying the NSM's visibility. Despite its unflattering portrayal, it provided free publicity, bolstered recruitment, and cost us nothing. My strategy was to position the NSM as a dominant street force. Clashes that erupted into street fights were exploited by Party propagandists to draw more fighters to the ranks. This set the NSM apart from groups that preferred to 'eat, meet, and retreat' rather than engage the enemy. To me, any leader or group that avoided street activism exuded cowardice.

In the 2000s, the NSM spearheaded major public demonstrations, reigniting neo-Nazi activism in the U.S. to levels unseen in decades. One notable event was the Valley Forge rally on September 25, 2004, where iconic American landmarks were leveraged for maximum symbolic impact. I crafted a speech laced with quotes from George Washington, aiming for historical resonance to boost recruitment. By this point, we had become experts at staying in the headlines.

The night before the rally, we gathered in the Philadelphia area. Large gatherings, especially when alcohol was involved, often led to trouble – and this night was no exception. An altercation erupted between one of our men and a hotel security guard. Though I didn't witness the fight, I saw its aftermath: the guard being wheeled into an ambulance, lights flashing against the night sky.

After the cops left empty-handed, I launched an internal investigation to determine who'd started the fight. Witnesses reported the incident began when the black security guard threatened our associate with mace. Our member had warned him not to raise a weapon, but things quickly escalated. According to witnesses, the guard began using racially charged, anti-white slurs while brandishing the mace, then shoved our guy aggressively. In self-defense, our member responded with a single punch, knocking the guard unconscious in the hotel lobby.

The next morning, we assembled a convoy at a truck stop outside the city before heading to a designated pickup point. From there, buses would shuttle us directly to the Valley Forge Amphitheater. With combined forces from the NSM and allied groups, our numbers swelled into the hundreds. Antifa was notorious for targeting vehicles at events – slashing tires, smashing windows, even ambushing isolated cars. Using buses helped maintain control and reduced the risk of attacks. By then, anticipating violence had become a necessary part of our planning.

The rally proceeded as intended, drawing a volatile mix of counter-protesters and supporters. At one point, someone in the audience unfurled an NSM flag, sparking a brief moment of tension, but overall the main event remained surprisingly peaceful. However, in the aftermath, reports surfaced of sporadic clashes erupting across the park as Antifa targeted individuals they suspected of being NSM supporters. In one disturbing instance, a wedding party for a U.S. soldier was reportedly harassed or assaulted. Another shocking report detailed a pregnant woman pushing a stroller who was threatened and spat upon. Elsewhere, a skirmish between skinheads and Antifa broke out, ending with Antifa deploying mace.

Following the event, the NSM released after-action reports declaring the rally a resounding success. Predictably, Antifa issued statements of their own, claiming victory over fascism. This ironic pattern – two diametrically opposed extremist factions both claiming triumph – became a familiar theme after events.

The post-rally party took place near an Amish settlement, creating a striking contrast. The tranquil sight of horse-drawn carriages, quiet farmhouses, and the simplicity of Amish life stood in surreal juxtaposition to the loud, raucous NSM gathering just down the road. It felt like two worlds colliding: one rooted in peace and tradition, the other in chaos and defiance. The contrast was jarring – almost haunting – highlighting just how far removed our reality was from theirs.

CHAPTER 25

TOLEDO RIOT

On October 15, 2005, a small NSM protest was underway in Toledo, Ohio. Tensions simmered long before the rally began, with Antifa circulating leaflets urging the community to "confront the Nazis." The stage was set for a clash of extremes, as if the entire city had become a powder keg, poised to explode.

Martin, an NSM leader in Ohio, later described the chaos. "It started like any other rally," he explained. "Counter-protesters were angry, but no one crossed the line – until a van pulled up." In a brazen display, Antifa piled out, openly handing out clubs, bats, and bricks to the crowd. In that instant, the tense standoff exploded into a full-blown riot.

Law enforcement knew Antifa often stashed weapons near protest sites, typically conducting sweeps beforehand to intercept these caches. This open, daylight distribution of weaponry, witnessed by Martin and others, was a dangerous escalation that blindsided everyone. It was unlike anything we'd ever encountered.

Desperate to defuse the violence, police ordered the NSM to leave. Instead of calming the crowd, they redirected their fury toward the officers themselves. The mob turned on the police, chanting the familiar Antifa mantra, "The Kops and Klan go hand in hand!" The mob surged forward, and control slipped away. Windows shattered, businesses were ransacked, and chaos spilled into the streets. Rioters hurled projectiles, set fires, and vandalized police cars and ambulances. A raw, primal energy tore through the city as Toledo descended into an orgy of violence and destruction.

By nightfall, the riot had made global headlines, sparking a surge in NSM recruitment. We seized the moment, issuing a press release that framed the chaos as validation of our message. The incident thrust the NSM onto the international stage, with Antifa's reckless actions serving as an unintended catalyst. Ironically, despite their stated mission to eradicate fascism and racism, Antifa's violent tactics only empowered the very groups they aimed to dismantle.

After Toledo, law enforcement agencies nationwide had no choice but to brace for riots and civil unrest whenever the NSM announced a rally.

CHAPTER 17

YORKTOWN AND SATAN

In June 2005, the NSM held a rally at Yorktown's historic Revolutionary War battlefield. Upon arrival, we were met by a government bureaucrat overseeing our rally permit. His unusually hostile demeanor set the tone immediately. Barking orders at both us and law enforcement officers, he attempted to micromanage every aspect of the rally. Among his more unreasonable demands was to limit our equipment truck to a single trip to the rally site. While law enforcement usually maintained respectful communication during events, this official seemed determined to antagonize us at every turn.

NSM policy permitted military veterans to display their service awards on their uniforms. Wild Bill, the NSM's Eastern Region Leader, wore his Purple Heart from the Korean War. Due to physical limitations, Bill requested a ride in the equipment truck to the rally site. Despite this reasonable request, the bureaucrat overseeing the event admonished Bill, shaking his finger in the veteran's face as if chastising a misbehaving child. In our world, respect was paramount; witnessing such blatant disrespect toward a senior citizen and war veteran was intolerable.

On the verge of losing all semblance of diplomacy, I confronted the bureaucrat, tone steady but firm. "Sir, lower your voice, calm down, and get your damn finger out of our Regional

Leader's face. What's the problem here?"

Red-faced and frothing at the mouth, the bureaucrat hissed, "How dare you speak to me like that! I'll revoke NSM's permit if you don't back off and get everyone moving down the trail right now."

A policeman intervened, attempting to defuse the situation, "Sir, why is this even an issue? A senior citizen collapsing could result in a medical emergency – and he's a Purple Heart veteran."

The bureaucrat sneered, his voice dripping with disdain. "I don't give a damn! Do I need to remind you who's in charge here?"

The officer's jaw dropped, stunned. He'd tried to deescalate the situation, only to become the target of this miserable little man's tirade.

Drake from NSM Security suggested a solution: two men could carry Wild Bill down the trail, linking arms to create a makeshift sling. Faced with the threat of losing our permit, we went with Drake's plan. The men alternated carrying Bill down the path to the rally site, each step a reminder of the bureaucrat's needling contempt. About a hundred yards out, Bill stopped them and insisted on walking the rest of the way himself. Though an old soldier well into his twilight years, he was determined not to show weakness.

Yorktown was considered a success by the NSM, with a solid turnout, commendable police conduct, and no violence. The only blemish was the unprofessional behavior of one bureaucrat, who allowed personal bias and anger to overshadow his responsibilities.

Looking back, there's a bitter irony in that encounter. Facing a government official whose intolerance mirrored my own felt like karma – or perhaps reaping what I'd sown. Disrespectful exchanges rarely lead anywhere constructive. While they might feel justified in the moment, they only deepen divides. Once dialogue breaks down, it fuels a vicious cycle, stifling any chance of understanding or personal growth.

THE NSM AND SATAN

The 2006 National Meeting was held near Lansing, Michigan. The night before, I was consumed with resolving internal disputes, notably a heated conflict between Rich, our Security Chief, and Will, a controversial new recruit who was a former communist. Despite my efforts to mediate, Rich refused to budge, ultimately boycotting the event in protest over Will's involvement. Tensions escalated further when several members confronted an interracial couple in the hotel parking lot, forcing our security team to intervene and order those involved back to their rooms.

The rally at the State Capitol proceeded as planned, starting with a press conference. Yet, the event was far from peaceful – fighting erupted in the spectator area between counter-protesters and supporters, adding to the day's unrest.

The NSM's rise marked a turning point for white nationalist groups in the U.S., finally overcoming the long-standing struggle to mobilize street forces. Yet, with increased visibility came an influx of critics, competitors, and adversaries determined to undermine us by any means necessary.

Among the detractors was the American Nazi Party

(ANP), a peculiar faction scavenging whatever scraps the NSM discarded. Despite its name, this group had no genuine ties to Rockwell's original ANP and consisted of a mere handful of individuals, shunned as pariahs by other organizations.

The ANP latched onto the fact that NSM's Chairman Emeritus, Cliff, shared a P.O. box with his wife, who led a group linked to Satanism. Within the NSM, religious beliefs were considered private matters, provided they didn't negatively impact the organization – a policy I'd codified in membership handbooks years earlier. Nonetheless, the ANP seized the opportunity to launch a smear campaign, circulating a doctored image of Cliff in a devil costume, falsely claiming the NSM was aligned with Satanism.

Their attempt to sow discord and prompt defections flopped spectacularly when they tried spreading dissent on white nationalist websites and forums. Undeterred, the ANP doubled-down, spreading their so-called 'NSM Satanism Exposé' across far-left platforms. By doing so, they crossed an unthinkable line, aligning with groups traditionally seen as enemies – something no legitimate white nationalist group would ever consider. In essence, they'd climbed into bed with the enemy.

The notion of a Satanism scandal within the NSM was utterly absurd to me. The Party's membership consisted of roughly 45% Christians, 45% Pagans, and 10% other religions, with known Satanists making up barely 1%. For most members, Satanism was considered degenerate and had no place in the organization.

Unable to wield influence on their own, the ANP's collaboration with Antifa accelerated the spread of outrageous claims that Satan was at the helm of the NSM. This manufactured Satan-Gate scandal opened doors for rival factions hoping to lure disillusioned Christians away. Among extremist groups vying for dominance, exploiting scandals and internal conflicts is a well-worn tactic to drain rivals of members and resources. The idea of a Satanic takeover within America's largest Nazi Party became ammunition for those who sought our downfall.

The so-called scandal soon caught the attention of far-right watchdog groups, who wildly exaggerated claims that the NSM was hemorrhaging members. In reality, only a handful resigned – and they were replaced within two weeks.

The ANP's treachery sank to new depths when they brazenly bragged online about leaking the location of an NSM meeting to Antifa. Nazis and Communists have historically been sworn enemies, making this act of collusion an unforgivable violation. For the first time, we had irrefutable proof of the ANP collaborating with the enemy – a line crossed that could never be undone. It wouldn't be the last.

CHAPTER 27

DEPORTATION: BANNED IN CANADA

The NSM's reach expanded rapidly, absorbing smaller groups and establishing branches worldwide. This growth raised alarm bells among governments, including Germany, which sent official notices declaring NSM Records' music banned for violating hate-speech laws. Ironically, these bans only fueled demand – the 'forbidden fruit' effect amplified the music's appeal, boosting sales across Europe.

The British Home Office formally banned me from entering the United Kingdom, citing concerns that my presence could incite riots and political unrest. At the time, I wore these bans like badges of honor – a testament to our growing influence on the global stage.

I discovered my ban from Canada unexpectedly during a visit from a New Zealand friend who held dual citizenship. We'd planned a trip to Thunder Bay, Canada, to explore his family roots, but first intended to visit the Northwest Angle – an isolated American exclave only accessible by boat across Minnesota's Lake of the Woods or by land through Canada.

At the border, Canadian authorities searched my vehicle and found some outdated, crumpled leaflets crammed beneath the stereo amp and speakers. I'd deliberately removed NSM materials before leaving, fully aware of Canada's strict hate-speech laws, but somehow overlooked these forgotten scraps.

Detained at the border, I tried reasoning with the guards, offering to turn around and return to the U.S. However, they informed us that the leaflets might violate Canadian law, requiring the Royal Canadian Mounted Police (RCMP) and an intelligence agency to drive from Winnipeg for further assessment. As hours dragged on and my patience wore thin, I began verbally lashing out at the guards, attempting to provoke them.

"Do you guys enjoy serving a communist country with no free speech? Are Soviet Commissars coming from Winnipeg to determine our fate?" I taunted.

The guards maintained their composure, politely refuting my claims about Canada. Eventually, tiring of my insolence, they stepped out. A Canadian civilian, who'd been chatting with the guards over coffee, leaned over and discreetly advised, "You should probably tone down the anti-Canada rhetoric. Those guys have the authority to confiscate your car."

The thought of the Fiero being impounded in Canada filled me with dread. After explaining to the civilian how I'd lost the car once before, I thanked him for the warning and ceased making inflammatory remarks.

Eventually, the RCMP arrived. As we sat on a bench in the waiting area, I overheard them pressing the border guards about why we hadn't been separated or handcuffed. The guards defended their approach, noting our cooperation. Observing this exchange shifted my perspective of the guards – they really weren't so bad after all. Watching the inter-agency dynamics also provided intriguing insight into their procedures.

Suddenly, the Mounties handcuffed us and led us into separate interrogation rooms, ordering us to strip down. Irritated, I unleashed some inappropriate comments about the strip-search. Surprisingly, afterward, the officers seemed more at ease. One remarked, "Jeff, you and your friend have completely opposite personalities."

Curious, I asked what he meant by that.

The guard smirked, "You were angry and defiant during the search, while your friend was dancing and playfully tossing his clothes around the room."

The mental image of my friend performing strip-tease in the interrogation room was hilarious, but I couldn't laugh. My mind was preoccupied with concerns of losing my freedom and the Fiero – again.

I mentioned the handcuffs were too tight, causing pain and discoloration. The officer apologized, offering to remove them if I promised not to flee. Ironically, moments later I was sitting on the same bench, handcuff-free, mirroring the exact scenario the border guards were reprimanded for earlier.

During detainment, they offered food and drinks, but I refused. Though irrational and paranoid, a deep-seated worry about being drugged simmered beneath the surface – a lasting scar from past experiences. My distrust of authority had been forged in trauma, from a court that celebrated my would-be assassin to the cop who threatened to shoot me in a police station. Such incidents convinced me of the U.S. government's malevolence, and I viewed Canada as even more oppressive. Paranoia had become a constant companion.

After nightfall, Canada's equivalent of the FBI arrived. Noticing I wasn't cuffed, they restrained me again. I was tempted to comment on the on-and-off handcuff routine but decided against it. The young agents began with the usual line of law enforcement questioning, but then the conversation took an odd turn. One agent remarked on how rare it was for them to apprehend someone like me, adding they'd much rather catch a terrorist on the scale of Osama Bin Laden.

I bristled. "Are you comparing me to a terrorist?"

The agent clarified. "No, we don't see you as a terrorist – but you are a notorious neo-Nazi, probably the most prominent figure ever detained at this remote border crossing."

Some of their more bizarre questions seemed to be drawn from pop culture references. One agent even asked, "Is the NSM anything like the movie American History X?"

I replied mockingly, "Do you believe everything you see in Hollywood films?"

After the interrogation, the agents explained that I was being deported, but first, they needed confirmation from the U.S. government that I was eligible for re-entry. A surge of panic hit me – what if this gave the U.S. an excuse to revoke my citizenship? Thoughts raced through my mind: which countries might offer asylum, or worse, would I be held indefinitely in a Canadian gulag? The agent wasn't gone long, but it felt like an eternity before he returned, confirming that my deportation had been cleared.

Relief set in; I believed the ordeal was nearly over and freedom was within reach. However, upon re-entering the U.S., we had to stop at the American border for additional paperwork due to my deportation status. At the checkpoint, we faced another round of vehicle searches and questioning. By this point, dehydration, hunger, and sheer exhaustion had worn me down, and my frustration boiled over. My belligerent attitude and foul language didn't sit well with the U.S. border agents.

The turning point came when the supervisor mentioned he'd been called in on his day off due to my deportation. Realizing the inconvenience I'd caused, I took a breath and offered a sincere apology. While it didn't excuse my behavior, I explained that my frustration partly stemmed from going over twenty-four hours without food or water.

The supervisor looked astonished, "You weren't offered any food or drinks by the Canadians?" My friend chimed in, listing everything he'd consumed that day, then turned to me, equally surprised.

"They did," I admitted, "but I refused because I was concerned it might be drugged."

The agents exchanged puzzled glances, clearly taken aback by my paranoia. A guard who'd previously been visibly irritated by my attitude seemed to soften. He stepped away briefly and returned holding sealed water bottles, handing them to me with a smirk. "Jeff, check it out, these are sealed. How about some water now?"

I thanked him, feeling the tension ease slightly. The other agents looked on – half-amused, half-incredulous – shaking their heads in disbelief.

Still uneasy about the possibility of being refused re-entry as an American citizen, I asked the border agents about the Canadians' cryptic statement. They reassured me it was nothing more than a formality, part of a routine warrant check.

With the deportation process finally behind us, we were released. As we headed out, a guard mentioned that if we hurried, we might catch a bar still open and serving food. We arrived just in time, with only minutes to spare. My friend may not have made it to Canada, but we had our freedom – and the Fiero hadn't been impounded. After the day we'd had, that alone felt like a small victory.

CHAPTER 28

MINNESOTA RAID

It was a crisp fall night. Leaves whispered in the wind outside, casting eerie shadows under the pale glow of streetlamps. Upstairs, the kids were tucked snugly in bed, lost in innocent dreams of the next day's school routine. I had long since numbed my mind with a few stiff vodkas and had collapsed into oblivion by 3:00 a.m.

Barely an hour later, a deafening crash shattered the fragile silence – like a bomb detonating in the heart of our home. My eyes flew open, my heart hammering violently against my ribcage. Heavy, deliberate footsteps thundered toward the basement bedroom door, each step louder, closer, relentless. I scrambled upright just as the locked door exploded inward, splintered wood flying in all directions.

Blinding beams from flashlights mounted atop rifles stabbed through the darkness, slicing straight at me, piercing my vision. Twisted shadows danced wildly across the walls, transforming the room into a sinister battlefield of light and dark. Figures stormed inside, clad head-to-toe in black military-style uniforms, armored, faces concealed behind helmets and masks. Their presence radiated pure menace.

"Put your hands up and don't make any sudden moves!" barked a voice – firm, commanding, lethal.

Time froze. My life flashed before me as I squinted into those piercing lights, confronted by the stark silhouettes of rifles aimed at my chest. None had identified themselves. No badges flashed, no warrants announced. In that chilling moment, rationality fled, replaced by terror-drenched paranoia.

If they weren't police, who were they? Antifa? Impossible – they lacked this kind of tactical precision and gear. Rival neo-Nazi factions wouldn't dare stage such a blatant assault, not with children sleeping upstairs. A cold, horrifying thought gripped my mind: Could it be Mossad? The secretive Israeli agency was the boogeyman whispered about within neo-Nazi circles – shadowy assassins sent to eliminate threats. Tonight, maybe they'd finally come for me.

Trapped in an extremist mindset, my thoughts raced to the darkest conclusions. This nightmare scenario had played out in my mind countless times; weapons were always within reach for this exact reason. Tonight, though, only a baseball bat and a knife were close at hand. Adrenaline surged, fueling a fierce, ancient defiance that burned in my veins. I'd defend my family with the same ferocity my Germanic ancestors had unleashed against Roman legions deep in the Teutoburg Forest. If this really was Mossad, then this basement would become my Alamo – a final, unyielding stand, no retreat, no surrender.

The armed intruders barked their commands again, louder, more insistent, guns trained on me with deadly precision. My fingers twitched toward the bat, muscles tensed, bracing for one last battle. Yet somewhere beneath the roaring adrenaline, a flicker of reason sparked through my clouded mind. What if I was wrong?

My voice defiantly tore through the unbearable tension:

"Who the fuck are you guys?"

"Police!" came the immediate, reply. "Put your hands up – now!"

Clarity slammed into me like a freight train. Once it was clear they were law enforcement, I surrendered without resistance, arms wrenched roughly behind my back as handcuffs bit deep into my wrists. The children's mother met the same fate, eyes wide with shock and terror.

Upstairs, the SWAT team had obliterated our front door with a battering ram; splintered wood lay scattered across the floor like debris in a warzone. Outside, an armored assault vehicle crouched menacingly, blue and red lights stabbing into the predawn darkness.

We were dragged out into the biting night air, bundled hastily into waiting police cars. But nothing – not the cuffs, not the shouted commands, nor the humiliation – matched the horror of seeing our terrified children. They sobbed uncontrollably, tiny faces pale with panic, clutching desperately to each other as armed strangers in body armor ransacked their home. The anguish in their cries pierced my soul deeper than any bullet ever could.

Though they turned our lives inside out, we were released without charges. The only explanation was the paperwork left behind – a no-knock warrant signed by a judge. For our children, however, the trauma lingered. Their trust in law enforcement was shattered, leaving them tormented by recurring nightmares. Words alone can't capture the heartache of hearing your kids wake up crying, haunted by fears that the police might return in the dead of night to take their parents away. Coming to terms with how my involvement in neo-Nazism scarred their innocent lives remains a crushing burden on my conscience.

After the raid, I made a calculated decision to keep the incident hidden within the NSM. I'd watched other leaders try to rally support in similar situations, only to see it backfire spectacularly. In extremist circles, vulnerabilities become ammunition; rival factions lie in wait, ready to pounce on any sign of weakness. I'd witnessed it too many times – groups crumbling as leaders became entangled in legal battles, exploited by those who saw suffering as an opportunity to advance their own interests. I refused to let my family's trauma become another pawn in the ruthless games of the movement.

Exploiting vulnerabilities for personal gain was something I always condemned. While some leaders shared my disdain for these underhanded tactics, many others were blinded by a short-sighted thirst for power, oblivious to the long-term damage they inflicted on their own credibility. They lacked foresight, failing to grasp that their quest for instant gratification came at the expense of honor and integrity – a price I refused to pay.

As a result, only the upper echelons of Party leadership were privy to information about raids or external pressures. Similarly, expulsions for criminal conduct or insubordination were handled with discretion, behind closed doors.

Mike, one of the few who knew about the raid, stopped by to survey the damage and scrutinize the warrant. He questioned the justification for such heavy-handed tactics, but I had no answers. Determined to get to the bottom of it, he stormed off to the police station – a concerning move, since diplomacy wasn't exactly Mike's strong suit. A few hours later, he returned with tools and parts, determined to fix the broken door himself.

When he confronted the police, they coldly told him it wasn't his business. Mike pushed back, declaring, "Raiding the Commander's home makes it NSM business, and I'm here on behalf of the organization." He argued that since the police had destroyed the door, they should bear responsibility for repairs. The officers flatly refused, insisting it wasn't their responsibility.

Refusing to back down, Mike pressed further. "How would you like it if I came to your homes at 4 AM and kicked your doors in?" he challenged. When they accused him of making threats, Mike replied calmly but firmly, "Of course not, Officer. If I were making threats, you'd know. I'm just asking a question."

After several tense exchanges, Mike wisely left before things escalated. Ultimately, no explanation for the raid ever materialized, and no charges were filed. We were left only with unanswered questions, broken trust, and the enduring scars it etched into my family's life.

Sensing our need for added security, a friend suggested we get a guard dog – she knew exactly where to find one. Soon, a white German Shepherd puppy named Justice joined our family. From the moment he arrived, Justice became more than just our protector; he became my constant companion, and best friend. For the next eighteen years, he stood by my side through every storm.

CHAPTER 29

ADOLF HITLER MEMORIAL MUSEUM

Tucked away deep in rural Wisconsin, the Adolf Hitler Memorial Museum stood like a ghostly relic of a bygone era, casting a haunting silhouette over the quiet landscape. Theo – a former Waffen SS soldier from Romania – had poured every ounce of his fading strength into this place, driven by an unshakable need to honor comrades who never returned home. Thick concrete walls rose from the hillside, their cold gray surfaces blending seamlessly into the rugged terrain. The building resembled a fortress trapped in time, an eerie sanctuary untouched by the changing world.

Long before whispers of his project reached the public, Theo had invited me to his home. Over a quiet dinner, lit by the soft glow of candlelight, he shared his vision. His voice was steady yet carried the raw, unmistakable pain of a man burdened by the ghosts of his past. To him, the museum was more than a memorial; it was his legacy – a place he imagined overflowing with exhibits and artifacts, a final gesture of remembrance.

My first visit inside revealed little more than a cavernous shell, empty and echoing with a somber silence. With each subsequent visit, Theo's vision took shape. Haunting displays filled the space: sculptures and a marble bust of Adolf Hitler, flanked by both Nazi and American flags.

The tour concluded on the rooftop, where the heart of Theo's vision loomed. There, beneath a wide-open Wisconsin sky, stood a massive marble gravestone – eight feet tall and stretching across the building's entire width. Carved deeply into its polished surface was a elaborate tribute to the Waffen SS, meticulously listing the countries from which the fallen soldiers had come, alongside the staggering numbers who had perished. The stone's heaviness chilled me; it felt as though it held the weight of thousands of restless souls, forever bound to this remote hillside.

Theo's ambitious dream of opening this museum to the public was derailed by endless zoning battles and bureaucratic red tape. When he passed away, his vision remained suspended in unfinished silence, the memorial museum fading quietly into obscurity.

Such a monument had never existed on American soil before – and likely never will again.

REBRANDING AND THE MARCH ON WASHINGTON DC

In April 2008, the NSM gathered for its National Meeting in Baltimore, Maryland, where we secured permits for what would become a landmark event: a march on Washington, D.C. Although turnout was much smaller than expected, the march marked a historic milestone. Adversaries had long insisted we would never dare set foot in the capital, yet there we were – marching down Constitution Avenue, flags unfurled, boots echoing sharply off the marble facades all the way to the Capitol lawn.

Behind this public display, an internal struggle simmered. At the meeting, I announced a major shift for the organization: we would retire the traditional brown shirts and swastika armbands that had defined the group since its inception in 1973 – and even earlier, dating back to the 1950s under Commander Rockwell. The meeting hall grew tense. I could feel resistance ripple through the crowd, eyes narrowing and breaths held in an uneasy silence, each person wrestling silently with the fear of losing symbols that had long formed our identity.

Yet my decision held firm. In place of the old uniforms, we adopted black BDUs, bearing the NSM patch on the shoulder. This rebranding wasn't merely cosmetic – it signaled the dawn of a new era, one we carried into the streets of Washington, D.C., that day.

RISING LIKE A PHOENIX

The NSM's activities in Phoenix, Arizona, included two major rallies. The first proceeded with relatively few issues; we used shields to block Antifa's projectiles, managing to avoid serious injuries. The second rally descended into chaos. Antifa had publicly vowed to "Smash the Fascists" and stop the march by any means necessary.

With columns formed, shields raised, and flags unfurled, we moved towards downtown, where our PA system was set-up. The opposition forces were massive. Antifa had rallied support from numerous far-left groups, including the Brown Berets, a militant Chicano organization we'd clashed with across the Southwest.

Chants of "The Police, Nazis, and Klan go hand in hand" echoed relentlessly as counter-demonstrators surged violently against police formations. In past confrontations, I'd witnessed Antifa charge forward only to scatter when officers pushed back – but this time was different. There was a raw, unhinged aggression in the air.

Suddenly, the sky filled with flying debris – chunks of concrete, shattered bottles, rocks, even projectiles embedded with nails – hurled indiscriminately toward us and the police lines. Makeshift barricades sprang up as Marxists dragged newspaper vending machines across streets, forming crude barriers before setting them ablaze. Thick plumes of black smoke spiraled skyward, darkening the midday sun and casting an apocalyptic shadow over downtown Phoenix.

Masked Antifa militants unleashed mace and pepper spray directly into the faces of police officers, who responded with a barrage of tear gas canisters. For a fleeting moment, relief swept through our ranks as dense, choking gas enveloped Antifa's front lines. But just as quickly, a gust of wind shifted direction, driving the toxic cloud straight back into our columns. On the sidewalks, self-designated medics among the counter-demonstrators tended to their injured.

The police struggled to hold their ground, their advance slowed by the ferocious onslaught from counter-demonstrators. Our shields barely withstood the relentless barrage of projectiles, and the risk of serious injury increased each time the police ground to a halt.

Amid the turmoil, I approached a police supervisor, urgently requesting permission for the NSM to bypass their lines. He stared at me incredulously, as if I'd lost my mind. Gesturing toward the violent melee, he stated the obvious – that the intensity of the counter-protest made crossing police lines far too dangerous. My request, flatly denied.

Seconds later, a chunk of concrete struck one of our women in the forehead, sending blood streaming down her face. That was the final straw. Some of our men were already bloodied from the relentless bombardment; now the women were suffering too. Rage surged through me, crystallizing into sheer determination.

I grabbed Charles, the leader of NSM's storm troop division, an imposing figure with a background in combat sports. As I studied the police formations, I noticed a small seam opening briefly as they advanced, only to close when they stopped. That fleeting gap was our only chance. I turned to Charles and said, "When that seam opens again, we're charging through – straight into their lines."

It was a bold, dangerous gamble, but protecting the group demanded it. Outnumbered by hundreds, hesitation was a luxury we couldn't afford – decisive action was the only path forward. Heart pounding, adrenaline surging, I briefed those around us. Moments later, the seam reappeared.

"Now!" I roared.

We charged through the gap – but only about ten of us made it, leaving most of our forces stranded behind police lines. Ahead loomed a mass of enraged counter-demonstrators, their numbers overwhelming. The bitter reality of a merciless beating, hospital visit, or worse hung thick in the air, but retreat was unthinkable. Summoning every ounce of courage, I rallied those who had broken through, shouting over the chaos, "Unleash your berserker rage and charge the enemy like lions!"

To our astonishment – and relief – the far-left hordes abruptly turned and bolted, sprinting away like Olympic runners. Our sheer resolve, mixed with wild-eyed fury, had somehow sent them reeling.

Moments earlier, urgent texts had come from troops at the rally site, reporting skirmishes as they struggled to defend our PA system from mounting opposition. With overwhelming forces bearing down on them, we didn't know how long they'd hold out – time was running short.

With empty streets now left by fleeing counter-protesters, we advanced the last two blocks unchallenged. For the remainder of the event, the opposition lingered behind their barricades, allowing the rally to proceed as planned.

Following rallies, after-parties had become tradition, and in Arizona, we gathered at a property known as Aryan Acres, easily recognized by its tall flagpole flying the NSM flag. Following the chaos of Phoenix, the atmosphere there shifted quickly from tense defiance to rowdy celebration, as skinhead bands took the stage, their music roaring into the desert night.

Before festivities kicked off, the host issued a peculiar warning over the PA system: beware of the "jumping cacti" scattered across the property. As drinks flowed and caution faded, one attendee – egged on by his mischievous brother – decided to test this curious warning. He approached a cactus cautiously at first, expecting some sort of movement. When nothing happened, his confidence soared. Boldly, he dropped his pants to taunt it further.

That's when the cactus retaliated.

Its spines embedded deep into his backside, triggering uproarious laughter as he ran through the crowd, pants tangled around his ankles, howling in agony, desperately pleading for help. The absurdity of the scene was exactly what we needed to break the day's tension, leaving even the toughest among us in tears of laughter.

No one was eager to deal with his bare-ass predicament, but since his brother had goaded him into playing with the cactus, it only seemed fitting that they share the burden of the consequences. Armed with needle-nose pliers, he painstakingly removed each spine, one by agonizing one, to everyone's amusement and the man's embarrassment. Each cactus spike, barbed like tiny arrows, tore mercilessly at his skin as they were extracted, making the process excruciatingly slow and painful.

That night, everyone learned a valuable lesson about jumping cacti: they're real, and you should never, ever show them your bare backside!

CHAPTER 30

THE ROAD TO DETROIT

After the relationship with my daughters' mother ended, I made the difficult decision to leave Minnesota and start over in Detroit, Michigan, with little more than a bag of clothes. It wasn't easy, but I found some solace in knowing we'd done everything possible to salvage an irreparable relationship, if only for the children's sake.

Back in Minnesota, my dad offered to gather my dog, Justice, and belongings with the help of Mike and a couple of friends. The plan was for me to meet Mike in Chicago, then continue on to Detroit. But there was one major hurdle – getting Justice into his travel kennel. Dad called to say that no one could get close to him without risking a serious mauling. At over 100 pounds and resembling an Arctic wolf, Justice was a force to be reckoned. The idea of leaving him behind was unthinkable, so I pleaded with Dad to try one last time. Reluctantly, he agreed, and after calmly reassuring Justice that he'd see me soon, he managed to coax him into the trailer.

As Mike drove toward Chicago, he called to say he was stopping for food and gas. He mentioned that Justice seemed calm and asked if he could let him out briefly for water and a burger.

"Oh my God, no! Absolutely not!" I shot back. "Don't

open that kennel under any circumstances. He'll be fine until I get there."

Mike, worried that Justice might be dehydrated, accused me of overreacting. I apologized for raising my voice, but stressed that opening the kennel could put him – and anyone nearby – in serious danger.

Mike then came up with a plan: he'd break the burger into pieces and push them through the kennel bars without opening it. I agreed it was a good solution. Fifteen minutes later, he called back, cussing mad.

"Jeff, I'd ditch this dog on the side of the road if he was anyone else's! With all due respect, Sir," Mike snapped. The sarcastic addition of "With all due respect, Sir" was his go-to whenever he was mad at me.

"What happened?" I asked.

Mike continued, "I gently offered him a piece of the burger, and the damn dog went for my hand instead of the meat, so I chucked the whole burger across the parking lot for him to see! What kind of dog refuses meat and tries to attack the person feeding him?" Imagining Mike's frustration as he flung the burger, I struggled not to burst out laughing.

That evening in Chicago, when I opened the kennel, everyone took a cautious step back. Justice, after our longest time apart, practically tackled me with excitement. Mike, still fuming, glared at Justice like he'd just encountered a new arch-nemesis.

Relocating to Detroit raised concerns that anti-racist organizations might target my family in my absence. In the NSM, we followed a mafia-like code that forbade targeting women and children, but there was no guarantee our opponents shared that restraint. My ex and I kept relationship issues private, knowing they could be exploited. Respected in the organization as a mother and activist, she sought advice from trusted members after the breakup.

The disclosure of our breakup led to a few members leaving the group. One regional leader resigned, accusing me of hypocrisy and of going against the NSM's principles of "Family, Race, and Nation." My appearance at events with other women shortly after the split didn't help matters – some saw it as a violation of the party's values.

Around that time, Jim, a member from the West Coast, relocated to Michigan to be closer to his girlfriend. Known for developing the NSM's first-person shooter games ZOG's Nightmare 1 & 2, Jim was also skilled in web development and podcasting. Despite his talents, most members disliked him, often questioning his mental stability. Yet, I valued his commitment and maintained a good working relationship.

Tensions flared after I appointed Jim's girlfriend as a moderator for the NSM's online forum. Soon after, Jim accused the Party's webmaster of making inappropriate advances toward her. I launched a thorough review, combing through their communications and speaking directly with both parties. The investigation showed their interactions were entirely professional – there was no hint of misconduct.

Despite the evidence, Jim's reaction spiraled out of control. He became enraged, demanding I purge the webmaster. When I refused, emphasizing that decisions had to be based on facts, not favoritism, his anger escalated into threats. Left with no choice, I expelled him from the Party. Furious, Jim launched a campaign of online harassment and doxxing, culminating in distributing fliers throughout the Detroit metro area, including our neighborhood. The fliers had photos of my new girlfriend and me, identified me as the leader of the Nazi Party, and exposed our address, names, and phone numbers.

We braced for violence at our doorstep – but Jim's attempt to incite hostility fell flat. Instead of widespread aggression, we faced just two angry fathers knocking angrily at our door, and a handful of anonymous hate calls. Most shocking, however, was the unexpected outpouring of concern from complete strangers worried about our safety. Even those offended by our beliefs condemned the leaflets.

Disgruntled ex-members had caused issues before, but few matched Jim's obsessive intensity. His behavior was bizarre, irrational, and illogical. Once again, someone I considered a friend had turned into an enemy over something trivial.

DETROIT

Detroit's descent from a beacon of innovation to a city marred by decay and crime was undeniable. Once celebrated as the Motor City, it had deteriorated into what many bitterly dubbed Murder City. The scars of the 1967 race riots still haunted its neighborhoods, and its economy rusting away into ruins. Charred remnants of abandoned homes dotted the landscape, and to me, Detroit seemed on the brink of collapse – an environment ripe for recruitment.

Within the movement, Detroit's decline was often wrongly attributed to its predominantly black population. After seeing cities like Atlanta thrive with similar demographics, I began to question that assumption. Detroit's challenges were rooted in economic mismanagement, political corruption, and the collapse of the auto industry – issues that transcended race.

Paradoxically, moving to Detroit didn't intensify my radical beliefs; instead, it became a catalyst for change. I began to fall in love with the city – the vibrant soul, rich history, and the music that pulsed through its streets. In a twist of fate, Detroit became central to my journey toward deradicalization. The empathy I began to feel for its people, regardless of race, slowly eroded the walls of intolerance I'd built over decades.

Though I started recognizing contradictions in my beliefs, it was difficult to accept that the ideology I had defended so fiercely was flawed. That realization planted seeds of change. Cracks formed in the ideological foundation I'd built, marking the beginning of a gradual but inevitable shift toward a worldview anchored in empathy and compassion.

NEIGHBORS

Living in the city introduced me to a diverse array of neighbors. Ironically, it was the white residents who caused the most drama. One woman, in particular, seemed determined to involve the police at every opportunity – whether we were barbecuing, had weeds in the yard, or the dogs barked. Her intense, irrational fear of dogs, lead to constant complaints about Justice and Chaos (my Rottweiler). No matter how much we tried to explain or reassure her about their training and purpose, she remained inflexible, thriving on conflict and painting herself as a perpetual victim.

Her boyfriend's daily routine revolved around alcohol – starting each morning and escalating as the day wore on. By afternoon, he was belligerent and reckless, taunting the dogs by sticking his arm into our yard, yanking it back at the last second before they could reach him. It was a dangerous game and only a matter of time before one of the dogs tore into his flesh. One afternoon, Justice came within an inch of sinking his teeth into him. I confronted the man and warned him to stop, but he took it as a threat, and – predictably – his girlfriend called the police again.

The dogs stood alert by the fence but ceased showing aggression when they saw me talking to him. As I turned to walk away, he spitefully poured his beer over the fence onto Justice. I went off like a stick of dynamite. Just then, the police rolled up.

Memories flooded back of an incident in Minnesota, where a roommate's German Shepherd had been euthanized after biting a neighbor. Fortunately, the police explained Michigan law to my neighbor, warning him that if he provoked the dogs by reaching over the fence and got bitten, it would be his fault. Knowing my dogs wouldn't be blamed if they defended themselves against this drunken fool set my mind at ease.

After the cops left, I turned to the neighbor. "If you pour anything on my dogs again," I warned, "you might just find out how much fun they are without a fence between you."

The neighborhood drama didn't stop there – it escalated, taking a darker turn with a particularly nasty woman living directly across the street. She spent her days spewing profanity from her porch. Whenever we stepped outside, she'd yell, "Fuck you Nazis, get out of our town." My girlfriend covered her five-year-old daughter's ears to shield her from the constant abuse as we hurried between the car and house. Disturbingly, the woman didn't spare the child, hurling vile insults at her whenever she played outside. Seeing her retreat indoors in tears, devastated by words no child should ever hear, demonstrated how unhinged this woman was – willing to target an innocent child with such venom.

A home should be a sanctuary, a place of peace and security, but ours was anything but that. The thought of leaving the house filled us with dread, caught in the crossfire between the woman across the street and the cop-calling couple next door. Due to our radical beliefs, we felt powerless to stop the harassment – certain if things escalated, we'd face criminal charges. The emotional toll was exhausting, and the abuse continued for as long as we lived there.

CHAPTER 31

COUNTERINTELLIGENCE OPS

In the neo-Nazi movement, staying vigilant against undercover operatives was a constant necessity. Though I mention a few in this memoir, the sheer number of informants exposed over the years is staggering – too many to document. Informants were so deeply embedded in extremist circles that trusting anyone became nearly impossible. You never knew whether the person next to you was a true believer, a government agent, or a desperate snitch trying to entrap someone to cut a deal.

To mitigate security risks, I implemented background checks. While not foolproof, certain red flags emerged – like recruits who faced unusually light consequences despite extensive criminal records. These checks also reinforced our strict no-entry policy for sex offenders, instituted after an ex-member humiliatingly appeared on a televised manhunt show. Another safeguard was the probationary period: recruits advocating illegal actions or displaying inappropriate behaviors were purged before becoming full members.

Infiltration tactics weren't exclusive to government agencies; watchdog groups and far-left activists had also mastered them. In contrast, far-right groups rarely conducted similar operations, instead relying on scattered intelligence. To address these shortcomings, I developed a counterintelligence strategy aimed at penetrating Antifa collectives nationwide. Our most effective operatives weren't white, making them far less likely to be suspected or detected. Though it may seem unusual for people of color to align with neo-Nazis, it isn't without precedent. Far-left extremists often failed to grasp that individuals who've fled communist or socialist regimes – and survived genuine oppression – harbor a visceral hatred for groups like Antifa. For many, aligning with Nazis felt safer than risking another communist nightmare – this time, in America.

One of our highest-stakes counterintelligence operations unfolded after intel surfaced that an Antifa affiliate had bragged about plans to shoot me and other NSM members at an upcoming rally. Despite the credible threat, we didn't involve law enforcement, opting to handle it internally. I provided our undercover operative with photos of the potential shooter and instructed him to scout the perimeter, focusing on areas where counter-protesters would gather.

During the rally, our operative texted me: target identified, concealing a pistol in the audience. My orders were clear – shadow him, and if he drew the gun, disarm and neutralize. The anticipated moment never came; the weapon stayed holstered. The irony was striking – the would-be shooter was white, while our undercover operative watching him was black.

Later that evening, as my girlfriend and I walked her dog near our hotel, a frantic call from an associate interrupted us. He warned us to avoid walking alone and get somewhere safe immediately. Confused, I asked, "How do you know we're alone?" Moments later, a photo arrived on my phone – taken by Antifa and posted online – showing us walking near the hotel. The angle suggested it had been snapped from the shadowy wooded area nearby. A chill ran down my spine; we were being stalked.

Years later, after I left neo-Nazism and began advocating against hate, the man who had carried a pistol to that rally reached out unexpectedly. He told me he'd left Antifa, distancing himself from all forms of extremism. Discovering that I'd made a similar journey surprised him. We spoke candidly about how our lives had improved since abandoning extremism – it felt surreal to share such a conversation with a former enemy.

Then, he disclosed that he had planned to target me at the rally – a threat I had anticipated and quietly prepared for. What he revealed next was bone-chilling: that same night he'd hidden in the woods near our hotel, rifle in hand, prepared to shoot. His finger stayed off the trigger only because his partner got cold feet at the last second. Learning about this close call, years after I'd believed the danger had passed, left me deeply unsettled – one squeeze of that trigger could have changed everything.

This revelation forced me to wonder just how many other near-misses had occurred over the years that I'll never know about. I am thankful for his courage – it takes remarkable strength to be so transparent. His honesty serves as a rare and sobering reminder of the transformative power of change – and how crucial it is to guard ourselves against our most destructive impulses.

CHAPTER 32

BETRAYALS, RAIDS AND INFORMANTS

The label informant was tossed around so loosely within the movement that nearly everyone faced the accusation at some point. On occasion those claims turned out to be true.

One afternoon, the leader of a small KKK faction reached out with a warning: one of our web developers, Eric, was supposedly an informant. Considering the severity of the accusation, I insisted on concrete proof before taking action to avoid an unjust expulsion. My insistence on evidence offended the Klansman, who declined to provide any, leaving us unprepared for the treachery that followed.

Eric wasn't just skilled in web development; he excelled at deception. While working on the NSM Record Store's website, he exploited his access to the business's bank account, siphoning thousands of dollars into his personal account. He took it further, hijacking NSM-affiliated domains, transferring ownership to himself. Then, on New Saxon, NSM's social network, he left a cryptic message stating "negotiations" were required to restore access.

When confronted, Eric played innocent, insisting the money was owed to him. Then he upped the stakes with an ultimatum: report the embezzlement and lose the domains, or stay silent and negotiate their return. He likely assumed I'd cut the losses – the domains held even greater value than the funds he'd stolen. But the moment he issued that ultimatum, his fate was sealed – I wasn't backing down.

I reported the fraud to both the bank and online payment processor. They refunded the stolen funds almost immediately, each confirming that Eric's actions constituted felony-level theft. The domain registrars were a different story. From their perspective, he was the rightful owner, having transferred the domains to himself. They refused to intervene.

Nevertheless, we recovered every stolen site through some rather unconventional methods – details I won't delve into here. Ironically, in the process, I gained control of Eric's own domains, including those tied to his business. Rather than retaliate by holding onto his sites, I washed my hands of the matter. Allegedly, his domains were dumped into the public sphere.

As the saying goes – he fucked around and got found out.

These events began while I was still living in Minnesota, but it wasn't until I moved to Michigan that the full extent of Eric's treachery came to light. That's when our home became the target of a massive law enforcement raid involving multiple agencies – BATF, FBI, IRS, and local police. They barricaded the entire street, flooding it with tactical units, transforming our neighborhood into what felt like the prelude to a Waco-style siege.

Inside, my girlfriend and I were handcuffed as agents methodically tore through our home. When they finished, we were released without charges – similar to the raid in Minnesota. This time, the warrant revealed that the raid was based on information obtained from a reliable confidential witness who'd previously been involved with the NSM Records website – it was unmistakably Eric.

Outside, our problematic neighbors had gathered, savoring the spectacle. Through the open windows, we heard their cheers, laughter, and applause – reveling in our humiliation, eager for a front-row seat to what they hoped would be our downfall. When we were released and the authorities began to disperse, their jubilation soured. Frustrated, they shouted, "Arrest the Nazis!" – as if their outrage alone could override due process.

Later, one of our other neighbors – an African-American family – shared that law enforcement had knocked on their door, asking if we'd ever threatened them or used racial slurs. The father shut them down immediately. He reprimanded the agents for turning the neighborhood into a war zone and assured them we hadn't caused any trouble.

This wasn't an isolated experience. My interactions with the black community in Detroit were generally positive and respectful, even when my politics were known.

I was no stranger to government scrutiny, raids and surveillance. That was the cost of being a political dissident. But realizing that this second raid had been orchestrated by someone we had expelled for criminal acts – embezzlement, fraud, hijacking websites – felt more insulting than a slap in the face. It reinforced my belief the system was corrupt, willing to align with criminals if it served their interests.

Simultaneously, as I began to see cracks in the shallow, race-based tribalism I'd long embraced, my hatred for the system burned hotter than ever.

TRIALS AND TRIBULATIONS

Custody disputes and divorce are enough to upend anyone's life. For me, the situation carried added weight, complicated by my infamy as a neo-Nazi leader. It was only a matter of time before the wreckage of that world collided with my personal life – like a runaway freight train.

As part of the custody proceedings, I was advised to undergo drug and alcohol evaluations and enroll in parenting classes. Though I'd never had issues with drugs and had overcome alcohol addiction after moving to Detroit, the parenting classes posed a unique challenge. It wasn't the classes themselves – it was the self-control required to sit in proximity to individuals with histories of child abuse. Though I completed the program, it took an emotional toll I hadn't anticipated.

From the outset, my lawyer had warned – gaining custody would be a long shot. Still, for the children's sake, I had to try. As I worked to prove I could provide a stable, safe, and loving home, something insidious was brewing behind the scenes.

At an Ohio NSM meeting held in a public library, I was the keynote speaker. The event was uneventful, even welcoming. Afterward, I was introduced to Ohio-Matt, the leader of a local skinhead crew. Our interaction was brief – a handshake and thank you for attending. These introductions were routine, and I always made a point to be polite and respectful.

Shortly after returning home, my phone lit up with shockingly explicit death threats from Matt – texts, voicemails, and calls filled with unrelenting graphic violence. These weren't the usual threats I'd grown accustomed to. Matt was different.

He wasn't just threatening me – he vowed to bomb our home, burn it to the ground, rape my girlfriend, and harm any children present.

Hearing someone so brazenly target women and children was appalling. In the skinhead scene, threats were sometimes exchanged between rivals, but families were strictly off-limits. Breaking this unspoken code would provoke severe consequences from any crew, regardless of affiliation – even prison-based crews didn't cross those lines.

As Matt's threats escalated, one thing became clear – he wasn't a neo-Nazi, nor was he Antifa. Neither side condoned rape or violence against children. His behavior was foreign to anything I'd encountered in extremist circles, a glaring sign that something was seriously wrong with him.

In an attempt to understand his motives, I called Matt. He accused me of disrespecting him at the library meeting, a claim that made no sense – our interaction had been nothing more than a cordial handshake. Despite my attempt to reason with him, his threats escalated, each more grotesque than the last. Then, to drive his point home, he recited our home address.

The most confrontational thing I said in response was, "It would not be in your best interest to show up at my home. It won't end well for you."

Then Matt did something strange – he taunted me for not retaliating verbally during that phone call. That immediately raised red flags. It was highly suspicious for someone to ask outright why I hadn't threatened them back. It was a deliberate provocation, he wanted me to say something incriminating. That's when I suspected he was an informant. After that, I stopped responding, but his deranged threats kept coming – voicemails, texts, each more unhinged than the last.

Anyone openly discussing murder, rape, bombings, arson, and harming children over the phone is either a lunatic or an informant protected by very powerful people. If Matt was simply a psychopath, he wasn't a major concern – especially in Michigan, where self-defense laws are robust. Any attempt on his part would quickly become his worst nightmare.

Not long after the threats began, a detective knocked on our door to inquire about them. The fact that law enforcement was aware of the situation only deepened my suspicion that Matt was working with them. Dripping with sarcasm, I pointed out the incompetence of their supposed informant, making it clear I wouldn't be lured into any entrapment scheme.

Despite my accusations, the detective remained professional, assuring me that Matt wasn't working for them. They even offered to pursue charges. That caught me off guard. If Matt was their guy, they wouldn't offer legal recourse. I declined, sticking to the code I lived by.

After the incident, I barely gave Matt or his threats any thought, chalking it up as another bizarre incident – until it resurfaced in my custody case.

The opposing counsel seized on the situation, framing it as gang warfare within the neo-Nazi movement. They cited a police report, threats against my life, and argued that my home was too dangerous for my children.

Months after the custody matter concluded, a lawsuit against a KKK group and its leader – whom I knew from past speaking engagements – made headlines. The case, brought by a well-known civil rights organization, was drawing widespread attention due to the KKK's involvement.

One evening, I was flipping through television news coverage of the trial when my breath caught. The screen cut to courtroom footage of a key witness for the prosecution. I stared in disbelief, as a wave of revulsion hit me.

Matt was perched like a Canary on the witness stand, smirking like he'd just won the lottery.

This so-called key witness – the man now posturing as a figure of credibility – was the same man who had flooded my phone with grotesque threats of bombings, rape, arson, and murder – every word documented in texts and voicemails. The same guy whose unhinged tirades were twisted in my custody case into supposed evidence of gang warfare.

To be clear, sharing this memory isn't to cast aspersions on the civil-rights group who propped Matt up as a witness in their lawsuit against the KKK; therefore, I'm not naming them. The public can draw its own conclusions about any ethical considerations at play.

One thing was certain. Months before Matt was grinning ear to ear on that witness stand, he'd been doing everything in his power to provoke and entrap me. I had no doubt that his testimony was just another scripted puppet act, orchestrated by his handlers – just like his previous attempts at entrapment.

It's often said that lies and hatred breed more of the same.

The hardships I had endured over the years hadn't broken me. If anything, every lash of the proverbial whip had deepened my radicalization, hardened my resolve.

Watching my adversaries use criminals like Matt to advance

their cause only reinforced my belief that their agenda was as unjust and corrupt as what they claimed to oppose.

Because the means by which a cause is pursued can tarnish the legitimacy of the cause itself.

Resorting to dishonorable tactics to achieve a goal is equivalent to moral bankruptcy.

In war, if one side commits genocide, it doesn't excuse the other from doing the same.

Genocide is always wrong – no matter the context.

CHAPTER 33

THE BATTLE OF TRENTON

The 2011 NSM National Meeting took place in New Jersey, followed by a rally in Trenton. As the women prepared dinner in a church meeting hall and members gathered for the evening's speeches, Jeff H, part of our security detail, burst inside, face drenched in pepper spray. "Antifa's outside – armed and smashing up vehicles in the parking lot," he reported.

I instructed the women, children, and elderly to stay inside for safety, while the rest of us moved to confront the attackers.

In the crowded hallway leading to the exit, Charles, Drake, and I grabbed folding chairs for improvised self-defense. Drake, the tip of the spear, pushed through the packed corridor to reach the enemy.

Outside, a masked Black Bloc mob awaited us, armed and causing mayhem. One of them, wielding a thick tree branch, smashed car windows with wild swings. Before he could raise it again, Drake lunged, landing a punch that sent him stumbling backward. The thug tried to counter with the branch but swung wide. It was an effective tool for vandalism – but useless in close-quarters combat.

Other Antifa militants were better equipped for violence, brandishing clubs, batons, knives, pepper-spray, and even a hammer. After forcing them back from our vehicles, the fighting spilled into the street.

I locked onto an obese masked man striking my friends with a baton. Adrenaline surging, I slammed a folding chair into him. He hit the ground hard, like a hog felled in a stockyard. My victory was short-lived. Another attacker blinded me, unleashing a torrent of pepper spray directly into my eyes. Disoriented, Duke from NSM security guided me back inside.

Inside, a nurse from our group flushed the chemicals from my eyes while tending to others with more severe injuries.

Outside, the street fight raged on, grinding traffic to a halt. Sirens wailed in the distance – police and ambulances closing in.

The moment the first squad cars arrived, Antifa scattered like cockroaches.

Several of our men stood drenched in blood, concern flickering over whether the police would arrest us instead of the attackers. Fortunately, NSM media captured footage of the assault. I gave the order to share it with the authorities – to prove we hadn't started this fight.

The aftermath was grim – blood stained the pavement, and remnants of the brawl littered the ground. Police recovered a blood-soaked knife dropped by Antifa during the battle. Several of our people sustained serious injuries and were rushed off in ambulances.

Drake suffered a devastating hammer blow to the face, shattering his cheekbone.

Later, as we reviewed photos and video footage, we spotted the masked Antifa thug wielding the hammer – a chilling reminder of how close we had come to losing lives that day. Swinging a hammer at someone's head isn't an act of protest. It's a lethal attack. There's no ambiguity – it should have been treated as attempted murder, no matter the attacker's beliefs or motivations.

The police apprehended some of the fleeing Antifa and charged a few, but from what I recall, the courts let them off without convictions.

Unfortunately, this was expected – far-left extremists seemed to get off with little more than a slap on the wrist, if anything at all, even when the police pursued charges. The lack of accountability was deeply disheartening, further eroding trust in the courts and fueling a growing sense of injustice. The glaring disparity in how justice was applied – one set of rules for the far-right and another for the far-left – radicalized thousands, myself included.

Forget ideology for a moment. Just look at the crime.

I've given plenty of examples where justice failed, but let's focus on this one. Video and photographic evidence was handed over to law enforcement. A bloodied knife was recovered. Multiple people were hospitalized.

Now, imagine if it was your loved one who had been struck in the face with a hammer. Imagine you had indisputable video evidence of the attack, only to watch the perpetrators walk away without consequence. How would you feel? How would it affect you emotionally? What about the victim, scarred for life, forced to live with the aftermath while their attacker faced nothing?

After the police departed, the meeting resumed. Despite the lingering sting of pepper-spray, I delivered a fiery speech, celebrating our enemies' retreat and honoring the courage of our men in the hospital. The crowd erupted in thunderous chants of "Hail Victory!" The battle had boosted morale, and reinforced commitment within the organization.

Later, back at the hotel, we gathered to review the fight footage. While our main cameras were indoors during the clash, recordings from NSM Media and some cellphones had captured parts of the altercation. Recognizing the video's potential to rally supporters nationwide, I prioritized its public release. Footage was later featured in two music videos as part of NSM's propaganda efforts.

As we analyzed the clips with about a dozen members present, something unexpected happened. Amid the chaos – fists flying, weapons clashing, bodies hitting the pavement – our camera operator had unknowingly caught a voice in the background.

"Excuse me, excuse me... where's the bathroom?"

Silence, then outrage. I slammed my fist on the table.

"Who the hell needed a bathroom break during a street fight?!"

We rewound the footage over and over, but couldn't identify the culprit.

Frustration boiled over.

"Bathroom guy is going to be held accountable. Either demotion or expulsion – depending on his excuse. I have zero tolerance for cowardice, and will make an example of him."

"A coward thinks he will ever live, If warfare he avoids; But old age will give him no peace, Though spears may spare him." Hávamál (stanza 16) – Thorpe Translation 1866.

In the middle of my tirade, Jeff H. walked in after tallying who was still in the hospital. He could hear me yelling from the hallway. I paused, hoping he could identify the voice behind the bathroom break question.

As the footage played, Jeff burst out laughing. Reminding me that during guard duty, he'd been pepper-sprayed by Antifa, forcing him indoors to rinse his eyes – as the rest of us countered the assault. Ironically, moments later, we were side by side in the same predicament, blinded by pepper-spray.

Jeff H was no coward – he was a respected front-line leader in the NSM. Yet, here I was, demanding bathroom guy be expelled – when it was him all along.

Once the misunderstanding cleared up, the room erupted in laughter – at my expense.

Jeff found it especially hilarious, given how often we spoke, and I didn't recognize his voice.

The next morning, we regrouped for the rally. Even those hospitalized the night before showed up, battered but defiant. I suggested they sit this one out and recover. They refused. One by one, they tore off their bandages. They'd show no weakness. Not to the public, the media, and definitely not to our enemies.

The rally remained peaceful, but reports surfaced afterwards that Antifa had vandalized businesses downtown.

THE CYCLE OF RADICALIZATION

Antifa's aggression, hostility toward law enforcement and support for initiatives like Defund the Police, inadvertently became one of our recruitment tools.

Their tactics – rioting, attacking police, destroying property – alienated everyone outside their circles. As public sentiment shifted, disillusioned people found themselves drawn toward far-right extremism.

This dynamic – reciprocal radicalization – is a vicious cycle. Extremism on one side fuels the other. As one group escalates, the opposing group grows in response. It doesn't matter whether the ideology is political or religious – at its core, radicalization thrives on intolerance.

That's why debating which form of extremism is worse is a waste of time.

Some forms may pose more immediate threats, but arguing based on personal bias or perceived harm only distracts from the broader issue: tackling all extremism without double standards.

If we ever want to break the cycle, we need to address radicalization fairly – not selectively. The moment we start treating one form of intolerance as more acceptable than another, we're not fighting extremism. We're feeding it.

CHAPTER 34

TRAGEDY STRIKES

Jeff H. and I had forged a friendship that extended beyond our roles in the NSM, strengthened by a shared sense of humor that lightened an otherwise serious atmosphere. His practical jokes were always creative. Once, he sent me a package, claiming it contained critical intel from NSM's Border Patrol operations. As I carefully unwrapped the overly secured box, sand poured out onto my floor. Inside, was a backpack, a single shoe, and a grimy shirt, along with a note joking about "treasures" uncovered during a Border Op. After cleaning up the mess, I jokingly told him those treasures were best left in the desert. He laughed and joked about sending more with his next report, and I vowed to return the favor if he tried.

At our National Meeting, I saw the perfect opportunity to prank him back. I told Jeff there had been an error on his rank promotion certificate – that he hadn't been promoted, but demoted. Handing him a "corrected" certificate, I watched as his expression shifted from confusion to disbelief. For a moment, he fell silent, his face turning pale, like he was going to be sick. Unable to keep a straight face, I burst out laughing and revealed the joke, watching the color return to his cheeks. These light-hearted moments provided a much-needed break from the intense seriousness that permeated our lives.

Jeff was a charismatic leader, always at the forefront.

When asked why he faced threats so boldly, he'd grin and say, "Someone's gotta be the tip of the spear."

During a particularly unsettling conversation, Jeff shared a haunting premonition – he believed he'd be martyred by our enemies. I tried to dispel his dark thoughts, telling him that thinking that way invited bad fortune. Despite my attempts, Jeff described it as a deep, unshakable feeling. He solemnly requested that if such a fate befell him, his ashes be scattered along the US-Mexico border. His request left me with a lingering sense of foreboding.

Though we all understood the risks inherent to our cause, we rarely discussed death. Some spoke of a glorious death in battle during Ragnarök, but Jeff's reflections carried a different tone – one of resignation. His words weren't driven by bravado but by a somber, melancholic acceptance, as if he believed his fate was sealed.

On May 1st, 2011, the phone wouldn't stop ringing. It was unusual to receive so many early morning calls, especially from Butch, NSM's Chief of Staff. A sense of dread settled in, and I braced for the worst. Was it a raid? An arrest? A shootout with cartels during a border op? My heart pounded as I returned the call.

Butch's voice was heavy with sorrow. "There's no easy way to say this – Jeff passed away."

I was stunned, mind racing. Just hours ago, Jeff and I had spoken on the phone. "What happened?" I asked, struggling to process.

"All I know is that Jeff was shot in the head while he slept. His son is in custody – the police believe he pulled the trigger."

The news shattered all semblance of normalcy. Absorbing the magnitude of the tragedy that had befallen Jeff's family felt inconceivable, as though time itself had frozen, the world suspended in a void of disbelief. Jeff's beloved ten-year-old son – his pride and joy – was at the center of an unfathomable catastrophe, facing legal consequences. Out of love and respect for Jeff's family, I won't delve into the details.

I struggled with whether or not to share this dark chapter, as many others have been left untold. After considerable reflection, I believe Jeff would have wanted one message to come through – that he loved his family deeply and despite the tragedy, his spirit will always remain with them as they move forward in life.

As arrangements for Jeff's funeral were underway, I was searching for reasons to avoid attending. It wasn't a lack of empathy; I struggled with the finality of saying goodbye at funerals.

During a call with Mike, who was stationed in Iraq, he expressed frustration over not being granted leave to attend. Then he asked if I had booked my flight. I hesitated before admitting that I hadn't planned on going. Knowing my aversion to funerals, Mike seemed to have expected that answer.

In all the years we'd known each other, Mike had almost never raised his voice at me, but that answer struck a nerve. "What the hell is wrong with you? How could you even say something like that? If it were your funeral, Jeff would've swam, walked, or done whatever it took to be there – and you're not doing the same for him?"

Somberly, I replied, "Yeah, you're right, but..."

Before I could finish, Mike's voice boomed. "Dammit! You're

going – no excuses! The Commander of the NSM should be there, period. In fact, I'm buying the plane ticket myself to make sure you show up!"

Besides Mike's push, I had promises to keep – like scattering Jeff's ashes at the border and finally taking up his challenge to learn how to surf and boogie board. Jeff had always teased me about never having surfed, insisting he'd teach me. Every time I visited California, he'd joke that I disappeared with the "latest flavor of the month." I'd laugh, saying, "Brother, you know I can't resist those Cali girls." But I swore that next time, we'd hit the waves together.

During the trip to California for his funeral, that promise was fulfilled in a meaningful way. A Party member whose family owned a surf shop helped arrange it. She and her ex-husband met us at the beach with surfboards in tow. On that emotional day, as we approached the ocean, we all felt Jeff's absence, yet sensed his presence, playfully chiding, "About time you guys showed up to surf with me!" Now, every time I see a surfer, memories of Jeff come rushing back.

The memorial service took place at a member's home, honoring Jeff's Odinist faith. Party members helped prepare the Funerary Rites, while I conducted the Rite of Passing. With Jeff's family present, I felt a responsibility to honor my friend with respect and sensitivity to his family's feelings.

Navigating these concerns, I led the Rite of Passing with heartfelt sincerity, concluding with a solemn farewell, "Until we meet again, Brother, see you in Valhalla." Thankfully, Jeff's family embraced the ceremony with understanding and grace.

In remembering those who have departed this world, we

grant them a form of immortality. By carrying their memories within us and sharing their stories, we keep their spirit alive. In this way, those who have passed on live eternal.

In Memoriam
Jeff H.
November 21, 1978 - May 1, 2011

CHAPTER 35

GUNNED DOWN IN ARIZONA

The NSM's border operations in Arizona quickly gained media coverage. Beyond street activism, we deployed heavily armed members to confront illegal immigration and drug trafficking, aiming to appeal to a new demographic by tackling issues that resonated with many Americans. Even so, these efforts were barely a drop in the bucket compared to the overwhelming scope of border issues.

The NSM distinguished itself from other border-patrolling groups by adopting a unique approach to engagement and visibility. I encouraged members to document their actions with photos and videos, sharing them across platforms to generate publicity and serve as a recruitment tool. This focus on strategic marketing aimed to position the NSM as a force to be reckoned with, distinct from groups that only posed as active online.

The online white nationalist scene was flooded with factions often consisting of little more than a guy operating from his mom's basement. These so-called groups misled people, causing them to waste time and resources on phantom organizations that offered nothing but empty promises. Recruits frequently shared their disillusionment after joining groups that collected donations without real activism. The NSM's boots-on-the-ground approach rekindled their enthusiasm. However, broadcasting our activities also drew unwanted attention from law enforcement and far-left activists.

As NSM Arizona expanded, internal conflicts and territorial disputes became inevitable. To manage personality clashes, I split conflicting members into separate NSM groups, allowing them to operate independently while uniting for major events. One such conflict involved JT, who I first met at an NSM protest outside the Mexican Consulate in Omaha, Nebraska. He approached me, eager to speak, and I saw in him the charisma and determination I valued in leaders. With a Marine Corps background, JT gravitated toward the NSM's militaristic approach. Eventually, though, his larger-than-life personality caused friction with Arizona's established organizers, leading me to assign him leadership of his own local group.

NSM Arizona was already dealing with internal problems, including rooting out an informant whose actions contributed to a prison sentence for someone accused of plotting to plant IEDs along drug trafficking routes. After the informant's identity was revealed, rumors circulated that he'd either gone into hiding or entered witness protection due to fears of retaliation. Compounding this, another associate was imprisoned after a stabbing incident. Any further missteps could heighten the risk of a full-scale government crackdown.

One evening, JT called to discuss a bold new idea: acquiring armor – not the wearable kind, but the type that runs on tracks and burns diesel. He was eager to buy a surplus tank for desert operations, assuring me it was legal as long as the tank had no functional weaponry. JT believed the tank would serve as a deterrent against cartels and illegal crossings into Arizona. But in light of recent arrests, JT's proposal seemed like a disaster waiting to happen. Transferring any armored vehicle, even demilitarized, would certainly attract scrutiny from the Bureau of Alcohol, Tobacco, Firearms, and Explosives (BATF). As our conversation ended, I made it clear that I couldn't support the plan. We parted amicably, but it was necessary to officially end his membership, allowing him to pursue the project independently, free from NSM's regulations and oversight.

Not long after, JT turned his focus to something more conventional – running for Sheriff. Inspired by Jeff H's electoral success with 27% of the vote in a previous race, he sought NSM's endorsement for his own campaign. An endorsement would provide him with manpower and support, while simultaneously strengthening NSM's foothold in the region. It seemed like a mutually beneficial endeavor.

Then, on May 2nd, 2012 – exactly one year and a day after Jeff H's death – tragedy struck again, this time at JT's home. In a horrific event that claimed five lives, JT's girlfriend, her daughter, and infant granddaughter were fatally shot inside their home. Outside, a family friend was gunned down in the yard, and JT was found dead by his bullet-riddled vehicle from a gunshot wound to the head. News reports concluded that JT had committed these heinous murders before turning the gun on himself.

Trying to come to terms with how anyone could commit such an atrocity was incomprehensible. I'd spoken with JT just days before the killings, and there had been no sign of depression, anger, or any hint that he was capable of such a despicable crime. It seemed impossible to fathom that he could harm his loved ones, especially a baby.

In the aftermath of these tragic murders, those who knew JT were plunged into a state of shock and disbelief. Speculation ran rampant, with many questioning whether JT could truly have been responsible for such monstrous acts. Alternative theories circulated – some suggested it was a cartel hit, a targeted assassination, or even a government cover-up. Personally, I found it hard to reconcile with the idea that someone we knew was even capable of such appalling actions.

The police concluded their investigation, ruling it a murder-suicide. This remains one of the most harrowing memories from my years of involvement, underscoring the grievous consequences of being immersed in extremism.

CHAPTER 36

LEITH, NORTH DAKOTA

Leith, North Dakota – a town that once bustled as a railroad stop in the early 1900s – had by 2013 faded into near-obscurity. A ghost town in all but name, with only a handful of residents keeping it on the map. Into this isolated silence stepped Craig, a longtime white nationalist, with an ambitious plan. Targeting remote properties, he enlisted the NSM for promotion and manpower, seeing an opportunity to establish a stronghold with minimal resistance. Soon, he secured a home and several plots of land in Leith, hoisting racialist banners across his property. The image of Nazis attempting to gain a foothold in rural North Dakota provoked a firestorm, and soon media outlets from around the globe descended on Leith to cover the story.

In a symbolic act, Craig transferred an old creamery building to the NSM for a single dollar. Confronted with minimal infrastructure – lacking a modern sewage system, and paved roads – Craig improvised, installing a makeshift shower and renovating an antiquated outhouse, adjusting to conditions straight out of a century-old homestead. Despite the primitive conditions, an NSM family with young children uprooted their lives to settle there and assist with the project.

As word of the project spread, so did a simmering fury among Leith's residents. They gathered in tense meetings, debating how to counter the sudden intrusion and protect their town from becoming a neo-Nazi outpost. Vandalism began targeting the NSM family's vehicles, each act of aggression fueling an already volatile situation.

Amid this charged environment, I reached out to Leith's mayor, hoping to find common ground before tensions escalated further. But instead of seeking resolution, he seemed intent on stoking the flames, issuing bold, inflammatory statements to the press about plans to "drive the Nazis out." Undeterred, I made multiple attempts – calls, letters, emails – all met with silence. There seemed to be no interest in an adult conversation, only a steady escalation of hostilities.

With no other option, I posted an open letter on the NSM website, formally requesting a meeting with the mayor to discuss a peaceful resolution. I warned that if he continued to ignore our calls for civil discourse, I'd organize a town-hall meeting to address the community directly. His refusal left me no choice but to follow through on that promise.

The arrival of the NSM Commander from Detroit for the town hall reignited a media frenzy, and Leith was thrust back into the national spotlight. The news didn't go unnoticed by Antifa, who mobilized to counter our presence.

On the way to Leith, Mike called, asking about possible resistance, especially from nearby reservations. Confidently, I explained that historically, American Indians had never taken a stand against us; they had no stake in this conflict. The NSM, after all, respected the sovereignty of Native reservations. I anticipated minimal opposition from them, if any.

That assumption was shattered as our convoy rolled into town. Alongside NSM supporters, there were farmers, a small group of Antifa, reporters from numerous media outlets, and, unexpectedly, a vast contingent of Native Americans. Adorned in traditional attire, their feathers and beads catching the sun. I hadn't seen Sioux Indians dancing with with ceremonial war drums since my childhood in rural Minnesota – it was a sight to behold.

Law enforcement had been deployed from across the state, with riot control teams prepared for potential unrest.

Walking through Leith, I encountered some locals who were willing to talk, though others – including the mayor – avoided eye contact. Outside the hall, an eerie symphony filled the air. Our friend Jimmy's Scottish bagpipes played mournful notes that mingled with the relentless rhythm of Sioux war drums. The two sounds, so different, blended into a haunting backdrop – a strange harmony that captured the surreal collision of clashing cultures, charged ideologies, and the heavy tension of that day.

Inside the hall, the Police Chief cautioned: the old wooden floors could only support around 100 people. Any more, and the structure risked collapse. As the crowd grew raucous, I directed NSM Security to remove anyone who became disruptive. The Police Chief quickly intervened, making it clear that law enforcement – not us – would manage any disturbances.

When Craig attempted to start the meeting, he was met with immediate hostility. Half the attendees booed and shouted him down, refusing to let him speak. Observing the blatant disrespect, I stepped forward and took control of the microphone, addressing the crowd with a firm, authoritative tone. I warned that any further childish outbursts would lead to removal from the premises. My declaration restored order, allowing the meeting to proceed in a more disciplined manner.

The only other disruption came when a man at the back, visibly intoxicated, began staggering forward, muttering some nonsense about pulling me off the stage. Several supporters rose to their feet, prepared to intervene. I held up a hand, signaling them to stand down, then addressed the man from the podium.

"Sir, you're clearly intoxicated," I said, my tone measured but unyielding. "I'm only warning you once – it would be in your best interest to return to your seat and behave."

Defying my warning, he continued advancing with drunken resolve. Though he couldn't have pulled me off the stage if he tried, his belligerence called for a decisive response – a reminder of who was in control. It warranted knocking him on his ass, putting him in his place to show that such unruly behavior wouldn't be tolerated. Fortunately, the police intervened and removed him before he crossed that line.

That night, we stayed at one of the only motels in the area. The guys had come prepared with homemade mead, moonshine, vodka, and beer. By this time, I rarely drank, but still occasionally indulged at after-parties. The evening was marred by a steady stream of threatening calls to the phone designated for the meeting. It wasn't out of the ordinary – death threats had become a routine aspect of our lives. One caller specifically mentioned our motel and threatened to shoot us if we didn't leave. Not one to back down, I invited him to try, saying he'd find out how well that would work out for him before hanging up. Still, we posted a guard as a precaution.

Later, Cacie, a charming young woman I'd met earlier that day, began massaging the tension from my shoulders. Wanting to get to know her better, I mentioned needing to make a call and invited her along. Once in the privacy of my motel room, she flashed a mischievous grin and suggested hopping in the shower while I handled my business.

Ten minutes later, she emerged wrapped in a towel, steam trailing behind her. With a sultry smile, she dropped to her knees to unlace my boots. As she rose, the towel slipped from her shoulders and fell to the floor. I pulled her close, running my fingers through her hair, as we kissed. With a smirk, I took her hand saying, "That towel was destined to end up on the floor – you're even more stunning without it."

This isn't an erotic tell-all, so I'll just say the night was filled with raw, intense passion that lasted until the light of dawn. When we woke, it was time to check out. Outside, Randy and Tony were waiting to say goodbye. When I asked how their night had gone, Tony just grumbled about not getting any sleep.

Randy, a mountain-sized man who'd previously been an enforcer in a 1%'er motorcycle club, laughed heartily, "Well, Boss, if you really wanna know why none of us got any sleep, it's because of the religious revival going on next door!"

Still half-asleep, I rubbed my eyes and asked what he was talking about. With a wicked grin, Randy imitated a womans voice, "Oh God, oh God, yes, oh Jesus, YES!"

He continued, "That revival didn't stop until 6AM! Sounded like they were having a whole spiritual awakening over there."

Once it dawned on me what he was referring to, I practically doubled over laughing.

My next trip to Leith, however, was under much graver circumstances. Craig and a colleague had been arrested after patrolling the area with rifles, following a verbal altercation. I attended their court hearing to offer support, but they were ultimately convicted on claims that their armed presence had instilled fear in a local resident. Craig's arrest marked the beginning of the end for the Leith project, setting off its eventual collapse.

CHAPTER 37

MISSISSIPPI BURNING AND THE NATIONAL CONVERSATION ON RACE

In 2013, a man named James left a message on the NSM Hotline, stating that he'd been referred directly by Edgar Ray Killen and requested to speak with me personally.

BACKGROUND

Edgar Ray Killen (January 17, 1925 – January 11, 2018) was an American Ku Klux Klan organizer who planned and directed the murders of James Chaney, Andrew Goodman, and Michael Schwerner, three civil rights activists participating in the Freedom Summer of 1964. He was found guilty in state court of three counts of manslaughter on June 21, 2005, the forty-first anniversary of the crime, and sentenced to 60 years in prison. He appealed the verdict, but the sentence was upheld on April 12, 2007, by the Supreme Court of Mississippi. He died in prison on January 11, 2018.

It wasn't uncommon for prisoners to refer people to us, but this particular call felt extraordinary – and nearly unbelievable – because James was black. His message piqued my curiosity immediately, and I was eager to hear his story. When I returned his call, James explained that he had been cellmates with none other than Edgar Ray Killen, the notorious Klansman, at Parchman Prison in Mississippi. The idea of a black man sharing a cell with one of the most infamous living Klansmen was beyond astonishing.

According to James, Edgar saw the KKK as a relic of the past, believing that the future of white nationalism belonged to the NSM. James described an unlikely friendship that had formed during their time together, even recounting an incident in which he claimed he was beaten severely for defending Edgar after other black inmates spat in the Klansman's food. His decision to stand up for Edgar, he explained, was driven by his principles and a strong sense of morality.

Listening to James talk about standing up for Edgar despite their profound differences resonated with me. After several conversations, I became convinced that James was an extraordinary individual – someone motivated by principles rather than financial gain, safety, or self-interest. In a world where such integrity feels increasingly rare, meeting someone committed to values – even when we didn't see eye to eye on everything – felt like discovering a kindred spirit.

James had become a Baptist minister and was said to have brokered peace agreements between well-known LA street gangs in the 1980s and 90s. Claiming to have drawn inspiration from Martin Luther King, he was passionate about addressing issues between black and white communities. Having previously worked with black organizations, he was now reaching out to the NSM to discuss racial matters. The idea intrigued me, particularly because there was historical precedent: Commander George Lincoln Rockwell, founder of the original American Nazi

Party, had met with Malcolm X and the Nation of Islam.

In 2014, James launched what became known as The National Conversation on Race. While a few tiny KKK factions had attempted publicity stunts by meeting with NAACP chapters, those Klans had no real influence, membership base, or credibility. A genuine dialogue between leaders of different races had been absent from the white nationalist movement for over half a century, and I was thrilled to be part of such a historic initiative.

The event was scheduled at a venue in Beverly Hills, California. The NSM delegation included Brian, the Public Relations Director; Matt on Security; and me.

Before the event, a group of us decided to grab lunch near the venue. On our way back, we encountered an all-too-familiar sight: a small, loud, and obnoxious group of frothing-at-the-mouth communists protesting outside, waving a Soviet flag. One protester demanded to know why the black leaders were meeting with Nazis, while spouting some nonsense about me being the American version of Hitler.

In response, one of the black leaders addressed them calmly, stating that they were fully aware of who they were meeting with and didn't appreciate the unsolicited disruption. Undeterred, the protesters persisted, insisting that the black leaders needed their help. In a powerful rebuttal, one of the women among the leaders spoke up, pointing out the arrogance of that assumption. She noted how offensive and hypocritical it was for a group of white protesters to presume that black leaders required their assistance. With eloquence, she highlighted the irony of people who claimed to oppose racism yet displayed racial bias by assuming black leaders couldn't navigate the situation on their own.

This interaction served as a learning experience, highlighting the complexities of racial dynamics and the importance of treating others with dignity. The woman who confronted the protesters stood out – intelligent, assertive, and tenacious. I admired her resolve, and she left a lasting impression.

Once we all went inside, however, things took a turn for the worse. The protesters outside began banging on the doors and windows of the black-owned venue. Some managed to slip in through a back door, shouting communist slogans and causing a disturbance. The business owner was visibly upset, clearly concerned that his establishment might be damaged in the chaos.

I suggested that the NSM handle the removal of the intruders. Drawing on past experience, I explained that the only response the far-left seemed to understand was meeting their aggression with an equally forceful hand. James disagreed, arguing that such an approach would only escalate tensions. Instead, we relocated the event to a nearby hotel meeting hall.

The communists claimed to oppose white supremacy, but their behavior demonstrated a different truth. Their callous disregard for a black business owner's property and their disruption of a discussion on race organized by black leaders ironically showed that racism is alive and well – under the hammer and sickle. They seemed hell-bent on sabotaging the first notable effort since the 1960s to bring ideologically opposed groups together for peaceful dialogue.

The far-left often misuses rhetoric to present itself as inclusive, but their actions toward those with differing views reveal an intolerance no different from the neo-Nazis and white supremacists they claim to oppose. The extreme far-right and the extreme far-left may seem worlds apart, but their actions show them as two sides of the same extremist coin.

During the event, listening to the black leaders provided insightful glimpses into their experiences, and they seemed equally curious about ours. As we exchanged perspectives, it became clear we shared more common ground than anticipated.

After the meeting, the event's PR coordinator arranged a series of radio interviews in Los Angeles. Once those wrapped up, the black security guard who'd been with us all day seemed to relax, and the conversation lightened, eventually shifting to Michael Jackson's iconic moonwalk. Standing nearly seven feet tall, the guard casually mentioned he could pull off the dance move.

I joked, expressing doubts given his imposing stature. With a confident snap of his fingers, he said, "Check this out." To everyone's amazement, he glided down the hallway, moonwalking as smoothly as Michael Jackson himself. We were all in awe – no one expected the big guy to move like that!

On the way back to the hotel, I asked him for a good BBQ spot recommendation. He grinned and quipped, "When it comes to BBQ, you're asking the right guy. Black folks know it best." Sure enough, his suggestion didn't disappoint – the meal was fantastic.

Early the next morning, as James drove us to the airport, he asked how everyone had slept. The guys said they felt great, while I admitted to being exhausted, having only managed about two hours of sleep. With a smirk, I added that the upside was waking up on the well-endowed chest of a beautiful woman – one of our local members who'd stayed the night – which had everyone laughing.

James and I kept in touch after the event, and I promised to participate in future National Conversations on Race.

CHAPTER 38

LOSING FAMILY

As 2015 drew to a close, I was struck by the fragility of human life in a way I'd never experienced before. A shadow of death loomed over our family, ushering in an era of loss that would persist for the next three years.

Until then, I'd often felt invincible, taking life's preciousness for granted. Our family had enjoyed long, healthy lives, and I'd grown accustomed to their steady presence, rarely stopping to appreciate just how fortunate we were. This all changed when close family members began to pass away, forcing me to confront the bitter reality of mortality and the true value of life.

PATERNAL GRANDPARENTS

Sundays after church were family time, with most of Dad's fourteen siblings and their families gathering at our grandparents' home. Each family brought a dish to the potluck, overseen by Grandma, who made everything seem effortless, while still finding time for each of her grandchildren. Grandfather, a model of hard work and resilience, kept the farm running despite losing one hand and crippling the other in a tractor accident.

The passing of my grandparents marked the end of an era for our family. My father, always stoic, bore the weight of their loss silently. Though I was young at the time, the warmth of those memories remains vivid. Thankfully, it would be decades before our family felt the sting of death again.

MATERNAL GRANDPARENTS

I was fortunate to share a lifetime of cherished memories with my Opa and Omi. My bond with Omi was especially strong; there was a deep, unspoken understanding between us.

When Omi entered hospice care in late 2015, Opa struggled to adjust to her absence from home. At the same time, my mother was fighting her own battle with cancer. Despite her health issues, Mom made the trip to say goodbye to her mother, accompanied by my sister and me.

Mom often felt stressed around her parents, largely due to their bickering, much of which stemmed from Opa's teasing and flirtatious behavior toward Omi. While Opa's humor had amused me since childhood, it often stressed others. With Mom battling cancer, it was essential to minimize her stress, so I did everything I could to be supportive.

Due to flight delays, we arrived at the hospice around midnight, well past visiting hours. Still, the staff kindly allowed us to see her, quietly informing us that Omi was asleep. I stepped into her dimly lit room and suggested we return in the morning to avoid disturbing her rest.

Suddenly, Omi's voice broke the silence. "Jeff! You're hours late. You come in here, look at me without saying anything, and now you're leaving?"

Grinning, I responded with a smart remark, "Why are you

pretending to be asleep in a dark, silent room?"

Earlier, Mom had mentioned that Opa visited Omi daily, staying by her side until the staff insisted he leave. His dedication moved me, so I shared those feelings with Omi. To my dismay, instead of appreciating the sentiment, she made some disparaging remarks about Opa, who was quietly sitting across the room.

Noticing the pain in his expression, I leaned in and whispered to Omi, "What you said about Opa isn't right, and he's right behind you, listening."

Unfazed, she doubled down, "What I said stands, and besides, he's hard of hearing."

Aware he heard, I asked softly, "Opa, did you hear what Omi said?"

His response was quiet but unmistakable, "I heard every word." The pain in his voice was undeniable. Slowly, he rose and left the room, with my mother following after him.

In an attempt to heal the rift, I spoke to Omi about the emotional toll her words had on Opa and my mother. Although we were close, she was notoriously stubborn and rarely accepted advice. Before leaving, I urged her to reconsider her statements, explaining that acknowledging Opa's presence, despite their differences, could help mend fences.

With a scowl and a heavy sigh, Omi replied, "Jeff, I'll think about what you've said overnight. I'm not making any promises, but I'll have an answer when you visit tomorrow."

For the first time that evening, I saw my mother's mood lift.

As we left, Mom confided, "Jeff, I have no idea how you got Omi to even consider apologizing, but if she follows through, you'll officially be the Omi whisperer."

The next day, during our visit, Omi motioned for Opa to come closer. In a rare, heartfelt tone, she apologized, expressed her love, and reassured him that he didn't need to be there every day. Opa's entire demeanor transformed instantly – his eyes welled with emotion as he responded, telling her he loved her and gently kissed her cheek. In all my life, I'd never once heard Omi tell Opa that she loved him. He practically bounced out of the room to get her favorite ice cream, like a teenager who had just received his first kiss. Omi mentioned that she'd reflected on our conversation and realized that making amends was the right thing to do.

This meant a great deal to my mother, and it was heartwarming to see some resolution between my grandparents before Omi passed away.

In the days before her passing, Omi kept asking about the date, which baffled everyone. Her younger sister and closest friend since childhood, had passed away a year earlier. Poignantly, Omi passed away on the exact one-year anniversary of her sister's death.

MOM

Mom had always been the person I turned to for advice – whether it was relationship troubles or anything else. She had an incredible knack for listening and offering thoughtful, sagely advice. As her battle with cancer intensified, I made a conscious decision not to burden her with my problems, knowing that stress could worsen her condition. Instead, I focused on being a source of positivity and support.

When she called to tell me that the doctors estimated she had about eight weeks left, it felt as if the whole world was collapsing around me. I struggled to keep it together and project strength. Just weeks earlier, she'd been talking about traveling to Mexico and even returning to work. Yet, in this devastating conversation, she remained eerily calm, asking if I still planned to show her Mackinac Island.

Upon hearing the doctors' prognosis, I cautiously proposed, "Mom, maybe you shouldn't travel to Michigan. I could come to Minnesota instead." That suggestion didn't land well. Disappointed, she replied, "Jeff, are you trying to cancel our plans?" Quickly, I backtracked, "No, just considering your health…" I paused, knowing that in our family, implying someone wasn't capable of something was never well received.

After my parents finalized their flights to Detroit, I checked the calendar. The appointment to euthanize my Rottweiler, Chaos – who was also battling cancer – was scheduled on the same day they were arriving. Brittany, my ex-fiancée, kindly offered to be there with Chaos, ensuring she wasn't alone as she crossed the rainbow bridge.

When my parents arrived, stress was overwhelming my father. The mental and physical toll seemed to be sapping the life from him, which was almost as difficult to witness as seeing Mom in such a frail state. As Dad worked tirelessly to ensure Mom's comfort, she grew agitated with him. The only tool I had to defuse the tension was humor, and it was a shot in the dark if it would work or backfire.

In a scolding but mocking tone, I interrupted Mom, saying,

"Alright children, if you keep misbehaving, there won't be any family trip to Mackinac tomorrow!"

It worked! Like a light switch, Mom paused, then burst out laughing. "Oh really Jeff?"

"Yep! When we were kids, that was always the threat. How does it feel now that the roles are reversed?" We all laughed together, and the tension dissipated.

The next morning, we set out on the five-hour drive to Mackinac, which concluded with a scenic ferry ride to the island. Mom was excited about spending a couple of nights there, and her spirits soared as we visited the butterfly house and explored the island. That trip would become one of my most cherished memories – a precious moment forever etched in my heart.

After our stay on Mackinac, my parents returned home. The following morning, I was jolted awake by an urgent call from my sister. "Jeff, you need to come home right away. Mom's about to pass away!" I was in shock, barely able to process her words. "But she seemed fine when she left Michigan yesterday," I stammered, feeling as though I were caught in a nightmare.

I rushed home and reached out to my children, making sure they could say goodbye to their grandmother. My eldest daughter, who shared a particularly close bond with her grandmother, made the long drive to rural Minnesota to gather her younger sisters. When we arrived, Mom couldn't speak, but we were certain she knew we were there, feeling the love that surrounded her in those final moments.

As the evening wore on, concerns grew within the family about my daughter's long drive home. True to her nature – strong, determined, and fiercely independent – she reassured us that she'd be safe but wanted to spend a few more precious moments with her grandmother.

About thirty minutes later, my second-to-youngest, a gentle and compassionate soul, held her grandmother close and softly announced that she had taken her final breath. The weight of the moment was unbearable. I'd always kept my emotions in check, never breaking down in front of my children, but witnessing three of my daughters consumed by sorrow, alongside the finality of my mother's passing, was too much to bear. I stepped away, trying to project strength amid the overwhelming grief.

Mom departed with what my dad and sister described as a peaceful, Mona Lisa-like smile on her face. It felt like her way of telling her granddaughters that she heard them and loved them until the very end. It was such a fitting echo of her character – much like her mother before her – in control of her fate until the last breath.

Since losing my mother, butterflies have taken on a special significance, evoking memories of her whenever they flutter into view. The metamorphosis of a butterfly, from its humble beginnings as a caterpillar to its flight on delicate wings, reflects her spirit's journey. Thank you, Mom, for your love, compassion, and never giving up or losing faith in me.

Words seem inadequate to convey the depth of sorrow and devastation that defined this period of my life. The years from 2015 through 2018 were marked by profound grief, with each loss leaving a lasting emotional scar. Gradually, I began to see the humanity in others and recognize life as the precious gift it is, prompting me to reflect deeply and reassess the path I was on. These life-altering events became catalysts for change, setting the wheels of transformation in motion.

Coming to terms with the painful truth that my past actions had caused harm to beloved family members, now gone, was a bitter realization. Though I hadn't yet freed myself from the mental prison of extremism, the seeds of change had been planted – and were slowly beginning to take root.

CHAPTER 39

SEEDS OF CHANGE

DARYL DAVIS:

In 2016, I was approached for a film interview, which wasn't unusual given my decades leading the NSM and frequent media appearances. What I didn't expect was how this particular meeting would profoundly alter the course of my life. Brittany, my fiancée at the time, and I arrived a bit early at the diner where the interview would take place. Shortly after, a car pulled up, and out stepped a black man with a warm, welcoming smile. He introduced himself as Daryl Davis, and we exchanged handshakes.

His name sounded familiar, but I couldn't place it immediately. Then it clicked – Daryl was known for his groundbreaking work engaging with members of the KKK, helping them abandon their racist beliefs and turn their lives around. I wasn't prepared to debate him, but figured this would be just another day at the office. I couldn't have been more wrong.

Our early arrival threw off the filmmaker's plans – they'd hoped to capture our first interaction on camera. When the cameras finally started rolling, the dynamic between us was anything but typical for an encounter between a black man and a neo-Nazi leader. Instead of tension, we connected like old friends, laughing and sharing stories. Daryl and I discovered common ground in unexpected places. As a world-renowned musician, he'd performed with legends such as Elvis Presley, Chuck Berry, and Little Richard – a dream I once pursued before abandoning it for the movement.

During the interview, I realized we were getting along perhaps a bit too well, so I shifted my tone and made a provocative statement about fighting for my people until the last bullet. Yet, Daryl's calm and authentic demeanor didn't falter. He continued with the same warmth and respect, refusing to be rattled. It struck me that genuine rapport wasn't something forced – it was earned through real, human connection. Daryl's calm, unflinching nature intrigued me. I'd never met anyone quite like him.

Daryl spoke candidly about the painful impact of racism on his childhood, recounting a traumatic experience at a Boy Scout parade where white adults hurled rocks at him solely because of his skin color. As the cameras rolled, I maintained a stoic expression, careful not to show any outward reaction. I chose not to reveal just how deeply his story bothered me.

For the first time in decades within the movement, someone was personally sharing how the doctrines I had championed had directly harmed them. It had always been easy to dismiss stories of racism when they were on the news or spoken about from a distance, but hearing Daryl's firsthand account was different – it struck a chord I didn't even know existed. It felt inherently wrong, and allowed me to see Daryl's humanity. He was instrumental in laying the foundation for re-humanizing a neo-Nazi who had spent years dehumanizing others.

Despite these seeds of doubt, I remained entrenched in the

movement, trying to convince both myself and others that our cause was righteous and virtuous. True change, however, rarely happens overnight; it is a gradual process, a slow unraveling of deeply held beliefs. Daryl's words didn't instantly revolutionize my worldview, but they acted as a spark – like Johnny Appleseed scattering seeds that would eventually grow into towering oaks.

Over time, those seeds of doubt and introspection planted by Daryl began to take root. They led me to question the very ideology I'd once so fervently embraced. This was the beginning of my metamorphosis – from radicalism to redemption.

DEEYAH KHAN

In 2017, another unexpected friend entered my life: Deeyah Khan.

Background: Deeyah Khan, a British-Norwegian documentary filmmaker, human rights advocate, and music composer, has left an indelible mark through impactful documentaries. Her body of work delves into complex issues like extremism, racism, and cultural identity, exposing the depths of these topics with unflinching courage.

With an impressive array of accolades, including the prestigious Emmy Award, Deeyah's films have earned widespread acclaim for their ability to bridge divides and foster understanding. Her commitment to exploring uncomfortable truths and challenging mainstream narratives has sparked crucial conversations about building a more inclusive and tolerant society. Her relentless advocacy for human-rights underscores the transformative power of storytelling in driving social change.

When Deeyah invited me to participate in her documentary *White Right: Meeting the Enemy*, I agreed on the condition that the interview wouldn't exceed thirty minutes. However, once we met, that brief conversation stretched into hours. Deeyah's approach to engagement was unlike anything I had encountered, except perhaps with Daryl Davis. What started as a single interview evolved into numerous conversations over several months.

As Deeyah shared her personal experiences with racism and hatred, I felt a deep empathy I hadn't anticipated. Her vulnerability and honesty had a profound effect on me. Several of these pivotal moments were captured on film and made it into the documentary, highlighting key turning points in my journey toward transformation.

When Deeyah said, "Jeff, the beliefs you stand for made a little girl feel unworthy, ugly, hated, and less than human," it felt like a sledgehammer to my defenses. The impenetrable walls within me – forged of concrete, brick, and steel – began to crumble. I could see the deep pain and sorrow in her eyes, and what made it even more unbearable was the unspoken heaviness that hung in the air. Watching this remarkable woman carry such sadness felt like being kicked in the chest by a horse. The cameraman zoomed in, capturing the intensity in my eyes as I fought to maintain a façade of toughness while breaking down inside.

For a quarter-century, I'd rationalized and compartmentalized my actions, clinging to a toxic belief system that perpetuated hatred and intolerance. Deeyah, broke through the barriers that had insulated me from seeing the humanity beyond my fortress of prejudice. She didn't use force, anger, or manipulation to dismantle those walls. Instead, she brought her authentic self

– a vulnerable heart, an open mind, and a genuine desire for understanding – and that resonated.

Much like Daryl Davis, Deeyah never outright told me I was wrong. Instead, she recognized the barriers and sought to understand them. Through compassion, empathy, and sharing lived experiences, these two extraordinary individuals gradually chipped away at the walls within me, allowing change to take hold where intolerance once flourished.

Off-camera, Deeyah and I had a recurring joke where I called her my bratty little sister because of her relentless questioning. After the last interview for her film, we shared a hug, and she looked at me in disbelief saying, "This is so weird! We're not supposed to be friends. How is this even happening?" I laughed and said, "Deeyah, even though I tease you about being a bratty sister, you've gained a brother for life."

We stayed in touch, and she became one of the few people – along with my father and a couple of others – who knew about my internal struggle with leaving the movement. By the time I officially left, a few other prominent NSM figures had already exited, partly because of their own interactions with Deeyah.

JULIE

Throughout my journey from radicalization to disengagement, others played a pivotal role in sowing the seeds of change, especially in the later years as I sought to liberate myself from the grip of Nazism. One of those people was Julie, an Orthodox Jewish woman who reached out while I was still involved in neo-Nazism. She approached with an open heart, eager to engage in dialogue despite knowing my beliefs. I inundated her with offensive, antisemitic questions, yet she never responded with anger. Instead, she offered patience, understanding, and compassion – qualities I hadn't expected and certainly didn't deserve at the time.

One day, during a text exchange, Julie asked what was new, and I casually mentioned that Antifa had doxxed my personal information – address, phone number, even my car's VIN – which was more of an annoyance than anything else. Her immediate response was concern, worried about my safety. I assured her it wasn't anything to worry about, as I was well-prepared to handle threats.

The next day, Julie mentioned that she'd spoken with her husband about what I was dealing with, and they offered me a place to stay for a few days to ensure my safety. Though deeply touched by their kindness, I declined the offer. I've never been one to abandon ship or seek safety from threats or danger. Yet, to this day, I am moved by the empathy shown by a Jewish woman who, despite barely knowing me, offered compassion to a neo-Nazi unworthy of such benevolence.

A couple of years later, when I shared with Julie that I'd left the movement, she expressed joy and immediately asked about my safety and well-being. She then said, "I always saw the person you are on the inside – not Jeff the Nazi, but the real person underneath all that."

Reflecting on crossing paths with people like Julie, I am filled with gratitude and strive to embody the same humanity that was shown to me when I deserved it the least.

GHETTO FABULOUS

Throughout my time in Detroit, I've had many notable interactions with the black community, but none as powerful as what happened just a few months before I left a lifetime of extremism behind.

After a night out with Tammy – a bubbly, stunning blonde half my age – we were driving back to my place around midnight. As we wound through one of Detroit's most dangerous neighborhoods, my sports car started sputtering, threatening to break down entirely. Tammy insisted we pull over immediately to avoid damaging the engine.

I protested, "We can't stop here. Nothing's open in the ghetto at midnight. If we leave the car, the rims and everything else will be gone in minutes. Plus, we risk getting shot."

Tammy, unfazed, replied with conviction, "Jeff, have some faith. It'll be fine. Trust me, don't ruin your car over this." Reluctantly, I gave in and took the next off-ramp.

"Pull over there," she pointed to the only place still open – a busy liquor store with people hanging out, drinking, and smoking.

The moment we pulled into the parking lot, smoke poured from under the hood, proving her right – the car wasn't going to make it home. Now we were stranded in one of Detroit's most dangerous neighborhoods, a place notorious for gang activity and violent crime. Here, even if you called the cops, they likely wouldn't show up until morning.

As I popped the hood to check the damage, a group of men began to gather around. They complimented the car and asked what was wrong with the engine. One of them mentioned how fortunate we were to have stopped there, as it was the only place open for miles.

To avoid drawing unnecessary attention, I urged Tammy to stay in the car while I handled the situation. In her skintight red dress, she looked like a Hollywood starlet, and considering we were the only white people, unarmed in gangland, I worried things could get dicey. Still, she was determined to go into the liquor store to find help.

To ensure her safety, I suggested we go in together, rather than her going alone.

Tammy leaned in and whispered, "Jeff, you look mean, intimidating, and dangerous. If we walk in together, no one will help us. Let me go alone – we'll have a better chance." Cautiously, I gave in, realizing she had a point.

With confidence, Tammy approached the crowd in the parking lot, calling out, "Are there any mechanics here?" A few more men gathered around to check the engine, though none were mechanics. Undeterred, Tammy strutted toward the liquor store, her high heels clicking on the pavement. The way her hips swayed in that little red dress commanded attention with every step.

Moments later, she returned triumphant, declaring, "I found a mechanic – clear a path, everyone!" Her charisma was off the charts, glowing with the thrill of success. I wasn't sure what was more awe inspiring: that she found a mechanic after midnight in a liquor store, or that everyone we encountered had been so friendly and willing to help.

The mechanic, a young black man with two children in tow, introduced himself and offered to help with the car. Astonished,

I glanced at Tammy, who playfully winked and stuck out her tongue. "Told ya I'd find help, silly boy!"

The mechanic skillfully resolved the issue, and when I offered him cash for his help, he politely declined. He explained that the repair was a temporary solution to get us home safely and advised against driving further until a replacement part was installed. He also emphasized the need to fill the radiator with antifreeze before driving. The crowd that had gathered around confirmed that nothing nearby was open at that hour.

An elderly man emerged from the crowd and asked, "Did someone say that ya'll need anti-freeze?" I nodded, explaining that everything nearby was closed. With a warm smile, he said, "Hang tight, I got this." His car, parked next to ours, looked like it served as his temporary home, with clothes and personal belongings packed to the roof in the backseat. He popped his trunk, rummaged through it, and held up a full gallon of antifreeze. "Here you go. This will get you home safely," he said, offering it with genuine warmth.

As my anxiety melted away, I was overwhelmed with gratitude, especially struck by the man's kindness given his own apparent hardships. When I tried to pay him for the antifreeze, he firmly declined, saying all he wanted to do was help. I insisted, feeling it was unjust to accept a gift from someone who clearly had so little, but he wouldn't budge.

We went back and forth – me trying to offer cash, and him refusing each time. Then, he looked me in the eyes and placed a hand on my shoulder. "Listen, young man, if the roles were reversed, I'm sure you'd have done the same for me." His words struck a chord, causing me to pause and reflect. With his hand still on my shoulder, he made a heartfelt appeal: "The next time you have the chance to help someone in a similar situation, do it." He called it paying it forward. Without hesitation, I gave him my word. It was a powerful lesson in humanity and humility, and my promise to him is one I've upheld ever since.

On the drive home, I admitted to Tammy that she'd been right to insist we stop – it likely saved the engine. The kindness we encountered that night unsettled me, but I kept those emotions buried. The entire experience clashed with the deeply ingrained beliefs I'd held for years, and I struggled to reconcile the internal conflict it stirred.

After we returned home, Tammy and I shared another night of intense passion. By morning, she was gone, leaving behind a note that made everything painfully clear. In it, she explained her decision to end our relationship, citing my racist beliefs as the reason. She pointed out that the kindness we'd experienced in one of Detroit's roughest neighborhoods should have made me question my views, yet I had stubbornly remained unchanged.

Initially, I felt hurt and angry over how Tammy left, but as time passed and I reflected, I realized she was right. Clinging to toxic beliefs had created a barrier, blinding me from seeing the world and its people for who they truly were.

The memory of that night lingers, and I often wonder about the man who helped us. Does he still face hardship, struggling on the streets, or has life changed for the better? I pray he's thriving and back on his feet. The compassion he offered complete strangers serves as a powerful reminder that a single act of kindness can create a ripple effect, changing lives in ways we may never fully comprehend.

A man's worth isn't measured by possessions, fame, or power, but by character, integrity, and how he treats others. That night, I met a man of immense character. Despite having so little, he selflessly gave what he could to help others – a lesson I carry with me to this day.

As the leader of the NSM, I was supposed to be the epitome of leadership. Yet here I was, receiving help from a community I had long advocated to be separated from. The hypocrisy was glaring. How could I claim to be honorable while judging people based on superficial traits they couldn't control – like race? This inner conflict ignited a crisis of conscience, forcing me to question my beliefs and integrity as a leader. True leadership demands equal treatment of all – a standard I upheld within my own circles but failed to extend to others. Choosing when and where to apply these principles reeked of false virtue.

The signs were becoming impossible to ignore: the path I'd devoted my life to was built on flawed foundations. Yet walking away felt overwhelming, unrealistic, almost impossible. Bound by past choices, I faced a rising tide of uncertainty, threatening to sweep away everything I'd spent a lifetime building.

CHAPTER 40

FAR-RIGHT vs ALT-RIGHT

A distinction that's never been established in the public's consciousness is the striking difference between the alt-right and the traditional hard-right. The alt-right emerged around 2010, a relative newcomer to the white nationalist scene. During my years in the movement, I aligned with the hard-right, as did most of my peers, and we held a strong disdain for the alt-right's leaders and ideologies.

In my view, the alt-right harbored an obsessive animosity toward women. Their entire trajectory felt unnatural and illogical, from bizarre discussions about concepts like 'white sharia' to other counterintuitive views. Born of a younger generation, the alt-right embraced provocative memes and so-called edgy humor. While cartoon frogs and internet memes might appeal to twelve-year-olds, for adults, its notably childish. In contrast, the hard-right was grounded in politics and history – committed to ideologies rooted in concrete beliefs, while the alt-right indulged in fantasies of fictitious realms such as 'Kek,' replaced ideology with fetishism.

Some might chalk up these differences to a generational divide, but I disagree. The cartoon memes, perhaps, but the anti-female rhetoric gave off militant homosexual cult vibes. Many alt-right leaders exuded an effeminate 'beta-male' aura and held a condescending attitude toward blue-collar people – a sharp contrast to the hard-right's predominantly working-class base.

Despite these differences, there were commonalities between the hard-right and alt-right, such as a focus on race and a set of shared enemies.

In 2017, a leader from a hard-right group reached out to ask if the NSM planned to attend an upcoming alt-right event called Unite the Right in Charlottesville, Virginia. Initially, I had no interest in attending anything affiliated with the alt-right. However, after learning that some allies were planning to go, I reconsidered and inquired about the possibility of being listed as a speaker.

I was given the contact information of the event's permit-holder, Jason – someone I'd never heard of. When I called him, he came across as somewhat awkward, and one of the first things he mentioned was that swastikas were forbidden at the rally. I explained that the NSM had rebranded the previous year and no longer used swastikas publicly. When I asked about being added to the speakers' list, he hesitated before explaining that having a National Socialist speaker might cause some alt-right groups to withdraw. It felt disrespectful and a waste of time to attend an event where our presence wasn't welcome.

Then, Jason proposed that the NSM provide security for the event. Throughout the conversation, I maintained professionalism, but when he suggested we provide security for the alt-right, I burst into laughter. The audacity of some alt-right newbie asking the NSM to serve as security was ludicrous and insulting. After ending the call, I decided against attending the event, especially since we weren't even welcome to speak. Later, though, the hype about a massive turnout caused me to second-guess that decision.

Since the NSM had no role in organizing or sponsoring the rally, I lacked any control over the permits, planning, or speaker lineup. When we hosted events, we didn't allow other groups to dictate the speakers. They could request a slot, and we often accommodated them, but sometimes we denied those requests. So, it wasn't fair to hold a grudge against Jason or the alt-right for excluding me from the speaker list at their event. This presented a dilemma: if the rally turned out to be a resounding success, what excuse would I have for not attending? I could either stay home and sulk over not being included as a speaker or attend as a guest alongside the other groups and individuals.

Unite the Right emerged as a direct response to the widespread removal of Confederate statues. Although I didn't support the Confederacy or condone slavery, I saw unsettling parallels between the removal of monuments and actions taken by oppressive regimes. For example, the Taliban's destruction of the Buddhas of Bamyan – cultural treasures with immense historical significance – or ISIS's obliteration of heritage sites in Syria and Iraq, both of which aimed to erase history itself. My concern was that removing Confederate statues might open the door to erasing other historical figures, like George Washington, or even memorials for military veterans.

After deciding to attend Unite the Right, I announced my intentions online, encouraging others to show up if they were interested. Since the NSM wasn't organizing, I was relieved of the typical responsibilities that came with planning rallies: handling permits, coordinating with city officials and law enforcement, setting up meet-up locations, arranging convoys, managing PA systems, scouting routes, organizing parking, and setting up security measures. Without the usual logistical tasks and with no speaking role, I anticipated this would be one of the simplest events I'd ever attended. My plan was straightforward: show up for the rally and leave afterward.

CHAPTER 41

CHARLOTTESVILLE

In August 2017, as I drove to Charlottesville, I never imagined that Unite the Right would become the most violent rally I'd ever attended in over two decades of neo-Nazi activism. To avoid potential clashes with Antifa, we booked a motel about an hour outside the city. That evening, I met Nikki, an adorable brunette whose presence drew me in like a moth to a flame. The chemistry between us was intense, and we spent a sleepless night together, passion burning so hot that dawn came far too soon.

By morning, exhaustion hit hard. After the long drive from Michigan and barely fifteen minutes of rest, I was relieved not to have the added burden of speaking or handling logistics.

As we assembled with other hard-right groups in a parking garage several blocks from the rally site, everything seemed routine. We formed into columns, just as we had countless times before. But the moment we stepped out of the garage, something felt gravely wrong – there were no police anywhere in sight. In my twenty-five years of attending rallies, law enforcement had always been present, typically in overwhelming numbers. Yet here, despite extensive media coverage and a large media turnout on the ground, the police were conspicuously absent. Their absence cast a shadow over the day, a dark and ominous prelude to what lay ahead.

Moments after leaving the parking garage, we were

confronted by an imposing throng of thousands of counter-protesters, and the largest hordes of Antifa militants I'd ever seen. Soviet flags waved above a sea of raised fists, with many in the crowd brandishing an array of weapons. Not all counter-protesters were armed, violent, or linked to far-left extremism; some were there to peacefully protest. But the situation quickly spiraled out of control. Projectiles hailed down on us from all sides, and thick clouds of pepper-spray filled the air. Chaos erupted as Antifa swarmed in from both sides of the street, transforming what should've been a routine walk to the rally into a maelstrom of violence.

As we neared the park, counter-demonstrators locked arms to block our path. While those linking arms engaged in non-violent resistance, Antifa contingents surrounding us launched an assault – rocks, chunks of concrete, bottles, urine-filled balloons, and chemical irritants rained down on us from every direction. The stench was nauseating. I was doused with a chemical that burned my skin like fire, and others nearby suffered similarly. Then a counter-protester attacked me directly; in self-defense, I responded with a punch that sent him plummeting to the pavement.

Those at the front of the column managed to push through the counter-protesters, sparing the rest of us from further injuries. Once their line was breached, counter-protesters retaliated by launching tear-gas canisters, filling the air with noxious fumes. The park entrance looked like a war zone, strewn with blood, piss, and the remnants of chemical attacks.

Inside the park, hard-right medics worked frantically to assist the wounded, many of whom were bleeding from weapon

Jeff, TM Garret, and Alison Pure-Slovin, Midwest Director of the Simon Wiesenthal Center speaking at a synagogue. Illinois, 2020.

The Veritas Forum, New York University, 2020.

California Assembly Select Committee on the State of Hate. California, 2019.

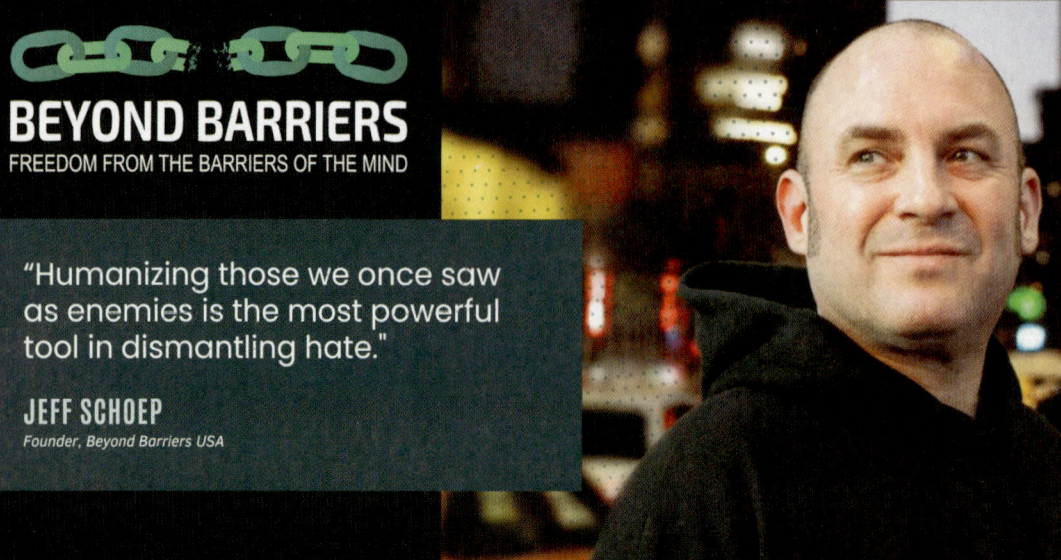

Photograph courtesy of David Scott Holloway, 2023.

Jeff and Greg Bura, President of Conscious Campus. NCORE, 2022.

Jeff speaks at the TLO Conference in California, 2021.

Below: Uprooting Prejudice with Daryl Davis, Jeff, and Scott Shepherd. Florida, 2022.

Jeff with Duke and Catherine Schneider. New York, 2021.

Sandy Teplitzky and Jeff. March, 2022.

"Combating Hate through Compassion and Dialogue" Jeff Schoep speaking to students at Riverdale Kingsbridge Academy in New York. March, 2025.

"Untangling Hate" with Illinois Senator Laura Fine and Jeff. Illinois, 2025.

Jeff speaks to students in Illinois with The Simon Wiesenthal Center, 2022.

The Simon Wiesenthal Center's Midwest Director Alison Pure-Slovin, Director of Research Rick Eaton, Jeff, and MAGEN Chicago, 2024.

Washington DC, 2024.

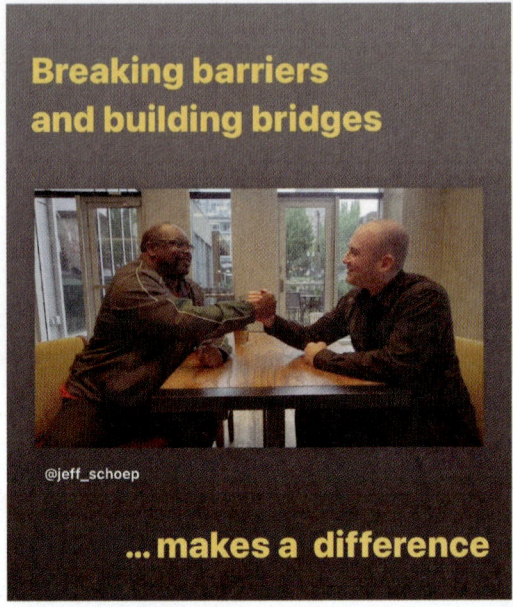
Rone Jones of Dialogues On Diversity and Jeff, 2022.

TM Garret, Juliana Taimoorazy, and Jeff. Assyrian Media Center. Illinois, 2020.

Pastor Jim Scudder of Quentin Road Baptist Church and Jeff. Illinois, 2025.

Jeff, Acacia, and Jeff's father.

SWC Director of Research, Rick Eaton and Jeff with California Assembly Select Committee Members, 2019.

Adrienne "Gammy" Banfield-Norris, Deeyah Khan, Jeff, Jada Pinkett-Smith, Willow Smith. Red Table Talk, 2022.

Below: Jeff speaks with Josh at The Simon Wiesenthal Center. California, 2021.

Skoll and Jeff - New Friendships Begin, 2023.

Below: Jeff and his father, 2024.

Jeff and Justice - Best Friends, (2002-2020).

Below: Jeff with his mother and grandfather (Opa).

Childhood photograph of Jeff and his sister.

Tomb of Tut Ankh Amun, Egypt, 2025.

Horseback riding in Roatan, Honduras, 2024.

Egypt, 2025.

New York City.
Photograph courtesy of David Scott Holloway, 2023.

Photograph courtesy of David Scott Holloway.

Below: Jeff and Daryl Davis. SWC Spirit of Courage Awards, 2024.

SOLIDARITY WITH ISRAEL

attacks. Others desperately flushed their eyes to clear the chemical irritants as the violence continued. Still, there was no sign of law enforcement.

An integral part of the NSM's self-defense strategy was the use of shields, each bearing scars from previous rallies like battlefield flak. Made from flexible plastic, these shields couldn't inflict harm but were effective at blocking incoming projectiles. I recall one rally where a shield deflected a brick thrown at me mid-speech; the impact buckled the shield and left its bearer with a sprained wrist. Time and again, these shields proved essential in preventing life-threatening injuries. In Charlottesville, their importance was undeniable as they intercepted projectiles hurled indiscriminately at attendees. Seeing someone take a chunk of concrete to the head or face drives home just how indispensable shields are for self-defense.

ABSENCE OF LAW ENFORCEMENT

The ongoing clashes underscored a glaring issue: the complete absence of law enforcement during a massive, high-profile rally that had drawn thousands of far-right and far-left extremists from across the country, now openly clashing in the streets. Just weeks prior, during a KKK rally in Charlottesville, police had deployed tear-gas and arrested counter-protesters, effectively preventing widespread violence. Now, that same police force was conspicuously absent.

With law enforcement nowhere in sight, militia troops attempted to maintain order but were quickly overrun by Antifa, with some in the Antifa ranks attempting to seize weapons from the militia. It was an unprecedented situation. Militias aren't trained or equipped for crowd control; they lacked shields and were perilously exposed.

One of our men, visibly shaken, asked if he could try to find the police, hoping they might intervene. I gave him permission, though I wasn't optimistic. When he returned, the look of despair on his face said it all. He reported finding a large police presence stationed somewhere behind the park, far from the violence, but they had ignored his request for help.

The park was enclosed by portable, waist-high metal fences. As counter-protesters attempted to topple them, the men at the front struggled to hold the barriers in place. Eventually, from the direction where our scout had spotted the police, a garbled announcement rang out, seemingly ordering everyone to disperse, followed by the sporadic whooping of police sirens.

Then, a voice from the alt-right side of the park, amplified by a PA system or bullhorn, announced that the rally was relocating. This only deepened the confusion – why were we abandoning a permitted event to move elsewhere?

What made the situation even worse was that the police were mobilizing behind us, far from where the violence was breaking out. Instead of addressing the clashes, they began clearing the park and funneled us down a narrow staircase directly into Antifa's front-lines. The exit became a bottleneck almost immediately, with hundreds of people surging forward at once. It felt like we were seconds away from being crushed – trapped between the crowd pressing from behind and a wall of bodies blocking the way ahead. Until that moment, I'd always thought stories of people being trampled in crowds were exaggerated or hard to imagine. But after being squeezed and immobilized on that staircase, it made perfect sense.

As we neared the choke-point, the source of the gridlock became horrifyingly clear: a counter-protester wielding an improvised flamethrower was attempting to set fire to people descending the stairs. Over the years, I had witnessed plenty of appalling acts at these events – Antifa attacking police horses, flinging manure at officers and attendees, and hurling their infamous urine-filled balloons – but seeing someone trying to burn people alive was a shocking escalation of violence I'd never encountered before Charlottesville.

STATE OF EMERGENCY

We relocated to a second park, waiting for instructions from the organizers on how the rally would proceed – but none ever came. The Virginia heat was blistering, and without water, many of us sought refuge under the shade of trees. Concerns quickly mounted over how we'd return to our vehicles, now surrounded by a sea of hostile counter-protesters. Exhausted, emotionally drained, and covered in chemicals and foul substances, our brief respite didn't last. A police vehicle arrived, announcing that a state of emergency had been declared. The National Guard had been deployed to manage the civil unrest, and everyone – on all sides – was ordered to vacate the streets and public areas immediately.

With no local guide to help us navigate back to the parking garage, we began forming columns to head toward our vehicles. Apparently, we weren't moving quickly enough. A police vehicle returned, reiterating the state of emergency with a stern warning:

anyone remaining on the streets would be arrested.

At that moment, a large white van carrying hard-right leaders arrived. Their plan was to evacuate the leadership first, with assurances that the van would return to shuttle everyone else. Offered the last seat, I hesitated, voicing concerns about the safety of the women and elderly still present. In good conscience, I couldn't prioritize my own safety while they remained in danger. I suggested Nikki and another woman take my place and stepped out of the van. Despite my insistence, both women refused to leave my side and wouldn't accept the seat. Instead, we found a senior citizen to take it.

Looking back, declining that seat wasn't the most practical decision, especially with the looming threat and the fact that Antifa had already singled me out by name. Still, my principles outweighed personal safety. The thought of women being attacked while I fled was a burden I couldn't bear. Besides, with about eighty people in the column, we had enough strength to repel attacks while heading to our vehicles.

As the column moved, several people struggled to keep pace. We stopped frequently to let them catch up, but as the delays mounted, my patience wore thin. Frustrated, I admonished them to move faster. Though guilt set in immediately, their slowness was jeopardizing the safety of the entire group. Meanwhile, the van continued shuttling people away, and our numbers gradually dwindled to just a couple dozen.

A block ahead, the streets were choked with hundreds of counter-protesters, openly defying the U.S. government's declared state of emergency and the mobilization of the National Guard. Many brandished weapons, their hostility cutting through the air like a knife as they stood between us and the safety of our vehicles. Our group – now reduced to just a couple dozen, including several women – had no choice but to pass through this gauntlet. Before attempting the perilous passage, I paused to let everyone gather their strength. The atmosphere was thick with tension, every breath heavy with the weight of what lay ahead. Every second felt like an eternity, but there was no turning back.

To boost morale, I spoke with conviction: "Brothers and sisters, steel your hearts and minds for what lies ahead. If we're attacked, fight like lions!"

As we prepared to advance, I glanced back and saw the stragglers who had repeatedly stalled the column trailing an entire city block behind. They'd slowed from a turtle's pace to a snail's crawl. Frustration surged, and I sprinted toward them, shouting, "We're facing hundreds of rabid commies ahead! If you're left behind, they will beat you to death. This is your last warning – move your asses now!"

It wasn't that I lacked empathy for their struggles to keep up; I simply couldn't understand why they hadn't taken the shuttle, given their obvious physical limitations. Their choice had cost us able-bodied men and left our already exhausted group with the added burden of protecting those unable to defend themselves.

Among the NSM security detail with me was Ken, a veteran who had served aboard a nuclear submarine in the Navy. His voice was steady, but the weight of his words was impossible to ignore. "Sir, I'm ready, but I feel like today might be our last battle. Still, it's been an honor serving with you."

There was no time to dwell on sentiment. His words hung heavy, but resolve was what we needed now. I looked him in the eye and replied, "Brother, we are lions. If they come for us, they'll regret it."

Despite battling heat exhaustion, Ken managed a weary smile and added, "No worries, I just hope God grants us peaceful passage this time."

I refused to show fear, but the reality was undeniable – it felt like we were walking a razor's edge, our lives hanging by a thread. How could this exhausted, injured group possibly navigate through such a hostile crowd? The odds couldn't have been worse.

As we neared the counter-protesters, a group of young Black men spotted us. One, wearing a Black Lives Matter shirt, shouted, "Look! It's the NSM! The REAL Nazis are headed this way! Let's take 'em down!" His rallying cry rippled through the crowd like a shockwave, and their numbers swelled as they closed in, blocking our path forward.

With another vanload gone, we were down to thirteen men and three women. It felt like this was it – our final stand. Surrounded, outnumbered, and facing an enraged mob, I mentally braced for what seemed like an inevitable, glorious death in battle. Yet, I clung to a sliver of hope that we might somehow survive.

Drawing on past experiences, I knew our survival depended on targeting the opposition's leaders, instigators, and main combatants. If we were attacked, our best chance was to ruthlessly punish their key figures and make an example of them. My focus locked on the man in the BLM shirt, the apparent ringleader. His eyes darted between the NSM standard and us, assessing the dynamics.

The standard was a potent symbol, modeled after the

banners of pre-World War II Germany. Handcrafted by a skilled woodworker, it featured a square NSM flag with gold fringes, mounted on a polished wooden pole. At the top, a meticulously carved wooden plaque bore the initials N-S-M, crowned by a golden eagle. Earlier that morning, amidst the chaos of street fighting, I'd overheard Antifa urging one another to seize the standard as a trophy. It was more than just a symbol – it was a target.

As we closed in, the man who had incited the mob suddenly stepped aside, allowing us to pass. Remarkably, the crowd followed his lead. As we moved through, I caught snippets of their conversations: "NSM are not the ones to mess with; these guys won't run like those alt-right kids." The air was thick with insults, but no one threw anything or attacked. It seemed our fierce reputation had preceded us – they knew we were an entirely different animal than the alt-right. Passing through unscathed felt like a miracle, and I prayed our good fortune wouldn't fade.

After clearing the crowd, I noticed a trendy outdoor shopping area cordoned off by riot police – an odd priority, considering the hundreds of armed counter-protesters still blocking the streets and openly defying the state of emergency. Hoping to comply with the emergency directives and find a clear route to the parking garage, I approached the officers. But just as our scout had experienced earlier, they were uncooperative. When I asked to speak to the officer in charge, one snarled, "Back away from us and figure out directions yourself!" Further attempts were met with threats of arrest, leaving us no choice but to bypass the police entirely.

Not long after circumventing the riot police guarding the

upscale shopping district, we finally located the parking ramp. The National Guard was mobilizing as we entered the garage, where others from the hard-right were waiting to ensure we got out safely. While ascending the ramps, Ken succumbed to heat exhaustion and collapsed. Running on fumes ourselves, we pulled him to his feet and pressed on toward our vehicles.

Leaving Charlottesville behind, we headed back to the motel, desperate to rid ourselves of the day's filth. The revolting stench of urine, blood, and chemicals clung to our skin, seeping into every pore. Exhausted in body, mind, and spirit, we longed to wash away the remnants of that brutal day.

THE AFTERMATH

Back at the motel, we turned on the TV, hoping for updates on the rally. What we saw was horrifying – every station was playing the same disturbing footage of a car plowing into a crowd. Stunned and emotionally drained, I asked for privacy, switched off the television, and sank down next to Nikki, burying my face in my hands.

How could this have happened? Why hadn't law enforcement kept both sides separated like they always had at every other rally? Why would someone drive into a crowd like that? My mind swirled with questions, racing through scenarios that offered no clear answers.

Later, the news confirmed the worst – Heather Heyer, a young woman, had died after being struck by the car, and two policemen lost their lives in a helicopter crash. The aftermath was heartbreaking: families in mourning, a community torn apart by hatred and violence.

Soon, footage surfaced of the driver, identifiable by the white polo shirt worn by the alt-right, deliberately ramming into the crowd. In court, he confessed to the crime. The realization was staggering. Initially, most of us, myself included, had assumed the tragedy might have been triggered by Antifa attacking the driver, panicking him into acting recklessly. But his confession shattered those assumptions, exposing an incomprehensible level of malevolence – a manifestation of pure evil.

How could anyone with even a shred of conscience commit such an atrocious act?

While entrenched in extremism, I had unknowingly developed a coping mechanism to process heinous crimes like mass shootings or bombings. I convinced myself that such actions were the result of mental illness in the perpetrators, never pausing to consider that the ideology itself might be the catalyst behind the violence. In moments of reflection, uncomfortable truths began to surface. The weight of the movement's long history of atrocities started to crush my conscience.

It became painfully clear that extremist ideologies don't just foment violence – they cultivate it. They offer a twisted justification, transforming hatred into a driving force for action and making atrocities seem acceptable in the name of a greater cause.

THE LAWSUIT

After Charlottesville, intense soul-searching revealed a war raging within me. The cause I'd devoted my life to no longer felt like the noble pursuit I once believed it to be. The desire to break free grew stronger, but the sheer magnitude of what that meant left me paralyzed. My entire adult life – friendships, career, and sense of identity – were intricately tied to the movement. I had power, influence, and a comfortable lifestyle. Walking away would mean losing everything: facing unemployment, societal rejection, and the permanent stigma of having led America's Nazi Party for decades.

Despite the storm of inner turmoil, I maintained a façade of strength, even as I felt utterly lost and despondent.

Time marched on, and not long after Charlottesville, I was served with a civil lawsuit accusing me, the NSM, and others of conspiring to incite racial violence at the rally. The lawsuit labeled me as an organizer – a claim I found both absurd and entirely baseless. My involvement had been attending the rally as a guest and inviting NSM members, not organizing the event. There's a clear distinction between participation and organization – or so I thought.

Much of the evidence cited in the filings came from discussions on Discord, the platform where the rally's planning had taken place. The filings detailed how the organizers allowed violent rhetoric to flourish in those chats. I was confident of being quickly dismissed from the lawsuit, as neither I nor the NSM had participated in any Discord discussions. Moreover, advocating for violence – whether at public rallies with cameras rolling or online where every word is potentially monitored – was strictly prohibited within the NSM. Over decades of involvement, whenever members advocated for violence or other illegal activities, they were given one warning: stop immediately, or face expulsion. These individuals were security risks – either informants or fools destined for prison – neither of which we could afford to tolerate.

Since its founding in the 1970s, the NSM maintained a strict policy of avoiding criminal behavior, which was essential to the organization's survival. To be clear, I'm not suggesting we were choirboys – far from it. Over the years, there was no shortage of violence, but it stemmed from internal conflicts or direct clashes with adversaries. Rallies were never a venue for instigating violence. With heavy law enforcement and media presence at every event, self-defense was permitted, but attacking first was strictly prohibited. My leadership record over 25 years reflects this standard without exception.

The case, however, painted a very different picture – portraying counter-protesters as peaceful advocates for unity and harmony, attacked without provocation by violent racists. It even claimed that the shields we carried were weapons rather than tools for self-defense, ignoring the well-documented history of violent aggression from far-left counter-protesters that had necessitated their use.

Had I broken any laws, I would have faced the consequences. My conduct in Charlottesville adhered to the same law-abiding standards I'd maintained at rallies for decades. Acting otherwise would have undoubtedly led to my arrest and criminal charges in the aftermath.

Let me be unequivocal – I do not justify the hateful language or harmful activities I once engaged in, nor do I defend the reprehensible events of Charlottesville. My decision to attend Unite the Right is a profound source of shame and regret that will haunt me forever.

Within the NSM, the lawsuit was met with bewilderment and outrage. Members were stunned to see us labeled as organizers, especially when it was public knowledge who the actual organizers were. The prevailing sentiment was that the lawsuit indiscriminately targeted prominent leaders and groups who attended, regardless of their roles. It was seen as a calculated act of lawfare against the NSM and its leadership, orchestrated by wealthy, privileged far-left radicals. In response, donations for our legal defense began pouring in.

Despite standing firm in my principles and denying any role in organizing the event or advocating violence, I remained ensnared in the lawsuit. The NSM's financial support for my legal defense made the decision to leave all the more agonizing. Walking away meant forfeiting my livelihood, financial security, and the resources to fight the lawsuit. Staying, however, meant betraying my conscience by remaining tied to an ideology I no longer believed in. I was caught in a moral and practical crisis, torn between two devastating paths.

CHAPTER 42

JAMES

In early winter of 2018, James called me to discuss organizing a second round of the National Conversation on Race. This time, he envisioned expanding its scope by including representatives from various minority communities, rather than focusing solely on Black and White groups. He emphasized the historical significance of our collaboration and how it could pave the way for broader racial dialogue. I eagerly agreed to participate once again.

After the first event, James and I stayed in touch. Though we came from opposing sides, we built a friendship grounded in mutual respect and understanding. As a Christian minister, James's trustworthiness and talent for fostering meaningful dialogue gave me the confidence to confide in him about my desire to leave the movement. His example inspired me to envision a different future – one where I could repurpose my skillset for peace-building and finally break free from the divisive ideologies of the past.

James seemed momentarily stunned by my confession and joked, "Wait, did I call the wrong number? Is this really Commander Schoep from the NSM?" We both laughed, easing the tension. Then he added, "Jeff, I've always believed God had a bigger plan for you than wasting your life in the movement."

After I shared my intention to leave, James proposed

an ambitious idea. Instead of organizing a second National Conversation on Race, we could embark on a joint peace-building mission. Together, we could transcend racial boundaries and create something extraordinary. A partnership between a Black civil-rights leader and a former neo-nazi leader had the potential to inspire meaningful change.

The idea was incredible and genuinely exciting, but I couldn't commit to starting right away. It would have to wait – though it seemed like a powerful plan for the future. When James asked who else knew about my intention to leave the NSM, I admitted that almost no one was aware. Nearly everyone I knew was still deeply entrenched in the movement.

James responded, "I've been praying for this day since the moment we met, believing you'd eventually choose a different path. Why hesitate? This is an incredible opportunity!"

For the first time, I told James about the lawsuit stemming from my attendance at Unite the Right. Leaving the movement would mean closing my business, losing my livelihood, and plunging into financial ruin without the resources to mount a legal defense. Beyond that, I'd face demonization, ostracism, and isolation from nearly everyone I'd known for decades. Leaving before resolving the lawsuit felt both impractical and unrealistic. Circumstances left me trapped.

 A few days later, James called again, insisting that my continued involvement with the NSM wasn't just a public disservice – it also lacked any meaningful purpose. He proposed contacting the plaintiffs' attorneys himself to inform them of my intent to leave the movement, even though I hadn't made the decision public yet. When I questioned why they would care,

James suggested that if the attorneys knew the NSM leader was stepping down, they could spin it as a victory, claiming their lawsuit had forced my decision.

I immediately interjected, clarifying that the truth was the exact opposite. The lawsuit hadn't pushed me to leave – it delayed my departure. I felt a moral obligation to fight it on principle. Abandoning a lifetime of involvement because of a lawsuit was the exact opposite of how I operated. Ideological extremists don't quit under pressure; if anything, it galvanizes them, emboldening their resolve – especially when they believe they're facing injustice, real or perceived. My entire life was definitive proof of how pushback only made me fight harder.

Only an ideological tourist – someone never truly invested – would buckle under the pressure of a lawsuit. After decades in leadership, the notion of abandoning the movement over such a matter was utterly ridiculous, especially since it wasn't my first time being sued.

James acknowledged my point and countered that, even if the plaintiffs' lawyers spun a narrative that their lawsuit drove me out, it wouldn't be lying on my part. Their spin wasn't within my control. "They've already painted you as an organizer of a violent conspiracy," James reasoned. "Would it really matter if they tossed a few more false equivalencies into the mix?"

Perhaps James had a point. A prominent Nazi leader leaving the movement could be a welcome development for the plaintiffs, especially if their lawsuit aimed to address racism.

A few days later, James called back with what he described as a detailed summary of his conversation with the plaintiffs' attorneys. According to him, they were open to the idea of removing me from the case. His intervention lifted my spirits and provided hope for an early departure from the movement – without the burden of fighting a lawsuit.

Then things started getting weird. After I expressed my gratitude, James suggested, "Jeff, when this is over, you could start a new white civil rights group – without the baggage of the NSM."

I was stunned. Had James misunderstood everything we'd talked about? Why would he propose such an idea?

"James," I clarified, "I plan to leave white nationalism entirely. Starting another group would contradict everything we've discussed. Why would I leave an organization I've built into the largest of its kind in the country just to create a new one?"

James backpedaled, reassuring me that he understood and emphasizing that we were on the same page. In our next conversation, he shared that he'd spoken further with the plaintiffs' attorneys. According to him, they recognized the futility of pursuing a lawsuit against someone walking away from hate. James explained that the attorneys believed my decision to leave the movement could serve as a powerful example, potentially inspiring others to follow suit.

"Forgiveness over vengeance," James said, "would send a far more impactful message to the public." He also mentioned that the attorneys were drafting formal paperwork for my dismissal from the case, which would be forthcoming.

CHAPTER 43

COURT MEDDLING & MEDIA CIRCUS

It's difficult to put into words what happened next, as this is the first time I'm publicly sharing my side of the story. But I'll do my best to explain what transpired.

James presented himself as a genuine friend, offering a doorway to a future free from extremism, hate, and division. It felt like a rare opportunity for a fresh start – one I was determined not to squander. While James had been a reliable and trustworthy ally in our previous interactions, my cautious nature led me to question his motives. Decades of involvement in neo-Nazism had sharpened my instincts, but had also ingrained a deep distrust of others. Over the years, the line between caution and paranoia often blurred, leaving countless relationships in ruins.

At a crossroads: I could remain bathed isolationist solitude or take a leap of faith and let others into my life. With the movement soon becoming a fading relic of my past, it was time to let go of the constant suspicion and embrace a new path forward.

In one conversation, I asked James, almost in disbelief, why he was so committed to helping me. His voice trembled with emotion as he replied, "Jeff, I know your heart. God has big plans for you. This is God's work, and there's a greater purpose behind our paths crossing. Assisting you on this journey to a new life is the right thing to do." His conviction that we were working together for a higher purpose struck a chord. Although I hadn't heard James preach in church, I could imagine his congregation was truly blessed.

This was my first real glimpse into a life beyond neo-Nazism – the first taste of what it might be like to break free from its suffocating grip. A flood of emotions washed over me – feelings of love, compassion, and a glimmer of hope for the future. The idea of walking away from everything I had once lived for was terrifying, requiring a level of courage I didn't even know existed. Yet the thought of a future surrounded by people like James brought a sense of peace, offering hope that there might still be a place for me in the wider world.

The excuses I'd clung to for so long began to dissolve, replaced by the exhilarating prospect of starting over with a renewed sense of purpose. For the first time in years, redemption felt not only possible but within reach, along with a path to attain it.

Or so I thought...

James soon provided what he claimed were documents from the plaintiffs' lawyers, signaling my release from the lawsuit. The paperwork looked legitimate – complete with attorney names, law firm details, and formal legal jargon. However, James cautioned not to disclose my plan to leave the movement – or his involvement with the plaintiffs' lawyers – to my attorney, suggesting this would ensure a smooth exit from the lawsuit. Despite my growing concerns as notices for an upcoming hearing continued to arrive, James reassured that the dismissal would be finalized before the court date.

As the hearing approached, James mentioned that the plaintiffs' attorneys insisted on speaking with me directly before filing the dismissal. Allegedly, they were unwilling to communicate through my lawyer. When I pressed for details, he claimed it was due to a conflict of interest – my lawyer represented multiple defendants in the case. To facilitate this direct communication, James advised that I fire my attorney.

Undergoing such immense changes had left me exceptionally vulnerable. I struggled to trust anyone outside the insular world I'd lived in for decades. Despite James's advice, I chose not to fire my lawyer. My intuition was screaming that something wasn't right, even as I tried to dismiss these feelings as residual paranoia – a byproduct of spending decades in the movement. Worst-case scenarios raced through my mind. Was James playing some sort of game? If so, why, and to what end? He was supposed to be a friend, a civil-rights leader, and a Christian minister devoted to peace-building.

As the hearing loomed, the situation grew increasingly convoluted and contradictory. The plaintiffs' attorneys filed a motion for sanctions against me, citing non-compliance – despite my submission of the requested documents months earlier. Alarmed, I reached out to James for clarity. His usual confidence had evaporated, replaced by nervous evasiveness. Then, in a baffling turn, he urged me to skip the court hearing altogether.

The red flags multiplied. I discovered James had contacted my attorney, falsely claiming to speak on my behalf, and told him he was fired. This miscommunication derailed my legal defense and directly led to sanctions.

The court hearing descended into chaos, unleashing a hurricane of havoc that tore through my life with ferocious intensity. In a surreal twist, James appeared on the court call, boldly declaring, "Your Honor, I am the leader of the NSM, and I plead guilty to all charges – guilty!" The sheer lunacy had escalated to insane asylum levels, leaving me stunned.

The judge intervened, explaining that pleading guilty was irrelevant since this was a hearing for a civil case, not a criminal one. Seeking clarification, the judge asked who this person was, suddenly claiming to represent the NSM. I immediately interjected, making it clear that James had no authority to speak for the organization. James, however, vehemently insisted that he was the rightful leader, his argument becoming increasingly unhinged. The judge quashed his claim, stating that James would need evidence and legal counsel to substantiate his position.

After granting sanctions against me due to the miscommunicated documents, the judge asked if I wanted to continue with my current attorney. Having lost faith, I chose to end the relationship. The judge allowed it but explained that, as an organization, the NSM was legally required to have an attorney. This was a law I hadn't been aware of. Now, I faced a strict deadline to secure new legal counsel – failure to do so would result in additional sanctions.

In the aftermath, it became painfully clear that the dismissal papers James had provided were forged. Falsifying legal documents wasn't just unethical – it was outright criminal. Despite years of leadership experience, tactical thinking, and preparing for worst-case scenarios, I'd been completely blindsided by this elaborate deception. Facing sanctions and without legal representation, I felt like a naïve fool trapped in a cruel web of lies.

Attempting to unravel James's motives for risking legal consequences by forging dismissal papers – complete with attorneys' names and law firm details – was stupefying. Yet, the immediate concern was finding a new lawyer. After an exhaustive search, I managed to secure new legal counsel, and the court barred James from any further interference in the case.

By March 2019, however, the damage was done. Media outlets erupted with sensational headlines such as, "Black Pastor Takes Control of neo-Nazi Group with Plans to Destroy It." Variations of this absurd and wildly inaccurate narrative spread rapidly across television, print, and online platforms. The ensuing media circus only intensified the chaos, making it even harder to move forward and leaving me to piece together the shattered remnants of my life.

After delving into the news stories, the mystery behind James's meddling in the lawsuit and forged dismissal papers began to unravel. His motives were laid bare, revealing an elaborate and calculated plot. The narrative spun by James was rife with deceit and exaggeration, peppered with just enough fragments of truth to appear credible – creating a preposterous yet captivating fairy-tale. The fact that James had never been in charge of the NSM, and that most of his claims were blatant lies, seemed irrelevant in the media's rush to amplify the story.

It became agonizingly clear that James had never intended to be a friend or partner in peace-building. Instead, he ruthlessly preyed on the one vulnerability I'd ever revealed – my desire to disengage from neo-Nazism. Vulnerability had no place in the world I'd inhabited for decades. I'd built mental, physical, and emotional defenses with impenetrable steel, ensuring no one could reach me. Yet, in a rare moment of trust, I let my guard down, hoping to find an ally who could help me step out of the darkness and reintegrate into society. Instead, James shattered that fragile trust, exploiting it for a fleeting fifteen minutes of fame.

Every hope, dream, and aspiration for a fresh start felt derailed. My intention to leave the movement had been twisted into a grotesque fairy-tale about a supposed takeover of the NSM – a brazen attempt to strip me of dignity and reduce me from a feared neo-Nazi leader to a target of ridicule and scorn. Being derided in the press was nothing new, but the shift from being feared to being mocked as an unintelligent buffoon outwitted by James, all while struggling to transform my life, was soul-crushing.

Normally, I could shrug off negative portrayals with indifference, but James's fabrications were recklessly dangerous and impossible to ignore. In the neo-Nazi scene, there was no higher level of leadership than what I had achieved, and my position within the movement remained secure despite the spin James was feeding to the press. I had weathered worse storms before and could have easily returned to 'business as usual.'

The real danger lay in my intention to leave the movement. Had I stood my ground and publicly countered James's claims – just as I had done with similar challenges throughout my 25 years in leadership – his allegations would have crumbled, withered, and faded into irrelevance.

It hurt deeply that one of the few people I knew outside the movement would resort to such a publicly humiliating form of betrayal. Ironically, James's treachery only reinforced the toxic stereotypes and prejudices I'd been striving to leave behind. Yet, I refused to let it derail my commitment to judging people by their character, not the color of their skin. Many in my position would have been driven back to neo-Nazism with a vengeance and renewed fervor, but I stood firm, committed to change.

Resigning from my position as the national leader of the NSM was no small feat. Walking away was difficult enough, but publicly denouncing racism afterward would set a historic precedent in the U.S. – no other prominent, nationally recognized neo-Nazi leader had ever made such a transition. I braced for the very real possibility of violent retaliation. Leaving was one thing; openly condemning racism would brand me a traitor in the eyes of many within the movement.

Another obstacle was the potential backlash from long-time adversaries on the far-left. Many would likely continue to label me a Nazi solely because I rejected their radical ideologies and refused to engage in harmful tactics like doxxing. There's a troubling tendency among some to indiscriminately brand anyone they disagree with – from devout Christians to conservatives – as Nazis. I anticipated that the cancel-culture drones would pin my past on me indefinitely and began preparing myself emotionally for that reality.

Once I decided to leave the movement, I'd be besieged by enemies from all sides, with no support system, and the burden of my past dragging me down like an anchor. Still, I held the reins to my own destiny, with a wide range of options at my disposal. Despite James's theatrical antics, I remained firmly in control of the NSM and wasn't about to relinquish that based on lies. My departure was imminent, but it would happen on my terms – not as part of some bizarre media circus casting me as the clown and James as the Party leader.

The fictional takeover of the NSM might have titillated the public's curiosity, but it gained no traction within the organization and held no basis in reality. Throughout its long history, the group had endured numerous controversies, some of which even led to resignations. Despite James's absurd claim of taking control of the largest Nazi party in the country making both national and international headlines, the NSM remained largely unaffected.

Regional and state NSM leaders reached out to me for an official response to the rumors circulating in the press. In total, the group lost only three members nationwide – one of whom issued a death threat against me, resulting in his immediate expulsion. The other two resigned impulsively, reacting to the headlines without bothering to verify their accuracy. If James had truly seized control, the group would have disbanded overnight. Yet, he continued to milk the story, perpetuating a fictitious narrative.

With a lenghty history of fiercely responding to such situations, my gut instinct was to retaliate with full force. The NSM wasn't a democracy; its members were steadfastly loyal, and my authority was unquestioned. Staying in power and maintaining influence within the movement seemed like the easiest and most practical path forward.

I stood at a crossroads: in one hand, the opportunity to preserve the legacy I'd built over decades; in the other, an uncertain future that had just been ruthlessly trampled. The choice was mine, but which path should I take?

Staying was practical, even tempting – familiarity, security, friendships, and my business were all deeply intertwined with the movement. But the problem with raising the sword to continue the fight was that I no longer believed in the cause.

As a man of principle, the thought of feigning allegiance and living a lie was unconscionable. Preserving one's honor and integrity cannot be reconciled with perpetuating a falsehood for the sake of self-preservation. To stay would mean betraying the core of who I was striving to become.

The ongoing lawsuit only added layers of complexity to an already fraught situation. Leaving the movement meant facing unemployment, societal exclusion, and the unshakable stigma of a highly publicized past. It also meant giving up my record store – a vital source of financial stability. Without an income, how could I possibly afford legal defense?

The internal conflict was agonizing, but I remained resolute in the decision to leave neo-Nazism. My first step was to issue a public statement on the NSM website, exposing James's scam and making it unequivocally clear that he had no authority or control over the organization or its assets. As Party leader, it was my legal and ethical obligation to safeguard the organization and its membership.

Some might argue that I should've burned the organization down on my way out, but such an act didn't align with my principles. The NSM wasn't mine to destroy, and doing so would've been both dishonorable and unlawful. Leaving the movement meant rejecting its ideology, not compromising my integrity.

James, however, escalated his fabrications to dangerous extremes, claiming he had access to NSM mailing lists, websites, and even my record store – all of which were blatant lies. Regrettably, some media outlets irresponsibly amplified these falsehoods. Had his claims been true, the repercussions would've been catastrophic: thousands of people doxxed, websites compromised, and me, quite literally, a dead man walking.

Internal matters were rarely addressed publicly on the NSM Party website, but the viral spread of James's lies left me with no alternative. I made the judgment call to confront the situation openly, dismantling his false narratives once and for all.

After considerable reflection, soul-searching, and heartfelt discussions with my father, I charted a path forward. Despite the inherent risks and obstacles ahead, I resolved to uphold my principles and take the difficult but necessary steps to do what was right.

I drafted a second announcement and press release for the NSM membership, its website, and the public. After twenty-five years as leader of the organization, I made the decision to retire.

The NSM's leadership structure didn't operate through self-selection or democratic elections; leaders were appointed. In cases of the Commander's incapacitation, retirement, assassination, or imprisonment, the Chief of Staff was designated as the successor. Factors such as rank, role, activism, and tenure were also considered in these appointments. I spoke with the Chief of Staff, a long-serving member, about assuming the role of Commander. Though initially hesitant, he agreed to step into the position.

The romanticized notion of being a prominent neo-Nazi leader, which may have seemed glamorous or enticing to younger members, was largely absent in the upper echelons of the NSM. Veteran members, particularly those in leadership roles, understood that leading the organization demanded immense effort and was fraught with dangers, challenges, and personal sacrifice.

Historically, white-supremacist groups across America often splintered into factions or collapsed entirely after the death, imprisonment, or departure of long-term leaders. The NSM, however, was relatively unique in its structure. It operated under a board of directors and functioned as a state-recognized nonprofit corporation, though it lacked federal recognition. Unlike skinhead crews, gangs, or loosely organized clubs, the NSM ran like a well-oiled machine, with a clearly defined hierarchy.

In civilian life, retiring after twenty-five years might conjure images of tranquility – a severance package or perhaps a symbolic gold watch. My retirement bore no resemblance to that. Which raises the question: Why did I retire rather than outright denounce the group the moment I left?

I envisioned a future dedicated to speaking out against racism and engaging in peace-building efforts. Yet, before embarking on that path, there were significant obstacles to overcome. Most people who leave such movements can make a clean break, severing ties and disappearing into anonymity. For me, however, it was far more complex. Leaving wasn't simply about walking away – it required untangling decades of deeply intertwined connections, influence, and responsibilities. Departing wasn't just a personal decision – it was a logistical and moral undertaking. Every thread of my life had been woven into the fabric of the movement, and unraveling it demanded a methodical, deliberate approach.

First, there was the ongoing lawsuit, which I was still actively defending. Taking a public stand against hate and racism while being named in court alongside movement groups and leaders created a precarious and potentially explosive situation. I also needed time to reflect, heal, and confront the gravity of my past actions. A period of introspection and reconciliation was essential before effectively and credibly advocating against racism.

James's relentless behavior further destabilized an already delicate situation, compounding the challenges I faced. His baseless claims of leading the NSM became more ludicrous with each passing day, yet certain media outlets persisted in entertaining his delusions. Just as coverage seemed to fade, James would resurface with fresh interviews, spinning even more outlandish tales.

The most disturbing aspect was James's calculated recklessness. With his background in negotiating gang truces, he was acutely aware of the dangers inherent in extremist circles – where a single misstep or inflammatory claim could have fatal consequences. I'm convinced he deliberately put my life in jeopardy after I left the NSM. He knew the risks because I had trusted him enough to share them. His actions weren't born of negligence; they were callous and intentional.

As media attention began to wane, James escalated his claims with a clear intent to cause harm. He falsely claimed control over NSM resources – everything from mailing lists, websites, and bank accounts, to membership data. He even extended these fabrications to include my personal business assets, such as the record store. Despite having no access to any of these resources, his lies spread across public interviews, gaining traction in sensational headlines. Then, in a sinister twist, James tweeted, "Jeff, you forget I know where all the dead bodies are," dragging the deception into macabre and dangerous territory.

Debunking James's claims about controlling NSM websites could have been done with a few quick clicks online. Despite my repeated appeals for the press to fact-check these easily disprovable lies, the disinformation spread like wildfire. I suspected James was banking on someone gullible enough to believe his nonsense and retaliate against me under the false premise that I had betrayed or harmed thousands of people. There was nothing in my personal history or character to support such vile accusations, but the real issue was trust: why would anyone in neo-Nazi circles believe me after I'd left the movement? That was the crux of the problem. Had I stayed on as Party leader or remained active, such rumors would have been dismissed outright. My disengagement, however, created a vacuum that allowed speculation and mistrust to flourish.

During my tenure as Party leader, the media eagerly covered NSM rallies and press conferences. While they understandably despised the NSM and its ideology, they treated me with a degree of personal respect. But when I left the movement, everything changed. Suddenly, I was portrayed as a low-brow ignoramus who'd been outwitted and duped by James. My public persona plummeted – from someone feared and, in some ways, begrudgingly respected, to becoming a source of ridicule and mockery.

Psychologically, it's hard to put into words what this does to someone. I felt lost, broken, and under siege, as if I were chained to a target at the end of a firing range, with everyone lining up to take their shots. What had begun as an effort to break free and build a better future now felt like an unending nightmare.

As James's stories grew increasingly unbelievable, his most outrageous claims – like accusing me of stashing bodies – never made it to publication. Media outlets had finally started fact-checking. Several reporters informed me that James had alleged I'd flown to California to threaten him with a gun at his home, where he supposedly overpowered, disarmed, and beat me up. Given his small stature, the idea of James engaging in such valiant heroics was laughable. Apparently, it was plausible for me to be painted as a low-IQ moron, but the notion of James overpowering and beating up the former leader of the Nazi Party was where the media drew the line – cue the fact-checking.

To cope with the mounting stress, I silenced my phone and ignored the flood of calls and emails. Most media outlets I spoke to didn't bother publishing my side of the story, and those that did included only insignificant snippets. One reporter, who claimed to know James personally, even berated me over the phone, insisting that James would never do what I had accused him of. Being branded a liar and scolded by a journalist was a first for me. Any fleeting hope that the public might hear the truth felt completely stripped away. Instead of walking away and starting over, it felt like I was sinking into a bottomless pit of quicksand – unable to defend myself while being mercilessly kicked every time I surfaced, gasping for air.

In a radio interview, James claimed I left the movement because the NSM wasn't paying me enough. The truth was,

I didn't draw a salary from the group – my livelihood came from running the store. His baseless accusations were clearly intended to stir the pot and provoke discontent. In neo-Nazi circles, accusations of financial opportunism and power struggles were almost a cliché. Throughout my years of involvement, I witnessed such claims being hurled at virtually every leader without exception. While some leaders were more adept at fundraising than others, the reality was that many accused of mercenary motives were barely scraping by, living precariously on the edge of financial viability. James's claims weren't just false – they were part of a tired but effective playbook of incitement.

The year I left the movement coincided with a period of unprecedented financial contributions to the NSM, driven primarily in response to the lawsuit. My business income had also remained consistently stable. If financial motivations had factored into my decision-making, staying involved would have been the logical choice. The bitter reality, however, was that leaving the movement obliterated the financial stability I'd relied on for years – almost overnight.

One of James's most perilous falsehoods was his claim that I was an informant or snitch. He knew all too well my deep-seated disdain for informants – a topic we'd discussed in depth. For decades, I'd been outspoken in my contempt, often repeating the phrase, "snitches end up in ditches." It's a well-established fact that I never ratted on anyone. Yet, if even one unhinged individual believed James's lies, my life could have been in serious danger.

Rather than succumbing to fear, I steeled myself as usual, and prepared to face whatever might come. My approach to threats is best summed up by the acronym FAFO – 'fuck around and find out.' I've tasted victory, endured defeat, and bear the scars of countless battles. A few more wouldn't make much difference.

James's allegations were not only baseless but also easily debunked. Had I been an informant, there would've been court proceedings, and prison sentences – evidence would've spread faster than a virus. If I'd handed over member lists, thousands of people would've been doxxed. If James had seized control of websites or businesses, it would have caused a public spectacle, exposing tens of thousands of customers worldwide. None of these scenarios materialized because none of his claims were true. His fabrications fell apart under scrutiny, leaving behind nothing but a trail of deception.

Being victimized while attempting to turn my life around was a torment I had not anticipated. The hardships, betrayals, and emotional toll were relentless – and they were only beginning. Adding to the pressure, I was served with another lawsuit, this one filed by James himself. Unlike criminal cases, civil suits don't provide public defenders, which forced me to hire a second lawyer, this time in California.

James's lawsuit targeted the NSM, myself as its former leader, the new Commander, and every board member, demanding exorbitant sums of money. Simultaneously, he engaged in questionable, and likely illegal, activities, such as tampering with Michigan's Department of Licensing and Regulatory Affairs (LARA) records, where incorporation documents for businesses and nonprofits are filed. He repeatedly claimed to be the rightful owner and representative of the NSM, even going so far as to list himself as several board members. The legitimate board was forced to expend time and resources correcting these falsified records to undo his meddling.

After my departure, there was no valid reason for the NSM to remain incorporated in Michigan, especially since the new Commander was based in another state. Consequently, the organization was officially dissolved, and state records were updated to reflect this change.

In the fall of 2019, James passed away, bringing this turbulent chapter to a close. While his passing ended the cycle of conflict, the emotional scars left behind lingered, raw and unhealed.

CHAPTER 44

EXITING EXTREMISM

Reflecting on my time with the NSM fills me with a profound sense of regret and shame. Several years before I left, seeds of doubt had already begun to sprout. I started to recognize that some of the group's beliefs no longer aligned with my evolving worldview. And yet, the thought of walking away wasn't just daunting – it felt impossible. Instead, I clung to the delusion that I could reform the organization, reshaping it into a white civil-rights group.

Looking back, I can see just how deeply flawed that idea truly was. At the time, it felt logical, even noble – like I was working toward something meaningful. In reality, it was an exercise in futility – a doomed attempt to mask the ugly Nazi ideology. My efforts to reframe those beliefs were little more than a desperate bid to convince myself and others that they weren't rooted in hatred, no different than putting lipstick on a pig. Like most extremists, I clung to the illusion of righteousness. When that façade crumbled, the truth was nearly unbearable.

Leaving extremism wasn't just about cutting ties with friends, a support network, and a sense of purpose. It also meant walking away from the financial stability and business I'd spent years building. The grim reality hit hard: my infamous past as a neo-Nazi leader rendered me virtually unemployable. As I grappled with an uncertain future, doubts crept in. Is this really what life is supposed to be like after leaving it all behind? Had I sacrificed my future on principle, only to fall upon my own sword?

For the first time in years, I was no longer consumed by the relentless demands of running the NSM. This newfound freedom gave me the space to focus on healing – but the process was far more difficult than I'd imagined. The weight of my past bore down on me, suffocating and inescapable. Haunted by the harm I had caused, I was constantly reminded of the damage my former life had inflicted. I kept wondering, How could I ever atone for it?

In those early days, I was utterly lost. The path toward redemption wasn't just unfamiliar – it seemed nonexistent. And yet, somehow, I had to find a way forward.

My phone and email were inundated with messages from NSM members urging me to reconsider leaving. They expressed disbelief, trying to pull me back in, asking, "When are you returning? We need you back and are behind you no matter what you're going through." Simultaneously, threats began pouring in from strangers, fueled by the false allegations James had spread in the media. The sheer volume of messages – and the emotional toll they inflicted – made responding impractical. I left 99% of them unanswered, reserving replies only for Party leaders regarding the two ongoing lawsuits and the return of NSM property, which I handled in line with my corporate and ethical obligations.

The period following my departure, which I refer to as the decompression phase, brought profound shifts in my perspective. Insights from outsiders that I had once dismissed as irrelevant suddenly became undeniable. Over the years, many of the women I had been in relationships with – who had seen the inner workings of the NSM firsthand – described it as cult-like. At the time, their comments provoked anger and defensiveness. I dismissed their observations as baseless, questioning my judgment in women rather than confronting the uncomfortable truths they were pointing out.

Stepping away from the echo chambers of extremism was like emerging from a cave into sunlight. The world outside seemed brighter, clearer, and sharper, as though reality itself was finally syncing into focus. It's a bitter pill to swallow when the full picture emerges, but reassessing your worldview from the outside is far easier than attempting to do so while still entrenched within it.

During the decompression phase, I gained invaluable insights into the challenges of leaving extremism behind. The painful transition brought clarity and a newfound sense of purpose. The lessons I learned – hard-fought and hard-earned – could be repurposed to help others striving to change their lives and break free from destructive paths.

Breaking free from the chains of neo-Nazism was one of the hardest battles I've ever fought. At my lowest, I was completely alone, drowning in isolation, and convinced that things couldn't possibly get worse. Hitting rock bottom has a way of stripping life down to its bare essentials – there's nothing left to lose and no further to sink. It felt as though I'd plunged to the depths of the Mariana Trench, but even there, I still had a choice: surrender to the abyss or fight my way back to the surface. I chose to fight, no matter how impossible it seemed.

Amidst the turmoil, an unexpected call from Daryl Davis

became a lifeline. His voice, filled with genuine concern, reached through the darkness: "Jeff, I've seen the news stories about you and wanted to make sure you're okay." His kindness and empathy were unwavering. "I always sensed our paths would cross again," he said. "I wasn't sure when, but it seems that time has come. How can I be of assistance?" Despite knowing only what the media reported, Daryl offered compassion and brotherhood.

On the verge of breaking down – an emotion I rarely allowed myself to feel – I was drowning in a sea of struggles, the weight of the world pressing down relentlessly. It felt as though everyone was determined to exact their pound of flesh, leaving me battered and breathless. Yet even in that suffocating darkness, a few pillars of support emerged: my father, Deeyah, a couple of girlfriends, and Daryl. Each one offered glimmers of hope when I needed them most.

Daryl became the cornerstone of a monumental transformation. I regret not telling him back in 2016 just how impactful our first meeting had been, but it wasn't until 2019 that I truly understood its significance. In my darkest hours, he extended a hand of genuine friendship, embodying the true spirit of camaraderie. Brotherhood and loyalty are forged through mutual support, and just as Daryl has been there for me, I am committed to being there for him.

Extraordinary individuals like Daryl guided me through one of the most turbulent phases of my life. Their presence was nothing short of a blessing, their support a steady anchor in the storm.

CHAPTER 45

FORMERS

When I finally decided to leave the movement, it never occurred to me to reach out to others who had once walked similar paths. In twenty-seven years deeply entrenched in the cause, I hadn't crossed paths with – nor even heard of – most of the former extremists who now spoke out against hate. Their voices were like ghosts, unheard in the insular world I inhabited.

As the leader of the NSM, I interacted with nearly every major figure in the white-nationalist movement across America. I traveled coast to coast, meeting thousands of people from all corners of the far-right spectrum – neo-Nazis, KKK members, skinheads, musicians, Identity Pastors, and Creators. The only branch I had limited interaction with was the alt-right, a newer faction that splashed onto the scene in the last few years of my involvement. I mostly avoided it, seeing it as distinct from the older, more traditional groups I was accustomed to.

Amid the media storm surrounding James and me, two men who had walked away from extremism reached out before I went public with my intentions to speak out. One of them was Jesse, a former Al-Qaeda propagandist who had since founded an organization to help others transition out of extremism. Though his past was rooted in a different form of radicalism, Jesse deeply understood the underlying forces that drove individuals into these dark spaces.

Jesse was the real deal – someone who had paid the price for his beliefs, served in the trenches, and did time in prison for his involvement with Al-Qaeda. His journey to redemption was nothing short of extraordinary. With unwavering dedication, sharp intellect, and a well-documented history in extremism, Jesse had become an empathetic listener and a catalyst for transformative change. His escape from the dark grip of extremism, achieved at immense personal risk, was living proof that even the most notorious extremists could turn their lives around and contribute meaningfully to the world.

Jesse's understanding of the psychological underpinnings of extremist ideologies was incisive. Under his mentorship, I began to let go of the anger and self-criticism that had weighed me down, replacing it with a mindset focused on healing and growth. Jesse also introduced me to former jihadists, survivors of hate-crimes, and members of the Jewish and Muslim communities, broadening my perspectives in ways I hadn't imagined. In return, I introduced him to some of my connections, mutually enriching our networks and the impact of our shared mission.

The other former extremist who reached out, whom I'll call Khristian, had a brief stint as a musician in a relatively unknown skinhead band during the 1990s. Our paths crossed only once, in Saint Paul, Minnesota, home to one of the top American skinhead bands at the time. Khristian was in town visiting them, and our interaction was fleeting – a handshake and a brief introduction. I wouldn't say I knew him; he was just one of the many faces that passed through the scene, leaving little impression. Not long after, he left the skinhead world, another transient figure who drifted in and then right back out, like so many others before him and countless more after.

In early 2019, as I struggled to claw my way back from rock bottom, Khristian's outreach offered a flicker of hope. His kindness and willingness to offer solidarity felt like a lifeline during one of the darkest periods of my life. During our conversation, he said, "Brother, you're not on this path alone. I've got your back and will stand by you throughout this journey." His words resonated deeply, and we soon made plans to meet in person.

At a local café, Khristian asked about my future plans. I shared my vision of peace-building and desire to help others exit extremism, similar to the work he was already doing. Leaning back, he said, "Wow, that's awesome! I'll share my knowledge and help guide you."

During our conversation, Khristian asked if I still held on to any residual beliefs from my time in the movement. In confidence, I admitted that, while I had abandoned racism entirely and had dated women of different racial backgrounds, I still harbored some skepticism about the number of lives lost in the Holocaust. This doubt was the result of decades of absorbing Holocaust revisionism – a textbook case of confirmation bias at play. These lingering doubts were the last remnants of twenty-seven years of indoctrination. Khristian assured me he would help address any misconceptions I had about the Holocaust. Then, shifting gears, he mentioned a TV show he had in development and invited me to participate.

In May 2019, Khristian and a film crew arrived to begin filming. The first day was straightforward, but on the second day, something felt off. We were sitting in Khristian's car, parked in a ramp, with cameras rolling. It seemed like one of those B-roll scenes, the kind of footage meant to complement the main content in post-production.

As we spoke, I emphasized my commitment to honesty. I'll never forget Khristian's reaction – his eyes lit up, as if he'd been waiting for the perfect moment. Then, out of nowhere, he asked, "Speaking of honesty, Jeff, what are your thoughts on the numbers in the Holocaust?" The question hit me like a punch to the gut, leaving me sick to my stomach. I had confided in him during our initial meeting – in strict confidence – that this was the final hurdle in my deradicalization process.

Disheartened, I couldn't understand why Khristian would exploit the one issue I had entrusted him with in private as a 'gotcha' moment on camera. I wasn't going to lie, but I refused to be manipulated, exploited, or taken advantage of. Shaking my head in disbelief, I asked Khristian if he was seriously posing that question. When he persisted, I stopped the filming and confronted him off camera, questioning why he would do such a thing.

Every time I voiced a question or concern to Khristian, his response was always the same: trust his process. He was adamant that anyone who wanted to be part of peace-building or deradicalization efforts had to follow his method without question. It was either trust his process or be excluded from doing meaningful work.

Something about the situation felt deeply off-kilter, but my determination to contribute to humanity kept me moving forward. Even though every instinct screamed at me to get as far away from Khristian as possible, I couldn't shake the thought: What if I'm wrong and his so-called process is right? I didn't have much experience navigating civilian life – maybe this was what it looked like. Perhaps I just needed to stop questioning and blindly put faith in Khristian's process, as he insisted over and over again, like a broken record. Against my better judgement, I pushed doubts aside and tried to follow his lead.

Red flags about Khristian's conduct continued to surface, and his so-called process had already failed to address the one issue I'd struggled with – aside from the exploitative moment on camera. Still, it seemed counterintuitive that someone claiming to help people leave extremism could harbor questionable motives.

Khristian's television show was set to air in August or September 2019, and he suggested my public announcement about peace-building should coincide with its debut. When a reporter reached out to me about an unrelated story, I felt the timing was right. In August 2019, weeks before Khristian's show aired, I went public – launching my website, social media, and a press release in which I renounced neo-Nazism and condemned racism. By then, I had resolved the lingering antisemitic doubts with Jesse's guidance.

Khristian had assured me that his show would be the perfect platform to launch my peace-building efforts. But when it aired, I was devastated to see the scene where he questioned me about the Holocaust included – and worse, it was framed in a way that made the issue appear ambiguously unresolved.

Afterward, I called Khristian to express how much it hurt, especially given the timing of my public announcement. He dismissed my concerns outright, insisting the show was fantastic and that I simply needed to trust his process. He brushed off my feelings, claiming that all former extremists went through this and that I was overreacting, worrying over nothing.

TURKEY

In the fall of 2019, Jesse invited me to speak alongside him and Jason, another former Al-Qaeda member, at the International Symposium on Radicalization and Extremism in Ankara, Turkey. Supported by the Turkish government and the European Union, the event brought together delegations from around the globe.

Right before the symposium, a social media dispute between Khristian and Jesse erupted into what can only be described as a child-like temper tantrum from Khristian. While en route to Turkey, I was bombarded with texts from Khristian demanding to know if I was associated with Jesse. When I confirmed that I was traveling to Turkey to speak alongside him, Khristian issued an ultimatum: sever ties with Jesse or lose his support and any future opportunities to work together.

Attempting to engage in a civil, adult conversation, I asked Khristian why it mattered so much who I associated with. Instead of offering a reasonable explanation, he reacted with hostility, hurling baseless accusations about Jesse. He then issued a warning: there would be consequences if I didn't heed his advice. When I pressed him on what that meant, he ominously replied, "You will find out!"

Over the course of decades in the movement, I never took orders from men driven by pettiness, insecurity, egomania, or narcissism – and I wasn't about to start bending a knee now. After Khristian's implicit threat, I remained professional and sent a final message politely expressing my disappointment in his decision to sever ties. That exchange in 2019 marked the last conversation we ever had.

Dealing with Khristian's petty drama on my way to Turkey was an unwelcome distraction. I was about to give my first public talk since leaving the movement, and the thought of speaking in front of international government officials and experts on extremism had my anxiety surging. I wasn't sure how they would receive me, knowing my past and the life I'd led for decades.

Thankfully, the symposium was a success. Jesse and Jason spoke about Islamic extremism, while I shared insights on far-right extremism.

During our time in Turkey, Jason and I carved out just enough time to visit two phenomenal sites: the historic Ankara Castle and Ataturk's Mausoleum. The castle was captivating – a place where people had lived within its ancient walls for centuries, preserving a tangible sense of living history. We indulged in Turkish coffee and marveled at the enchanting view from the castle's peak. The panoramic vista stretched endlessly across the city, made all the more surreal by the Islamic call to prayer, its ethereal echoes cascading off the surrounding mountains.

Visiting a predominantly Islamic country for the first time, I was deeply moved by the hauntingly beautiful prayer reverberating across the landscape – it left a lasting impression.

Next, we visited Ataturk's Mausoleum, a breathtaking complex that radiated grandeur. The towering columns and architecture evoked the majesty of ancient Rome. Inside, we explored a vast museum filled with artifacts from President Ataturk and Turkey's rich history – intricate battle dioramas, exquisite art, and walkways lined with statues of lions standing guard. The sunlight reflecting off the polished stone underscored the craftsmanship and meticulous attention to detail.

The mausoleum far exceeded all expectations, leaving us both in awe. It was a fitting tribute to the legacy of Turkey's first president and one of the most magnificent man-made structures I've ever encountered.

THE CAMPAIGN

In the fall of 2019, as I focused on rebuilding my life and contributing to peace-building efforts, Khristian followed through on his threats by launching a targeted campaign to discredit me. He began by contacting individuals within the peace-building community and journalists, spreading claims that I wasn't ready to contribute meaningfully to the fight against violent extremism. While everyone is entitled to their opinions, the extent of his efforts to undermine was staggering.

Privately maligning me apparently wasn't enough. Khristian took to social media, where he escalated his attacks with public denunciations. A handful of his friends – some claiming to be former extremists – joined in, parroting his accusations. Predictably, all of them seemed aligned with radical far-left ideologies. What bothered me most was that none of these individuals had ever met or spoken to me, yet they felt justified in publicly undermining my recovery, healing, and commitment to helping others. Their behavior bore a striking resemblance to the cliquish infighting and divisiveness I had witnessed countless times within extremist groups.

What began as mild criticism quickly descended into vicious and defamatory attacks. Khristian soon resorted to calling me an active Nazi and spreading outright falsehoods. On Twitter, he told a spokesperson involved with the Charlottesville lawsuit that I had approached him for help but was rejected for being insincere. The truth, however, is that Khristian had contacted me first, and our communication ended only after I refused his demand to cut ties with Jesse. Ironically, he admitted on his own TV show that he initiated contact, making it easy to debunk his fabricated narrative.

I've preserved text messages and screenshots as documented proof of my interactions with Khristian. His actions revealed a troubling misuse of influence, as he weaponized his standing in the deradicalization space to inflict lasting, irreparable harm on my reputation. This was not only a betrayal of the community's mission but also an alarming abuse of trust within a community dedicated to fostering peace and redemption.

Despite being the target of ongoing public defamation, I remained steadfast in my commitment to advocating against racism on both national and international levels, while supporting others on their journey out of extremism. Meanwhile, Khristian's campaign of defamation sank to a shocking new low when he falsely and publicly labeled Acacia – someone I care about deeply – as an active Nazi.

After leaving the movement, I had assisted Acacia in severing her ties as well. Once a webmaster and propagandist for the

NSM, she had been fully transparent about her past and was working diligently to rebuild her life. During the filming of Khristian's TV show, I introduced her to him, trusting in his professed commitment to helping others. Instead, he weaponized her past against her, falsely accusing her on social media of actively running Nazi websites. His baseless and malicious claims came at a time when Acacia was already navigating the difficult process of rebuilding her life, compounding her struggles with the weight of public humiliation.

Khristian's actions weren't just morally reprehensible – they were slanderous and libelous. His deliberate attempt to destroy Acacia's reputation during such a vulnerable phase of her healing revealed an appalling level of malice. The emotional toll was devastating – Acacia was left shattered, drowning in inconsolable tears and consumed by a paralyzing sense of hopelessness.

To falsely label any former Nazi as an active Nazi – especially someone working tirelessly to distance themselves from that identity – is an act of profound cruelty. It shows a gross disregard for the immense courage and struggle required to leave such a past behind, inflicting severe psychological harm and emotional trauma on someone striving for redemption.

The public accusations on social media, where Khristian called Acacia and me Nazis, were just the tip of the iceberg in his bizarre vendetta. He went even further, emailing my employer to shame him for allegedly platforming a so-called Nazi and contacting others in my professional network to spread similar false claims. Despite us having no communication since 2019, Khristian's animosity and hostility only escalated in the years that followed.

Reintegrating into civilian life and finding work was already an uphill battle. The added burden of being stalked and harassed by someone who claimed to have left extremism but acted otherwise pushed me to my limits. It felt like I was nearing a breaking point. In the world I'd left behind, Khristian's actions would have triggered swift and brutal consequences. But having moved on from that life, I was determined to handle things differently.

Reluctantly, I pursued legal action and sent Khristian a cease-and-desist letter, as ignoring his harassment had only emboldened him. His lawyer's response was absurd, accusing me of harassment for sending the letter – a blatant and truly ironic misrepresentation. I wasn't seeking compensation or damages; I just wanted the harassment to stop.

The entire situation was bewildering. I'd never confronted Khristian aggressively or caused him any harm, yet I became the target of his prolonged and irrational hostility. It all seemed to stem from one decision: my refusal to cut ties with Jesse in 2019. The experience was so surreal and nonsensical that I struggled to make any sense of it.

Advice from others suggested that Khristian's behavior wasn't directly tied to me or his conflict with Jesse. Instead, they pointed to personal insecurities – his fragile ego and low self-esteem – as likely root causes. Some speculated that he viewed my involvement in countering extremism, along with my leadership experience, as a threat to his status and opportunities.

While plausible, it seems unlikely that insecurities alone could sustain such intense hostility for years. I suspect the true cause of Khristian's behavior lies in unresolved mental health issues, likely intertwined with narcissistic and sociopathic tendencies. Allowing someone with these traits access to vulnerable individuals seeking to escape extremism is like handling a venomous cobra while blindfolded – it's dangerous and reckless.

The severity of the situation became even more apparent when others, also targeted by Khristian, reached out after seeing his disparaging posts about Acacia and me online. Their support was heartening but revealed a painful truth: his actions had inflicted unnecessary harm on others.

Change is inherently challenging, often marked by setbacks and struggles. It's deeply unjust for those seeking reformation to endure harm from individuals who present themselves as allies. In a world where some prey on the vulnerabilities of others, I remain committed to providing genuine support – offering encouragement, friendship, and understanding to those working toward a better future.

CHAPTER 46

NAZI HUNTERS

After launching jeffschoep.com in August 2019 and publicly declaring my commitment to peace-building, my inbox was inundated with responses. Old friends reconnected, curiosity seekers asked questions, and many reached out for help escaping extremism. However, there was also a darker side – hate mail, threats, and accusations of betrayal for renouncing racism.

Among the many emails, one stood out: it was from Rick Eaton, Director of Research at The Simon Wiesenthal Center, an organization renowned for tracking down war criminals after World War II. Rick mentioned he'd seen my website and proposed a meeting. My initial reaction was a mix of curiosity and anxiety. Could the Wiesenthal Center be pursuing me now that I was isolated, without the backing of the NSM? Would Mossad agents attempt to abduct and haul me off to Israel to stand trial like a Nazi war criminal?

These were irrational echoes of the paranoia ingrained in my past – especially since I hadn't committed any crimes. As the apprehension faded, curiosity took over. Still, I shared the meeting details with Acacia – just in case the unlikely happened and I found myself facing an involuntary extradition to Israel.

A few days later, Rick arrived in Detroit, and we met in a public setting. We spoke for hours, and any lingering anxiety melted away. I shared my committment to being a voice for peace and firmly opposing racism. The conversation was invigorating, with a genuine sense of positive synergy developing between us.

Once the Wiesenthal Center validated my authenticity through their vetting process in 2019, they invited me to speak alongside elected officials at a California legislative session on hate crimes. Their support, following my return from Turkey, became instrumental in paving the way for my advocacy against racism and extremism nationwide.

When Rick and I first discussed my intentions to speak out, he asked if I felt ready for the challenge. Confidently, I replied, "Public speaking has been my forte for decades; it's what I do. Only now, my goal is to unite and heal, not divide and spread hatred."

Rick raised an eyebrow. "Jeff, it might not be as easy as you think. You're used to speaking about the movement. This will be much different. You'll be speaking about yourself."

I shrugged off Rick's caution, certain it wouldn't be as difficult as he implied. Armed with a notecard of key points, I felt nervous but prepared. However, as the government officials at the California legislative session began delivering their speeches, the weight of my past hit me like a freight train. This area had been a hotspot for NSM operations not long ago. Sitting on the panel, I felt an overwhelming flood of guilt, shame, and regret wash over me. Dammit, this is what Rick meant when he said it wasn't going to be easy!

Fidgeting with a pen, I remembered the phrase, "Speak from the heart or forever hold your tongue." Emotions surged, and my voice quivered as I fought to maintain composure. This moment was unlike anything I'd ever faced. Decades of public speaking had prepared me for many things, but exposing vulnerabilities and confronting the mistakes of my past was an entirely different ordeal. Still, the overwhelming desire to make amends eclipsed the discomfort of self-exposure. I spoke from the heart, offering a sincere apology and acknowledging the pain and trauma my actions had inflicted on the community.

Rick's wisdom was undeniable – talking about myself was far harder than I'd imagined. As the Commander of the NSM, I had never stood before an audience to discuss my faults, much less admit to being wrong. I had been considered a figure of unyielding authority, untouchable and incapable of error. Vulnerability and remorse were traits I'd once viewed as weaknesses, emotions I refused to entertain. Yet, on that panel, those emotions swept over me like a tidal wave, impossible to ignore, demanding to be addressed.

SIMON WIESENTHAL CENTER

Despite having directed much of my vitriol toward Jewish people in the past, they were among the first to extend compassion, acceptance, and forgiveness. Their willingness to engage and offer understanding, despite my history, taught me invaluable lessons about humanity and the transformative power of reconciliation. Meeting Rick and the others at the Simon Wiesenthal Center (SWC) was a turning point, providing me with a path to atone for a regrettable past. Words cannot fully express my gratitude for this opportunity at redemption. Through the SWC, I became part of an incredible community dedicated to human-rights, peace, and the fight against racism.

The SWC could have easily dismissed me as an irredeemable former Nazi, but instead, they chose a path of compassion and mentorship. Their guidance opened doors to new experiences and allowed me to engage meaningfully with communities I had once misunderstood and vilified. Among these connections was TM Garret, a remarkable former extremist whose journey and work deeply enriched my path toward healing and transformation.

TM, a former skinhead from Germany, underwent a profound personal transformation after moving to the United States. Now, he devotes his life to speaking out against hate and guiding others out of extremism, offering empathy, wisdom, and steadfast support. It's often said that a person's character is defined by how they treat others, and TM embodies this ethos. He shines as a beacon of compassion, and anyone seeking to leave extremism would be fortunate to have his guidance.

In 2020, TM invited me to speak with him in Skokie, Illinois. It was a momentous occasion for many reasons – one being that I'd never set foot inside a Synagogue before. Anxiety coursed through me as I wondered how we'd be received, given my past actions. Back in 2009, I had sent NSM members to protest the opening of a Holocaust Museum in Skokie. Now, over a decade later, I was speaking in the same community alongside TM. It felt surreal, almost too much to process. But I knew it must have been a hundred times more difficult for those in the audience. Accompanying us that evening were Acacia and Ken, two former NSM members who, like me, had never visited a synagogue before.

TM couldn't hide his amusement at our nervousness. His smile was reassuring as he confidently predicted we would be accepted and grow from the experience. He shared how our apprehension mirrored his own journey years earlier. Throughout the evening, TM's attentiveness never wavered. He frequently checked in on us, offering quiet words of encouragement and understanding the significance of the moment, not just for the audience but for us as well.

Before our talk, Rabbi Ari delivered a heartfelt introduction, commending the courage it took for us to leave our pasts behind. His words pierced through me, evoking waves of regret and sorrow. Standing among Holocaust survivors and their descendants – the very people we had once vilified – was truly humbling. Yet, in that sacred space, the Rabbi welcomed us as brothers. His gesture wasn't merely symbolic; it was transformative. When he showed us the synagogue's holy scrolls, the depth of his compassion and forgiveness became almost overwhelming. That moment forever redefined my understanding of reconciliation and acceptance.

After the talk, members of the congregation came forward to warmly embrace us. I don't think I've ever received so many hugs in a single day. It was a powerful testament to the strength of human connection, the healing power of forgiveness, and the resilience of the human spirit to overcome even the deepest wounds.

Reflecting on my past, I often question how and why I harbored such unfounded hostility toward an entire group of people without ever truly knowing or understanding them. I'd been deeply entrenched in the belief that Jews were inherently evil, casting them as super-villains hell-bent on world domination through enslavement and subjugation. One of the hardest truths to confront has been my failure to critically examine these antisemitic myths.

Despite priding myself on fairness and meticulousness during my time as leader of the NSM – where major decisions were supposedly grounded in careful investigation – I inexplicably abandoned that same rigor when it came to the so-called 'Jewish question.' The glaring contradiction between my calculated approach to leadership and the blind acceptance of prejudiced beliefs has been one of the most difficult realities to reconcile.

After deradicalizing, I learned about confirmation bias, which illuminated many of those past behaviors. It helped me understand why I failed to critically analyze facts. Subconsciously, I sought out information that reinforced the movement's ideology while ignoring anything that contradicted it. Once you become aware of confirmation bias, it becomes easier to recognize and challenge. By applying emotional intelligence, it's possible to address unconscious biases, reevaluate entrenched beliefs, and approach information with a more balanced and objective perspective. This understanding is crucial for developing informed and empathetic viewpoints.

Through the SWC, I also had the privilege of meeting Tim Zaal, one of the first former neo-Nazis in America to speak out against hate. Tim's approach is raw, unfiltered, and infused with a sharp sense of humor that immediately puts others at ease. Talking with him reminded me of my mother's side of the family, who were equally direct and candid. If Tim and I had crossed paths in the past, there's no doubt we would've been the best of friends.

TM and Tim held each other in high regard, exemplifying the belief that former extremists should uplift and support one another. While agreement on every issue isn't necessary, we all share a steadfast commitment to never causing harm again.

During our trip to Skokie, TM introduced Acacia and me to Alison Pure-Slovin, the Midwest Director of the SWC. Alison hadn't been fully briefed on my history within the neo-Nazi movement, so when TM disclosed who I was, her demeanor shifted instantly. Her sharp, scrutinizing gaze felt like it could see straight through me, and her expressions carried a familiarity I couldn't immediately pinpoint. Then, it hit me – that was the same look my mother gave when she was skeptical or sizing someone up.

Alison didn't mince words. She launched into a series of pointed questions with a directness that felt like an interrogation. I glanced at TM; who was smirking, attempting not to giggle, which was a good sign. Meanwhile, Alison was all business, laser-focused on verifying my authenticity. To leave no stone unturned, she pulled out her phone and called Rick Eaton at the SWC – right in front of us. TM's face turned bright red as he struggled not to burst out laughing, as if he were witnessing a scene from a sitcom.

After ending the call, Alison stepped closer, looked me up and down once more before declaring, "Well, Rick says you're kosher, so that's good enough for me."

On our next trip to Chicago, Alison warmly invited Acacia and me to her home for Shabbat, the Jewish Sabbath. As someone who practices Orthodox Judaism, Alison has been instrumental in teaching us about Jewish traditions and culture.

She even invited us to celebrate Purim with her, a holiday I had grotesquely misunderstood during my time in the movement. Experiencing Purim firsthand was eye-opening – it's a joyous celebration filled with costumes, music, and festivities. It shattered the twisted myths I once believed, replacing them with an appreciation for the vibrancy and beauty of Jewish culture.

Exploring Purim's religious significance by attending a synagogue service was both enlightening and nerve-wracking. My curiosity was laced with apprehension, particularly because of the Orthodox tradition of separating genders during worship – something I hadn't considered until Alison casually mentioned it. The thought of sitting alone, with my past affiliations weighing heavily on me, felt unsettling. En route to the service, my anxiety manifested in nail-biting. Being as perceptive as she is, Alison immediately picked up on my unease. We both enjoy joking, so this was an opportune moment to really get me.

She began quizzing me on my knowledge of Purim, and when I admitted knowing very little, she shared the Biblical story of Esther and Haman, emphasizing Haman's role as the villain. Just before we arrived, she glanced over with a sly smile and said, "You know, Jeff, the story of Haman should really resonate with you." Curiously, I asked, "Why's that?" With perfect comedic timing, she replied, "Well, you sure were a lot like Haman in the past."

Her lighthearted teasing cut through my tension. She wasn't wrong, and I couldn't help but laugh at the fair comparison. Alison's wit and ability to balance humor with sincerity is one of the many reasons she has become such a beloved part of our lives, and is like family to us. Through her, we've also been introduced to an incredible community in Chicago, forging deep and lasting friendships that we cherish.

The painful irony of once believing Jewish people harbored nefarious intentions for world domination weighs heavily on my soul. That misconception stemmed from a woeful ignorance of their culture and traditions. Now, as I embrace the richness of those traditions and the friendships I missed out on for decades, the loss feels immeasurable. The remorse I carry for unjustly maligning an entire community runs deep, but it also drives my unwavering commitment to fostering understanding, reconciliation, and lasting peace.

REFLECTIONS

Reflecting on Alison's open-hearted welcome of Acacia and me into her life and home, I'm humbled by the depth of kindness and trust she extended to us – kindness we certainly didn't deserve. Yet Alison chose to look beyond our pasts, embracing us with the courage and grace that define her extraordinary character.

Understanding others often requires placing ourselves in their shoes – a principle that has become central in my conversations with other formers. If the roles were reversed, and we were Jewish, would we have the capacity to extend the same compassion to former neo-Nazis that Alison has shown us? It's an uncomfortable question with no easy answer, but it underscores the exceptional compassion and humanity Alison embodies. Her example shines as a beacon for fostering understanding and building a more empathetic world.

Former extremists frequently navigate a tumultuous sea of guilt, shame, regret, and introspection. These emotions aren't imposed by others; they arise from an internal reckoning over past actions. Forgiveness and acceptance, especially from those we've wronged, possess an extraordinary power to transform. They forge bonds of loyalty and friendship that leave an indelible mark on the soul.

At its core, humanity is bound by shared threads, even in the shadow of evil. Most people are inherently good, making it unjust to define entire groups by the actions of a few. This universal truth transcends religion, race, and ethnicity. Alison, and others like her, have illuminated my journey with lessons and insights that the years before never provided.

The words 'thank you' feel inadequate to express the depth of gratitude I hold for the remarkable people who now fill my life. They've shown me the power of grace, the resilience of forgiveness, and the infinite potential of human connection to heal even the deepest wounds.

The extraordinary individuals I've encountered through the Simon Wiesenthal Center have been an enduring source of inspiration. At the forefront is Rabbi Abraham Cooper, who exemplifies the highest standard of global human rights advocacy. His leadership is characterized by wisdom, compassion, and an unparalleled vision that inspires countless individuals worldwide. It's a true honor to call Rabbi Cooper a friend. His tireless efforts not only address the pressing issues of today but also ensure a legacy that will echo throughout the ages.

Simon Wiesenthal's timeless mission lives on through the impactful work of the SWC. With steadfast dedication, the

Center continues to advocate for tolerance, understanding, and a brighter future for all humanity, anchored in the unwavering principles of justice and equality.

"For evil to flourish, it only requires good men to do nothing."
    Simon Wiesenthal

CHAPTER 47

JUSTICE

Throughout my life, I've built relationships with many people – family, friends, and lovers. Yet, aside from family, one of the closest bonds I ever formed was with my best friend, Justice. In 2002, after the raid on our home, my children's mother brought home a white German Shepherd puppy, small enough to cradle in one hand. Our children suggested all kinds of adorable names – Snowball, Cotton, and other snow-themed ideas. Teasingly, I countered with more fearsome names like Snow Beast or Ice Monster, which, unsurprisingly, didn't go over well. We struggled with naming him, until their mother suggested Justice, an ironic choice considering the puppy's lineage came from a working-bloodline employed by police departments.

One weekend, during a visit to my parents' home, our family went into town for the afternoon, leaving Justice securely locked in the garage with his bed, food, water, and a window slightly open for ventilation. A few hours later, we returned to find Justice casually sitting on the front steps, sporting his usual confident German Shepherd grin. My mind raced: How did he escape? How many people had been mauled? I'd trained him as a guard dog, and he wasn't exactly fond of strangers. It was as if a loaded gun had sprouted legs and decided to patrol the neighborhood, ready to confront anything resembling a threat.

That was the vibe with Justice.

The mystery of his escape remains unsolved to this day. The garage's only exit was a window over five feet off the ground, cracked open just enough for airflow. Beyond that window was a nine-foot drop. Yet, there he was, proudly perched on the front steps as if his Houdini act was an everyday occurrence.

Another time, Justice and I were walking along the edge of a farmer's field when we spotted a doe about 100 yards away. Justice locked eyes with the deer, and I thought this might be the perfect way for him to burn off some energy. Without a second thought, I unclipped his leash and said, "Get 'em!" Never in my wildest dreams did I expect him to catch up with a fleeing deer from that distance. But Justice was built for the chase – he closed the gap astonishingly fast and began pulling her down.

I sprinted toward them, shouting at the top of my lungs, "Justice, Halt! Halt! Halt!" Amazingly, he released the doe and watched as it bounded off into the forest. When Justice returned, his ears were lowered as if he'd done something wrong. However, he'd followed commands and wasn't in trouble; instead, he received praise. That day, I learned an important lesson – never let him chase deer, no matter the distance. I couldn't help but think: while some folks train their dogs to retrieve birds, mine could single-handedly take down a deer.

Justice's vigilance, though admirable, wasn't always appreciated by the rest of the family. Whenever I took the kids swimming, they preferred that he stay home. During the day, when the lake was crowded, he'd remain behind, but in the evenings, when it was deserted, he'd join us. Justice was fiercely protective of the children, and to him, deep water meant danger.

If they ventured too far out, he'd swim after them, grab hold, and tow them back to shallower water where their feet could touch. It was awe-inspiring to witness, but there was one downside – his claws would inadvertently scratch them during these impromptu 'rescues.' However, there was a silver lining: if the kids didn't want leave the lake, the mere mention of Justice's 'rescue mission' was enough to get them scrambling for the shore.

Justice was truly a sight to behold. Weighing over 100 pounds, he was a powerhouse of pure muscle, with a coat as white as freshly fallen Minnesota snow. His eyes reflected his emotions, changing subtly depending on his mood. His understanding of language was nothing short of remarkable – he knew far more words and phrases than I ever thought a dog could comprehend. Walking him was always an adventure. People often crossed to the other side of the street, nervously calling out, "Is that a wolf?" as they kept a wary distance.

One unforgettable Fourth of July, I was setting off bottle rockets using a beer bottle, but Justice had other plans. Each time I tried to light a rocket, he'd knock the bottle over, making it clear he wasn't a fan of fireworks. When my girlfriend arrived, I explained that Justice had been temporarily banished indoors because of his interference. Skeptical, she raised an eyebrow, so I decided to prove it. I set an unlit rocket in the bottle and let Justice out. True to form, he marched straight over and knocked the bottle down. My girlfriend stared in disbelief, then admitted she'd never seen anything like it.

We laughed, and I reset the bottle. This time, Justice upped the ante – not only did he topple the bottle, but this time he pressed his paw down with enough force to shatter it into pieces.

Then, he looked up at me, his eyes gleaming with triumph, as if to say, "Try that again, I dare you." It was a striking display of his intelligence, determination, and problem-solving skills, wrapped up in one unforgettable moment.

Not all of Justice's escapades were so lighthearted. A more troubling incident occurred during a backyard play session with my Rottweiler, Chaos. The two were roughhousing as usual when Chaos accidentally scratched Justice just below the eye, leaving a deep gash that required stitches. Despite it being after hours, our veterinarian and his assistant kindly agreed to stay late to treat him. They administered a heavy dose of sedative to put him under for the procedure, but Justice barely seemed affected. After a second dose, his eyes finally started to droop.

As the assistant, understandably nervous around Justice, leaned in to help me lift him onto the operating table, his eyes suddenly snapped open. A low, menacing growl rumbled from his chest as he bared his teeth. She jumped back in fear. The veterinarian shook his head in disbelief. "I've never seen a dog stand up after a double dose of sedative," he said. It wasn't until they administered a third dose that Justice finally went under, leaving everyone stunned by his sheer resilience.

The vet mentioned it would be hours before Justice woke up from surgery and suggested I head home, promising to call when he began stirring. A couple of hours later, the assistant phoned, assuring me Justice would likely wake in about an hour, but he'd be groggy and disoriented for a while. "No need to rush," she said. Knowing Justice, though, I couldn't shake the feeling that I needed to get there – immediately.

As I walked into the clinic, chaos erupted. A scream tore

through the air as the assistant came flying into the reception area, slamming a waist-high door behind her, gasping for breath.

Alarmed, I rushed over, asking, "Are you okay? What's going on?"

Hyperventilating and visibly rattled, she managed to blurt out, "Thank God you got here early. He woke up!"

I couldn't help but laugh. "Justice waking up caused you to scream and run into the waiting room? Isn't that a bit dramatic?"

Her wide eyes and trembling hand pointing toward the office suggested otherwise. "Go see for yourself!" she stammered.

Curious, I peeked inside. There was Justice, charging around the office in a frenzy, ears pinned back, on the hunt for someone or something.

"Justice!" I called out.

At the sound of my voice, he froze in his tracks. His ears perked up, and he gave me a look that said, Finally. Let's go home.

Justice and I shared an unbreakable bond, built over years of loyalty and companionship. But one day, everything changed. When I came home, Justice nudged me persistently, signaling that something was wrong. He was unsteady on his feet, his balance faltering. Alarmed, I rushed him to the vet, where his mobility deteriorated rapidly before my eyes. The diagnosis was devastating: degenerative myelopathy, an incurable spinal condition that progressively robs dogs of their ability to walk. The prognosis was grim, and the vet gently urged me to prepare for the inevitable.

The next day was even worse – Justice couldn't walk at all. His pain was visible, and he refused to eat. A second trip to the vet confirmed my worst fears: his chances of walking again were slim to none. The vet compassionately explained the extent of his suffering, describing the brutal reality of his condition. My heart broke, but I wasn't ready to give up. Determined to exhaust every option, I asked about alternative treatments before considering euthanasia.

The vet suggested trying chiropractic care as a last resort. The dog chiropractor recommended six to eight weeks of treatment, cautioning that if there was no improvement by the end, euthanasia might be the most humane choice. It was a devastating prospect, but the thought of prolonging Justice's pain because I couldn't let go felt even worse.

Though his front legs remained strong, his back legs were paralyzed and without sensation, a cruel effect of the spinal condition. Caring for him became physically and emotionally demanding. Justice wasn't a small dog; every time I helped him outside, I used a makeshift sling to support his hind legs, allowing him to move forward with his powerful front legs. It was a grueling routine, but I was determined to give him every chance.

Weeks passed, and Justice fought valiantly, but by the eighth week, there was no improvement. The moment I had been dreading had arrived.

On Justice's final day, I took him outside and gently laid him on the grass, where he could feel the warmth of the sun one last time. He rested on the far side of the yard while I sat slumped on the concrete patio, close enough for us to see each other. In the midst of an emotional breakdown, I tried to convince myself that letting go was the right thing to do – holding on any longer would be selfish. I needed to summon the courage to accept that this day had been coming and release him from suffering.

As I sat there, lost in grief, Justice fixed his gaze on me, as attentive as ever. In my mind, I told him how much he was loved and that this was goodbye. I needed him to understand that what I was about to do was an act of mercy. It was agonizing, knowing that the next morning I would call the vet to schedule his euthanasia. Just as I resolved internally to let him go, and as I finished bidding him a mental farewell, something extraordinary happened. Our eyes locked, and for the first time in eight weeks, Justice stood up and walked across the yard to me. There's no other way to describe it except to call it a miracle. Having recently lost my mother, grandparents, and my Rottweiler, Chaos, it seemed like a cruel pattern for death to claim my best friend too. Somehow, against all odds, Justice defied death. Emotionally, I was already in shambles, after my mother's passing. I can't say whether it was fate, destiny, or a miracle that Justice stood up at the precise moment I'd come to terms with letting him go, but the timing was undeniably beyond coincidence.

Even the veterinary office had assumed Justice passed away. They sent a sympathy card signed by all the staff, expressing condolences for the loss of both Justice and Chaos. Justice had been on prescription thyroid medication for years, which I picked up monthly. The first time I picked up his prescription after his presumed death, the employees exchanged concerned glances but filled the script. The following month, however, they hesitated.

"Mr. Schoep," one of them said, "the doctor needs to see Justice before we can refill this prescription again."

When Justice walked into the clinic for his appointment, it was as though the entire staff had seen a ghost. An employee hurried to alert the vet, who emerged from the back and stared in disbelief. "I didn't even see your car pull in!" he exclaimed. I explained that we'd walked a mile from home. The vet, clearly astonished that Justice could not only stand but walk, immediately instructed his team to prepare Justice's prescription.

Seizing the moment, the vet conducted a more thorough examination. To his amazement, Justice still had no sensation in one hind leg and limited feeling in the other. Shaking his head in disbelief, he reiterated the degenerative nature of myelopathy and admitted there was no medical explanation for Justice's miraculous recovery.

For me, the reason behind Justice's resurgence didn't matter. I was simply grateful for the extra time we were given. Those additional years were a precious gift, allowing us to create more memories I'll cherish forever. But as much as Justice had defied the odds, time eventually caught up with him. At eighteen years old – a long life for any large dog – his spinal condition worsened, and he once again lost the ability to walk.

When the time came to say goodbye, I reached out to the women who had loved him. Several ex-girlfriends came by, each bringing Justice his favorite treats, ensuring his final day was filled with love and affection before he crossed the rainbow bridge. As the day wore on, my dear friend Kristin gently urged me to stay by Justice's side until the end.

Though the thought of seeing my best friend lifeless felt unbearable, Kristin's kind and compassionate words reminded me of the importance of being there for Justice – just as he had always been there for me. Her encouragement gave me the strength to honor our unbreakable bond and ensure that Justice felt loved in his final moments.

Heeding Kristin's advice was one of the most heart-wrenching decisions I've ever made, but it was also one of the most meaningful – a final act of devotion to my best friend of eighteen years. Justice's passing was, in so many ways, a reflection of his life – absolutely extraordinary. I had dreaded this day for years, knowing that even in his final moments, Justice would refuse to let go without a fight.

Once again, it took three doses of sedative. Justice fought valiantly to remain alert, his eyes locked onto mine in a silent display of willpower. As the third dose began to take hold, his eyes blurred, and he started sniffing the air, searching for me. I moved closer, and he seemed to find solace, knowing I was still by his side. Even then, his indomitable spirit refused to yield as the final drugs were administered.

The vet, clearly moved, remarked on how exceptionally strong Justice's heart was, fighting with everything it had. Leaning in close, my voice trembling with emotion, I whispered, "It's okay, Justice. You have to go now. I'll see you again on the other side; we'll be together again."

Moments later, he was gone.

CHAPTER 48

CIVILIAN LIFE

Leaving neo-Nazism felt like emerging from a war zone. For years, I had thrived in high-stress, conflict-ridden environments where survival depended on precision and focus. Adjusting to a peaceful existence was an entirely different challenge. As Commander of the NSM, my dedication had honed my skills to a razor's edge. I had stability, ran a successful business, commanded respect, and held a position of power at the heart of a community that relied on my leadership. Yet, despite the familiarity and security, staying involved would have been neither moral nor honorable. Walking away was the only choice.

Starting over wasn't just difficult – it was disorienting. Life outside extremism brought its own battles, few more daunting than the skepticism I faced in public discourse. One instance stands out vividly. A leading newspaper reached out to me for an interview about my transformation. I saw it as an opportunity to showcase my commitment to reconciliation and change. To illustrate the depth of my reform, I invited the reporter to a session at the California Assembly, where I spoke alongside lawmakers, elected officials, and representatives from the Simon Wiesenthal Center (SWC), the international human rights organization that had rigorously vetted my reform.

When the article was published, however, my association with the SWC was conspicuously absent. Instead, the headline provocatively asked, 'Do You Believe Him?' The focus wasn't on my transformation or the hope it could inspire – it seemed intent on casting doubt.

On a personal level, this portrayal was deeply hurtful. But more troubling was the broader message it sent to others contemplating leaving extremism. Many extremists harbor a quiet curiosity about life beyond their insular worlds, but seeing others walk away only to face ridicule or suspicion can extinguish that curiosity. It sends a dangerous signal: leaving may not be worth the cost.

Transformation is a fragile and deeply personal process. It demands navigating internal battles while withstanding external pressures. For those standing on the brink of change, public doubt can be more than discouraging – it can be paralyzing. If leaving means enduring relentless scrutiny and suspicion, many will never take that crucial first step.

The stakes couldn't be higher. Those who leave extremist ideologies behind are uniquely positioned to save lives. A single reformed extremist – particularly a leader with influence – can deter others from violence, preventing tragedies like mass shootings or bombings that devastate families and communities. The ripple effects of such transformations are immeasurable.

Skepticism is natural, but when it overshadows progress, it does far more harm than good. Instead of asking, 'Do you believe him?' the better question is, 'How can we help others leave?' Every defection from hate strengthens the fabric of a more compassionate society.

It was disheartening to see the news article overlook the significance of my collaboration with the SWC and engagement with elected officials to combat racism at the governmental level. These partnerships are vital in the fight against intolerance, offering a pathway toward a more peaceful and inclusive world. By focusing on doubt instead of progress, the article missed an opportunity to highlight the collective impact of these efforts.

In hindsight, I can understand some of the skepticism surrounding my departure from a prominent neo-Nazi role. Transforming from a figure synonymous with hate to one advocating for peace and reconciliation is a dramatic and extraordinary shift – one that's understandably difficult for many to grasp. The inner workings of extremist groups are often shrouded in secrecy, and few realize that once you publicly denounce those affiliations, there is no turning back.

Reading a headline that questioned my sincerity was psychologically devastating. It felt as though all my efforts to atone for the past and help others escape extremism were dismissed as meaningless. After dedicating myself to a path of reform and reconciliation, facing such public doubt was profoundly discouraging. Without strong internal resolve, that level of scrutiny could have completely derailed my efforts.

I pray that future generations of those who leave extremism and strive to make amends face less skepticism than I did. The journey out of hate is arduous, fraught with personal struggles, sacrifices, and risks. Adding doubt and suspicion only compounds the challenge, potentially pushing some to their breaking point. While blind trust in transformation is unwise, careful vetting ensures authenticity. Once someone has demonstrated their commitment to change, they deserve support – not suspicion. That encouragement can empower them to create ripples of change, inspiring others and reshaping communities for the better.

After renouncing racism, I was prepared for backlash from neo-Nazi circles – and it came swiftly. What I didn't foresee was hostility from factions on the far-left. Though I neither sought nor desired their approval, it was unsettling to see them persist in labeling me a Nazi, even after I had unequivocally denounced radical ideologies. In hindsight, my initial naiveté failed to account for the psychological dynamics and rigid dichotomies that underpin extremism. My reputation as a fierce opponent who had clashed with communists in the streets for decades, coupled with extremists' binary worldviews – right versus left, black versus white – made me a convenient target for their vilification. Because I didn't embrace far-left ideologies, I didn't fit their narrative of what a reformed extremist should look like.

The far-right harbors similar misconceptions, often assuming that anyone who leaves their ranks must have joined the far-left. This belief is reinforced when individuals who transition from far-right to far-left extremism are publicly celebrated as reformed, perpetuating the polarized thinking that traps both sides. My critique isn't of the broader political right or left but of the radical, intolerant factions on both ends that sustain division and hatred.

True deradicalization isn't about switching allegiances from one extreme to another – it's about rejecting extremism in all its forms. It's about choosing humanity over hate, peace over conflict, and reconciliation over vengeance. Remaining in the movement might have been the easier choice, and flipping to the far-left might have earned me public praise and validation from those who enable such behaviors. But neither option aligned with my conscience.

Instead, I chose a different path – a harder, lonelier path, but the only one that leads to genuine and lasting change.

OTHER COMPLICATIONS

Leaving the movement while the Charlottesville lawsuit was ongoing added yet another layer of complexity to an already difficult journey. The plaintiffs' lawyers, aware of my renunciation of neo-Nazism, asked during a video conference if I had any information to support their case. I told them the truth: I had no knowledge of any organizers planning violence. If I had, I wouldn't have attended. While I'd spent 25 years organizing far-right demonstrations, Charlottesville was different – I attended as a participant, not an organizer.

I also pointed to my verifiable record of participating in rallies where, although confrontations often occurred, neither I nor NSM members were ever arrested. Arrests were consistently on the opposing side, as we adhered strictly to a framework of self-defense. Maintaining this level of discipline was no small feat – especially within a hate group, where chaos often reigns. Over 25 years of rallies, not a single arrest among my ranks spoke volumes about the rigid discipline I upheld. Such consistency over decades is virtually unheard of in extremist circles.

It defied logic to suggest that, after decades of

demonstrations without incident, I would suddenly embrace violence at Charlottesville – particularly when such behavior had never been tolerated under my leadership. The media presence that day was overwhelming, with cameras capturing every moment, some of which was later used in criminal trials. If I had acted unlawfully, there would be no shortage of evidence. My actions in Charlottesville were entirely consistent with my history: self-defense only.

Equally offensive was the notion that I might falsely accuse others to protect myself from legal consequences. Dishonesty and cowardice are antithetical to my values. Harming others to spare myself isn't just morally indefensible – it's utterly repugnant.

Shortly afterward, a spokesperson affiliated with the plaintiffs began posting on social media, accusing me of still being a Nazi, fabricating my transformation, and claiming I'd left the movement because of their lawsuit. These allegations were outright falsehoods. I'd been sued before while in the movement and didn't leave then. In fact, walking away from the NSM left me financially ruined. The reality couldn't have been further from the narrative they spun. Seeing my efforts toward reconciliation derided with such malice was profoundly painful. Everyone is entitled to opinions, but presenting baseless accusations as facts is both unethical and harmful.

To defend my reputation, I sent the spokesperson a cease-and-desist letter, asking her to stop falsely labeling me a Nazi. Her lawyer responded by claiming my letter constituted harassment and intimidation, even threatening legal action if I contacted her again.

When I sent the cease-and-desist letter to Khristian, his

lawyer mocked me by referencing the earlier letter I had sent to the spokesperson involved in the Charlottesville lawsuit, claiming that what his client said about me was accurate and therefore not defamatory. He sarcastically remarked that I hadn't "learned my lesson" about sending what both attorneys referred to as 'harassing' letters. This comment revealed that Khristian or his lawyer and the parties connected to the lawsuit were in communication, as no one outside of my legal counsel was aware of the letters. The identical language used by both attorneys, combined with the mocking remark from Khristian's lawyer, strongly suggests a coordinated effort to discredit my attempts to defend my reputation and counter the ongoing defamation. Notably, both Khristian and the spokesperson were each served a single cease-and-desist notice – these were not part of any repeated or ongoing correspondence.

Cease-and-desist letters are a legitimate legal tool – not a form of harassment or intimidation. Both letters I sent, to Khristian and the spokesperson involved in the lawsuit, were carefully reviewed by legal counsel to ensure they were lawful and appropriate. Over the years, I've rarely resorted to such measures, even during decades in the movement. On the rare occasions I did, it was to address unauthorized attempts to use the NSM name. Those disputes, even within the hostile environment of hardcore neo-Nazi factions, were resolved without escalation.

Ironically, after leaving neo-Nazism, I issued two cease-and-desist letters with one straightforward request: stop falsely labeling me a Nazi. In both cases, the recipients defied the requests and continued their public defamation. Confronted by what felt like overwhelming wealth, privilege, lawfare, and abuse of power, I ultimately chose to let the matter go rather than engage in prolonged conflict, despite the emotional pain and psychological toll it inflicted.

In sharing these personal struggles, my goal is to encourage a more empathetic approach toward those seeking to change their lives. No one undergoing such a transformation should have to endure the scorn and derision I faced. Instead, I pray others find a community that embraces them with understanding, kindness, and the support needed to foster meaningful change.

Initially, I was hesitant to discuss the struggles I encountered after leaving neo-Nazism, worried that revealing these realities might discourage others from leaving or give them an excuse to stay. But after careful reflection, I realized that staying silent about the cruelty and indifference I faced would be disingenuous. I'm not sharing these experiences to seek sympathy – I neither need nor deserve it – but to inspire empathy and understanding for those who have made mistakes yet are working hard to make amends.

Every journey toward transformation is unique. While I encountered hostility along the way, the kindness and compassion I received from others far outweighed the negative. It is that kindness – not the cruelty – that truly defines what it means to embrace change.

To those who find my journey intimidating or view it as a reason to avoid change, let me assure you: leaving was the best decision I've ever made. If you're considering making a change, remember this – you're not alone. Many of us, myself included, are here to support you on your path forward.

In 2020, I had the incredible opportunity to collaborate

with Daryl Davis for several talks – a partnership that proved to be as educational as it was inspiring. One highlight came when CNN invited Daryl to appear on Kamau Bell's United Shades of America. True to his generous spirit, Daryl suggested that TM Garrett, Arno, and I join him for the segment.

After the interview with Kamau, we headed to a club in Pittsburgh where Daryl was performing. Knowing that TM, Arno, and I had musical backgrounds, Daryl invited us on stage to sing backup vocals. The energy in the hall was electric – a full-circle moment that brought me back to the long-haired rock-and-roll days I had left behind in the throes of extremism. It felt like a symbolic rebirth, like a phoenix rising from the ashes, reigniting the passions I'd abandoned so long ago. Surrounded by Daryl and the guys, the night became a powerful fusion of past and present – a celebration of healing and brotherhood.

After Pittsburgh, Daryl and I traveled to New York University, where we spoke to a packed auditorium of curious and engaged students. Sharing my story required a level of vulnerability I had rarely shown before. It meant stepping out from behind the hardened persona I'd cultivated during my time in the movement and exposing the humanity I had once denied in others. Though exposing my past was deeply uncomfortable, it was necessary. Transparency and accountability are vital for building trust – especially with communities I had once dehumanized.

For many, meeting a former neo-Nazi leader is unsettling. After my talks, people often approach me, confessing that they initially felt uneasy or even afraid. But as they hear my story, their discomfort often transforms into compassion. These encounters – often ending with handshakes, hugs, and heartfelt encouragement – are a testament to the power of change and the human capacity for understanding and reconciliation.

The most profound moments come from those who share their own experiences with racism. Their stories resonate deeply, offering powerful reminders of why this work is so vital. In a world often divided by fear and misunderstanding, their courage and vulnerability illuminate the possibility of healing. These connections reaffirm my belief that, no matter how daunting the journey may seem, meaningful change is always within reach.

To anyone contemplating a life change or feeling uncertain about the challenges ahead, remember this: transformation is rarely easy, and acceptance from others isn't guaranteed. People's perceptions are shaped by their own experiences, traumas, and the echo chambers they inhabit – echo chambers that may mirror the ones you're striving to leave behind. Confirmation bias and cognitive dissonance can further distort their understanding of your efforts. Even so, the decision to change is yours alone. While the path may be difficult and fraught with obstacles, it's also the most rewarding journey you can take.

If you're working to overcome extremism, addiction, gang involvement, a cult, or other obstacles, don't let the skepticism or judgement of others deter you. Universal approval is never guaranteed, no matter what hardships you've endured. Others may not fully understand your journey – just as you may not understand theirs. What matters is that you are in control of your destiny, and that power belongs to you alone.

Anyone undergoing a life-altering transformation will inevitably face tribulations. Struggles don't vanish overnight, and meaningful change requires consistent effort and determination. Those who step up to the plate and take a swing at life's challenges are destined for greatness. Conversely, those who surrender, capitulate, or abandon their goals often find themselves on the losing end of the equation – whether they deserve it or not.

The key takeaway is this: always choose to do what's right, even when it feels impossibly hard. A life burdened by regret – no matter how comfortable or easy it may appear – is never the right path. Believe in yourself, remain steadfast, and there are no limits to what you can achieve when you dedicate your heart, mind, and soul to your goals.

CHAPTER 49

NOT THE END, BUT A GATEWAY TO THE FUTURE

This memoir captures just a fraction of the harrowing experiences I've lived through – moments where split-second decisions could have led to imprisonment or death. What you'll find in these pages barely scratches the surface. Countless memories remain untold, left to the dustbin of history after countless hours of emotional reflection about what to include.

Throughout my journey, I've crossed paths with thousands of people. Some left the movement alongside me or shortly after, while others had broken free years before. Tragically, many still remain trapped in the cycle of extremism, though I hold onto hope that one day they will find the strength to break free.

To those who are still engaged, I implore you to reflect deeply. Consider the consequences of your actions: the lives lost, the people imprisoned. Think about the toll it's taken on your own life: the jobs you've lost, the friendships and family bonds you've severed, the impact on your children. Has this path truly brought any meaningful achievements? Does your cause justify the harm it inflicts, and is that morally defensible? These are difficult but necessary questions, especially if you believe your cause is righteous.

One moment stands out in my memory. My brother, Chris

Drake, once asked me a question I never anticipated: "How many people in the church down the street do you think know a murderer?" Caught off guard, I responded, "Probably none. Why?"

Drake continued, "How many people do we know who have taken a life?" The silence that followed was deafening. His question framed our past in a way I had never considered, drawing a stark line between our experiences and those of the general population. It highlighted the grim reality of the world we had lived in – a reality that most people could never imagine.

Avoiding painful memories may seem like a way to cope, but it doesn't erase the past. Surviving the chaos I've endured is statistically unlikely. Each day spent making excuses to stay on that path is another day wasted, pulling you further down a dead-end road. The internal justifications that keep you tethered to extremism – the belief that your life is worth less than the cause – are the same ones that once haunted me. That kind of blind loyalty is a trap, one that can only be escaped by confronting the truth.

It's imperative to understand that adopting an extremist mindset doesn't just harm you – it devastates the lives of your loved ones, your community, and your nation. You become like a grenade thrown into a crowd, raining shrapnel into the lives of innocent people. There is no moral justification for causing such collateral damage or traumatizing others in pursuit of a cause. You may be willing to sacrifice yourself, but what about the scorched earth you leave behind?

Guiding others away from harmful ideologies and toward positive change has become my driving purpose. Diverting even one person from a dangerous path not only saves their life but also creates a ripple effect, preventing harm to countless others. The potential to prevent tragedies, like mass shootings, fuels my dedication to this cause. Every life steered away from extremism is a victory that reverberates far beyond the individual.

After leaving neo-Nazism, I faced a slew of challenges, including deliberate sabotage from a handful of individuals with malicious intent. These obstacles compounded an already grueling journey, making it far more difficult than it should have been. Such barriers can easily discourage others or, worse, push them back into the clutches of extremism. This underscores the critical need for robust, supportive systems to help those breaking free from destructive ideologies. Without that support, the road to change can feel insurmountable.

Preventing harm starts with understanding and empathy. Breaking the cycle of extremism requires building bridges for those ready to leave and offering them a clear path to healing. Only through these efforts can we begin to repair the damage caused and create a future rooted in compassion rather than hatred.

In response, I've dedicated myself to ensuring that no one needlessly suffers on their journey toward reconciliation. Choosing to change takes immense courage and is unequivocally the right decision. This is why I am committed to guiding others through their transformations – support that is vital not only for their personal growth but also for the broader societal impact it fosters.

When I started speaking out against racism, I hoped my experience as a former white nationalist leader would be recognized as a valuable resource for organizations combating extremism. My background, though heavy with its share of baggage, carried rare insights into the inner workings of these movements – insights that could save lives. However, despite an active social media presence and high-profile speaking engagements, opportunities for collaboration were disappointingly scarce. Whether due to lingering skepticism about my past or the relentless false accusations from a so-called former extremist who labeled me a current Nazi, I found myself navigating constant uphill battles.

Thankfully, the Simon Wiesenthal Center saw beyond the noise and recognized my sincerity and potential. With their support, I was able to share my story with students, community leaders, and law enforcement, leveraging my lived experiences to educate and inspire meaningful change. Their trust in my transformation underscored the critical importance of providing spaces where individuals breaking free from extremism can rediscover their purpose and help steer others away from destructive paths.

Starting an organization to counter extremism was never my intention. However, as more people began reaching out for guidance, it became impossible to manage alone. Without an existing counter-extremism organization to collaborate with or learn from, I faced a difficult choice: either create something new or turn away those seeking help – a decision I simply couldn't morally accept.

One of the most common questions I received from those seeking to leave far-right extremism was whether I had any ties to Antifa. On the surface, the question seemed surprising – there was nothing in my past or present to suggest any connection to far-left extremism. Yet the concern was valid. It's a known phenomenon that some individuals leaving far-right ideologies end up flipping to far-left extremism. For those genuinely trying to disengage, this pattern is a glaring red flag. Anyone who transitions from one extreme to another not only risks their own path to recovery but also poses a significant threat to the integrity of legitimate deradicalization efforts. Such individuals should be kept far away from those sincerely seeking to change their lives.

People leaving extremist movements emerge from an environment bathed in paranoia and distrust. Before reaching out, many conduct extensive research on formers or deradicalization groups, meticulously analyzing online posts, affiliations, and reputations to determine credibility and trustworthiness. Naturally, those leaving the far-right are wary of engaging with individuals or groups associated with far-left extremism, such as Antifa, which they perceive as aligning with their former enemies. Beyond the optics, Antifa's reputation for doxxing and engaging in violence makes such affiliations inherently problematic. Exposing someone trying to leave far-right extremism to individuals or ideologies linked to the far-left doesn't support their transition – it risks re-radicalizing them into another destructive ideology.

True deradicalization is about moving away from all forms of extremism, not simply swapping one extreme for another. For those sincerely seeking to escape the toxic cycle, aligning them with far-left extremism, intentionally or not, undermines their progress and society's broader efforts to combat radicalization. It's critical that deradicalization initiatives remain neutral, credible, and committed to fostering genuine transformation rather than perpetuating a cycle of extremism in another guise.

It would be utterly absurd for someone leaving far-left extremism to seek guidance from Nazis to disengage from their ideology. Similarly, it's just as nonsensical to expect far-left radicals to effectively help someone exiting far-right extremism. Yet, despite this glaring contradiction, some organizations persist in involving radical far-left activists in deradicalization efforts. This approach is not only reckless but also counterproductive – it undermines trust and alienates those who are genuinely seeking to break free from extremist ideologies. Ignoring this issue doesn't make it disappear; it exacerbates the problem. Addressing and rectifying this fundamental flaw is imperative for any counter-extremism initiative to succeed.

As a former neo-Nazi, it is both frustrating and disheartening to have to point out such glaring oversights in American deradicalization programs. By highlighting these shortcomings, I open myself to scrutiny and backlash from those complicit in perpetuating these misguided approaches. If self-preservation or career comfort were my priorities, silence would be the easier path. But having seen firsthand how these ineffective methods fail those who need help the most, I feel an obligation to speak out.

For the sake of those genuinely seeking transformation – and for the countless well-meaning individuals disillusioned by the inefficacy of current programs – it's vital to challenge the status quo and demand better. Only by addressing these systemic flaws can we create pathways that truly help people escape the destructive cycles of extremism and rebuild their lives with purpose and integrity.

Considering my perspective could prove invaluable, as I stand to lose far more by challenging entrenched systems and exposing these flaws than I could ever hope to gain, my critique is not an attack on sincere efforts; rather, it is a call to refine and improve them, ensuring they truly support those striving to break free from extremism and build meaningful lives.

It's important to recognize that individuals leaving far-right extremism often retain conservative or right-leaning political views, while others may gravitate toward liberal or left-leaning ideologies. What truly matters is their rejection of hate, racism, and extremism, regardless of where they land politically afterward.

A recurring concern among those seeking guidance is the presence of former extremists who share Antifa-related content on social media. For individuals who have been targeted by Antifa – whether through doxxing, violence, or other confrontations – this can be deeply unsettling and creates significant barriers to trust and engagement.

Imagine asking a victim of assault to seek counseling from their attacker. The absurdity of such a scenario perfectly illustrates the problem. It's not just inappropriate – it's harmful and counterproductive. In the same vein, expecting individuals leaving far-right extremism to feel safe engaging with those perceived as aligned with far-left extremist groups is unrealistic. This dynamic erodes trust, deters participation, and severely hampers the success of deradicalization efforts.

Resolving this issue should be simple, yet it remains a

persistent thorn in the side of some programs. Addressing it directly would dismantle barriers, foster wider engagement, and greatly enhance the effectiveness of these initiatives. If we are genuinely committed to achieving meaningful change, we must confront these challenges head-on. By prioritizing the concerns and well-being of those seeking to leave extremism, we can create a neutral, supportive, and secure environment that lays the foundation for genuine transformation and lasting progress.

Some formers choose not to publicize their political leanings online – a thoughtful strategy that enhances their ability to assist others. By remaining neutral, they create a safe and inclusive environment for individuals who are still exploring their own ideological shifts. This approach fosters a more open and effective path to deradicalization, where individuals feel welcome regardless of their political evolution.

In 2020, despite my reluctance to establish a new organization, I joined forces with other formers and experts, including Daryl Davis, to establish Beyond Barriers, a 501(c)(3) non-profit. Our mission is rooted in Relational Dialogue, a method pioneered by Daryl that has helped countless individuals, including myself, leave extremism behind. Beyond Barriers operates with a strictly non-partisan ethos, a cornerstone of its effectiveness in today's highly polarized climate. Our aim is not to direct people toward any specific ideology but to empower them to think critically, independently, and free from the constraints of group-think.

At Beyond Barriers, we are driven by a fundamental principle: true change cannot be forced. Change that is imposed tends to be shallow, fleeting, and devoid of genuine commitment. Authentic transformation, on the other hand, arises from within – born of personal reflection, insight, and conviction. Our mission is not to dictate change but to equip individuals with the tools, support, and guidance they need to embark on their own journeys of growth.

We believe that the individual must be the architect of their own transformation. At Beyond Barriers, our role is to act as facilitators – helping to clear the path, offer encouragement, and provide resources along the way. This personalized, non-coercive approach ensures that the change is not only meaningful but also enduring. True transformation, rooted in self-driven realization, has the power to create lasting impact for individuals and their communities.

While I've shared some assessments, I want to emphasize that I am not insinuating there is a lack of support for those seeking to leave extremism. Many dedicated individuals and organizations are doing extraordinary, life-saving work to help people disengage from hate-fueled ideologies. These evaluations are not critiques of the Countering Violent Extremism (CVE) field or the tireless efforts of those driving positive change. Rather, my intention is to highlight specific areas where constructive improvements could be made with relatively simple adjustments. These enhancements would not only increase overall effectiveness but also better serve those striving for lasting transformation. I remain confident that these initiatives will continue to grow and evolve, creating an even greater impact in the years to come. I hope these insights will prove valuable to practitioners in the field.

Having spent decades immersed in extremism, my long

journey toward redemption and reconciliation transcends the personal – it underscores the urgent need to address the polarization that continues to pull individuals into extremist ideologies. This memoir is intended to serve as a resource, offering a window into the mindset of a former extremist. In writing it, I've endeavored to be as candid and transparent as possible, sharing my experiences with unflinching honesty. While I have changed some names and omitted specific details to respect privacy, every event described has been presented factually and accurately to the best of my memory.

To those still involved in extremism or considering joining a hate group, I hope this memoir speaks to you. If my story deters even one person from making harmful choices, then revisiting these painful memories will have been worth it. My goal is to provide a cautionary tale that discourages others from walking a destructive path and offers a beacon of hope for transformation.

For everyone else, may this memoir inspire and motivate you to make a positive impact in the lives of others. May love, compassion, and understanding guide your path.

In Service to Humanity,
        Jeff Schoep

GLOSSARY

1. **Doxxing (or Dox):** The act of publicly sharing private or personal information about someone online, often without their consent, typically to harass, threaten, or intimidate.

2. **Skinheads:** A subculture that emerged in 1960s Britain, originally associated with working-class youth, reggae, and ska music. While not inherently racist, the term is often linked to far-right, neo-Nazi groups that gained prominence in the 1980s. Skinhead culture is commonly identified by distinctive attire, including shaved heads, boots, braces, and flight jackets.

3. **S.H.A.R.P. (Skinheads Against Racial Prejudice):** A far-left, anti-racist skinhead movement that emerged in the late 1980s in response to the rise of neo-Nazi skinheads. While advocating against racism, some S.H.A.R.P. factions have engaged in violent confrontations with far-right groups.

4. **Nazism (National Socialism):** The totalitarian ideology of the Nazi Party, which ruled Germany under Adolf Hitler from 1933 to 1945. It promoted extreme nationalism, racial supremacy, and antisemitism, leading to the systematic persecution and genocide of Jews and other targeted groups. Nazism dismantled democratic institutions, seized assets, stripped civil rights, and established ghettos and concentration camps, culminating in the Holocaust.

5. **Neo-Nazis:** Far-right extremists who support modern adaptations of Nazi ideology, promoting white supremacy, racism, and antisemitism. Some neo-Nazi groups advocate for or engage in acts of violence against perceived enemies.

6. **Antifa:** A far-left extremist movement with roots in the communist and socialist movements of 1920s and 1930s Europe. Modern Antifa groups align with Marxist and anarchist ideologies, actively opposing capitalism and fascism through direct action, protests, and violent confrontations. Known for using black bloc tactics, vandalism, and physical assaults against ideological opponents, Antifa justifies its actions as a form of resistance against perceived oppression.

7. **A.R.A. (Anti-Racist Action):** A U.S.-based anti-racist movement founded in the late 1980s in Minneapolis, Minnesota. Often considered a precursor to modern Antifa, A.R.A. was known for aggressively confronting white supremacist groups, often through violent clashes, vandalism, and organized disruptions of far-right events.

8. **Christian Identity:** A religious and political ideology that merges elements of Christianity with white supremacist beliefs. Adherents claim that white people are the true descendants of the biblical Israelites, rejecting mainstream Christianity while promoting racist, antisemitic, and separatist views. Some Christian Identity groups have been tied to acts of terrorism and hate crimes.

9. **Black Hebrew Israelites:** A movement of African Americans who believe they are the descendants of the ancient Israelites. While beliefs vary, some factions espouse racist and antisemitic ideologies, often targeting Jewish and white communities. Certain extremist Black Hebrew Israelite groups have been linked to violent rhetoric and attacks.

10. **Mossad:** Israel's national intelligence agency, responsible for intelligence gathering, covert operations, and counterintelligence. Known for its secrecy, Mossad has played a key role in high-profile missions, including tracking Nazi war criminals, countering global terrorism, and confronting threats to Israel's security.

ACKNOWLEDGEMENTS

This book exists because of the strength, resilience, and grace of many. While I can't name you all, you know who you are. Your presence – whether in moments of chaos or calm – carried me farther than I could have walked alone.

To my family – father, late mother, sister, children, and grandparents – I dragged you through fire. Still, you loved me. You showed up when I didn't deserve it. You held the line when I was too far gone to see it. You are my greatest blessing and the foundation this redemption rests on.

To Acacia – thank you for your patience, empathy, and gentle strength. Walking beside me through the years it took to bring this story to life wasn't easy. I know the memories took a toll. As an empath, you carried more than your share of the weight. I saw the sorrow in your eyes, felt the heaviness in your heart. Thank you for holding space for my healing while quietly enduring your own.

To the Simon Wiesenthal Center and Museum of Tolerance – Rick, Alison, Rabbi Cooper, and the incredible team: you extended a hand when I least expected it. You taught me about Teshuva, Tikkun Olam, and opened the door to a world I had only known through hatred and ignorance. That door led to forgiveness, learning, and humanity. I still marvel at the irony – that those I once demonized the most became the ones who offered me the most grace. Your work changes lives. It changed mine.

To Daryl Davis and Deeyah Khan – you shattered the last of my blindness, not with judgment, but with compassion. You led with humanity. You showed me truth. Thank you for changing the lens through which I see the world.

To Chris Drake – thank you for helping me build the bones of this book when it was still just a whisper. We've stood shoulder to shoulder through countless battles – both literal and symbolic. You are living proof that brotherhood outlasts war. A true warrior in heart and soul. *"One's back is vulnerable unless one has a brother."* – Hávamál

To all my friends, past and present – especially those who've clawed their way back from extremism to humanity. I've seen your battles, and know the cost. It takes a kind of strength most people will never understand. The world needs you.

To all the beautiful women who put up with me over the years – thank you for trying – delicately, often persistently – to show me that a life of war and constant conflict wasn't the only path.

To Michael Wilkinson and the entire team at Wilkinson Publishing – you believed in a story that many were afraid to touch. You backed it with courage, conviction, and boldness. Thank you for giving this book a stage – and a spine.

In the end, this is not a story of hate – it's the story of a phoenix rising from the ashes, scarred by fire, but reborn in truth.